Jacques Derrida's Cambridge Affair

Futures of the Archive: Theory, Criticism, Crisis

Series Editors: Arthur Bradley and Simon Swift

What will be the future of critical theory's past? This series offers a set of radical interdisciplinary interventions which explore how the history of critical theory can contribute to an understanding of the contemporary. By returning to classic critical debates in philosophy, politics, aesthetics, religion and more, the volumes in this series seek to provide a new insight into the crises of our present moment: capitalism, revolution, biopolitics, human rights, the Anthropocene. In this way, Futures of the Archive shows that the past – and in particular critical theory's own past – is not a dead letter, but an archive to which we still belong and which continues to shape our present and future.

Titles in the Series

The Labour of Subjectivity: Foucault on Biopolitics, Economy, Critique
Andrea Rossi

The Aesthetics of Violence: Art, Fiction, Drama and Film
Robert Appelbaum

Ontology and Perversion: Deleuze, Agamben, Lacan
Boštjan Nedoh

Jacques Derrida's Cambridge Affair: Deconstruction, Philosophy and Institutionality
Niall Gildea

Jacques Derrida's Cambridge Affair

Deconstruction, Philosophy and Institutionality

Niall Gildea

ROWMAN &
LITTLEFIELD
———INTERNATIONAL

London • New York

Published by Rowman & Littlefield International Ltd
6 Tinworth Street, London, SE11 5AL, United Kingdom
www.rowmaninternational.com

Rowman & Littlefield International Ltd.is an affiliate of Rowman & Littlefield
4501 Forbes Boulevard, Suite 200, Lanham, Maryland 20706, USA
With additional offices in Boulder, New York, Toronto (Canada), and Plymouth (UK)
www.rowman.com

Copyright © 2020 by Niall Gildea

All rights reserved. No part of this book may be reproduced in any form or by any electronic or mechanical means, including information storage and retrieval systems, without written permission from the publisher, except by a reviewer who may quote passages in a review.

British Library Cataloguing in Publication Data

A catalogue record for this book is available from the British Library

ISBN: HB 978-1-78661-260-1

Library of Congress Cataloging-in-Publication Data

Names: Gildea, Niall, author.
Title: Jacques Derrida's Cambridge Affair / Niall Gildea.
Description: Lanham : Rowman & Littlefield International, 2019. | Series: Futures of the archive | Includes bibliographical references and index.
Identifiers: LCCN 2019038363 (print) | LCCN 2019038364 (ebook) |
  ISBN 9781786612601 (cloth) | ISBN 9781786612618 (epub)
  ISBN 9781538148129 (pbk)
Subjects: LCSH: Derrida, Jacques. | University of Cambridge—Degrees. | Degrees, Academic.
Classification: LCC B2430.D484 G55 2019 (print) | LCC B2430.D484 (ebook) | DDC 194—dc23
LC record available at https://lccn.loc.gov/2019038363
LC ebook record available at https://lccn.loc.gov/2019038364

Contents

Introduction   vii

PART 1   1

1   Reprising the Cambridge Affair   3
     Deconstruction and 'the University'   6
     Prince Philip and the Flysheets   9
     Responses to the Cambridge Affair   16
     The Orator   33

PART 2   45

2   Some Kantian Stereotypes: (The Conflict of) *The Conflict of the Faculties*   47
     The Ethics of Authenticity   51
     'Free Play'   58
     Grafting Philosophy   64
     (The Conflict of) *The Conflict of the Faculties*   66

3   The Place of Philosophy   77
     The Cambridge Affair in the History of Philosophy   78
     Impossible Grammar   85
     Impossible Worlds   91
     Interiority Complex   96
     The Philosopher and the Inside   102

4   Repudiations: Derrida and Thatcher   121
     Philosophy in Rehab   121

Philistines 127
Derrida and Thatcher 134

PART 3 **143**

5 'Préférance' 145
   Preference 1: Martin Hägglund 146
   Preference 2: J. Hillis Miller 153
   Preference 3: Ernesto Laclau 159

6 Dénégations 165
   Negative Theology, Deconstruction, and Exemplarity 165
   The Three Paradigms 170
      1: Greek 170
      2: Christian 172
      3: Other 178
   Ailleurs 183

Afterword 195

Bibliography 199

Index 215

About the Author 217

Introduction

On Wednesday, March 18, 1992, in the *Cambridge University Reporter*, Cambridge's Vice-Chancellor announces the nine individuals on whom Honorary Degrees are to be conferred that year. For the title 'Doctor of Letters, *honoris causa*', Jacques Derrida's name was given, in the form of a 'Grace to be submitted to the Regent House at a Congregation on 21 March 1992 [. . .] That the title of the Degree of Doctor of Letters, *honoris causa*, be conferred under Statute B, IV upon JACQUES DERRIDA, Directeur d'Études, École des Hautes Études en Sciences Sociales, Paris. [. . .] It is expected that admission to the title of the degree will take place at a Congregation to be held on Friday, 12 June 1992'.[1]

A week later, the Vice-Chancellor announces the following:

> The Graces for the conferment of Honorary Degrees in 1992 were published in the *Reporter* on 18 March and were submitted to the Regent House at the Congregation on 21 March. At the Congregation notice of *non placet* was given in respect of Grace 5, for the conferment of the Honorary Degree of Doctor of Letters on M. Jacques Derrida, Directeur d'Études, École des Hautes Études en Sciences Sociales, Paris. Under the provisions of Regulation 17 for the conduct of business the Grace was withdrawn; the Vice-Chancellor gives notice that a Congregation will be held at 2 p.m. on Saturday, 16 May 1992, when the Grace will be resubmitted and a vote will be taken. Voting will be in person at the Congregation.[2]

This notice of *non placet* ('It is not pleasing'), and the announcement that a vote would have to be taken on Derrida's Honorary Doctorate, marked the beginning of an academic debate now known as the 'Cambridge Affair'. Derrida's work – and, occasionally, more personal matters – were weighed against concepts as diverse as Cambridge's institutional reputation, the nobility of the discipline of philosophy, and creeping neoliberalism in the British university.

Derrida would be awarded his Honorary by a majority of 336 to 204. This is really not that large, given how many of these degrees are formalities, and/or attempts by universities to signal their awareness of wider cultural trends by putting gowns on DJs, retired footballers and famous gardeners. The irony of the Cambridge Affair is that Honorary Degrees are with due respect often very trivial matters, which would not usually be seen as saying anything very profound about the values of the awarding institution.

Between the *non placet* notice of March 1992, and the final article written on the Affair, in June 1993, a group of academics mostly from one university argued over whether a third party's oeuvre was truly worthy of the name 'Philosophy'. Derrida's is a body of work that questions with uncommon force the presuppositions underpinning such a debate. As will become clear, the question of philosophy is really where the Affair begins and ends. Derrida's nomination had been made by members of Cambridge's English and modern languages faculties, and the fact that this had happened without the say-so of the philosophy faculty produced the point of contention from which all others followed.

Many believed that if the nomination ought to have come from anyone, it ought to have come from the philosophy faculty – and if it did not come from them, then it should not have come at all. This demand squarely to identify Derrida as part of one already existing discipline, with already existing contours, is of a piece with the kind of positivism that is at present handicapping many junior researchers in the humanities and posing a threat to academic meritocracy. And it certainly is doing no favours for the study of philosophy. For all that humanities departments tubthump about 'interdisciplinarity', researchers whose profiles do not already situate them safely within a given discipline are at a major disadvantage in the accurately named 'academic job *market*'. I remember being advised by a very senior Professor of Renaissance Studies that my research on Derrida would enjoy greater 'impact' were I to get into the habit of referring to him as a 'mad Frenchman'. And this at a time when many literature departments in Britain believe that just about anyone could teach a bit of theory on the side.

But at the same time, a serious reading of the ideas of philosophy – the *philosophies* of philosophy – invoked in this debate shows that this imagined disciplinary stability is a kind of fantasy. The more that the absolute facticity of philosophy is insisted upon in the Cambridge Affair, the more the philosophical archive to which this insistence appeals buckles under the weight of this quasi-theological claim. If this book were condensed into one statement, that would be it. In my view, this makes the Affair a highly useful case study that highlights, for instance, problems both with absolute defences of existing canons and with facetious claims to be in the business of 'busting' or 'decolonizing' them.

Have I therefore sought to 'deconstruct' the Cambridge Affair in this book? No – people who claim to have 'deconstructed' this or that tend to have done nothing of the kind. I don't think Derrida ever announced that he had successfully finished deconstructing anything. What I have done is to try to understand the Affair according to an ethics of nuanced reading that Derrida certainly *did* practise, even if whether what he was doing was deconstruction itself, or but one dimension of a more thoroughgoing deconstruction, or something else entirely, remains an open question.

The book is divided into three parts. Part 1 recaps thoroughly and prosaically the substance of the Cambridge Affair, whose details will be unfamiliar to many readers. I wouldn't advise reading any other parts of the book until you have read that one. I will warn conspiracy theorists now that there is no great secret at the heart of the Affair – no major antagonist, nothing like that. There is, however, a quite extraordinary debate over the nature of philosophy, through which the broader philosophical past reverberates uncannily. This is the focus of the three chapters that comprise part 2. Chapter 2 is about Kant's *Conflict of the Faculties* and how it both underpins and undermines the *non placet* case. Chapter 3 looks at the appeal to an 'inside' proper to philosophy, and at the philosophical history of this appeal. Chapter 4 focuses on the claim made during the Affair that Derrida's work bore some resemblance to Thatcherite conservatism and represented a similar threat to the university institution at large. Part 3 comprises two chapters that interrogate the major blind spot of the Affair on both sides of the debate: the desirability, and the straightforwardness, of belonging to an institution. Chapter 5 examines three attempts to make Derrida 'belong' (to atheism, to deconstruction, to Marxism), and chapter 6 reads Derrida's great text on institutions, 'How to Avoid Speaking: Denials', as a rigorous thesis on belonging that comprehends the Cambridge Affair six years in advance.

NOTES

1. *Cambridge University Reporter*, Vol. 122, No. 22 (Wednesday March 18 1992), 509.
2. *Reporter*, Vol. 122, No. 23 (Wednesday March 25 1992), 514.

Part 1

Chapter 1

Reprising the Cambridge Affair

There was this terrible honorary degree crisis in Cambridge.[1]

Inevitably, it will be known as 'the Derrida affair', though [. . .] it might from another perspective be more justly denominated '*l'affaire Cambridge*'.[2]

. . . leaving aside the Cambridge affair. . .[3]

'The Cambridge Affair' is the name given to the debate concerning Jacques Derrida's proposed, and ultimately awarded, honorary doctorate of letters at Cambridge University in 1992. It is referred to frequently in biographies of and introductions to Derrida, but always in adumbration.[4] Retrospective accounts of the Affair tend to be only schematic narratives or foot- or endnotes. The brevity of these synopses has produced the oversimplification of two principal interpretations. The first views the Affair as one episode of many in the 'Theory Wars' of the final three decades of the twentieth century.[5] The second – an interpretation rejected by Derrida[6] – regards it as emblematic of a longer-term enmity between British and French philosophy going back at least as far as the eighteenth century.[7]

This simplification perhaps follows from the fact that Derrida himself refrained from subjecting the Affair to a thoroughgoing analysis, stating more than once that he had 'abstained' from writing a polemical text about the Affair. Accepting an honorary doctorate from the University of Silesia in Katowice in December 1997, Derrida referred to 'a polemic [about the Affair] from which I have always abstained',[8] and in his honorary doctorate acceptance address at the University of Coimbra in November 2003, this phrase and his broader summary of the Affair were rehearsed verbatim.[9] Whatever the reasons for Derrida's abstinence, one of its effects has been that outright critics of Derrida have expended more words on the topic of the Affair than have those supportive of his work. I maintain throughout this book that the Cambridge Affair was neither simply symptomatic of the Theory Wars, nor of intellectual jingoism, but is best understood as a debate in which the question of philosophical propriety, proper-to-philosophy, was debated and determined (not to mention cathected) from several perspectives.

I show in chapter 2 that the debate elaborates the logic of Immanuel Kant's late text, *The Conflict of the Faculties*. The university becomes the institution in which Kant's ideal of scholarship – articulated most succinctly in 'What Is Enlightenment?' – practically can be realized.[10] For Kant, the 'lower faculty' of philosophy has no civic obligation (its research does not answer to state imperatives), but it can be of civic use: The onus is on the state to 'listen to', to *hear* (*höre*) the philosopher,[11] whilst promising to the philosophy faculty an unimpeachable autonomy and autotely; hence philosophy's contrast to the 'higher faculties' of law, medicine, and theology, whose ends are the training of students for civic positions in those fields. It is valid to object that the philosophy faculty's autonomy *already* may have been impeached by this contract with the state; Derrida has illustrated this constitutive paradox of Kant's model.[12] In the present chapter, I prepare this relation to Kant's text by describing the Cambridge Affair in detail. But there are other important contexts for the Affair, which are worth going over here; they are discussed more thoroughly in the chapters that follow.

The first is the immediate political context. The Affair played out alongside the run-up to the general election of 1992, which saw John Major's Conservatives defeat Neil Kinnock's Labour Party. Although there were few explicit references to the election (those that were made are outlined in chapter 4), many parallels were made by Derrida's opponents between the Thatcherite interference in academia throughout the 1980s and the growing influence in the university of 'Continental' (predominantly French) philosophy and theory, for which Derrida was considered a synecdoche. To preview only the most overt juxtaposition here, Brian Hebblethwaite, whose retrospective article on the Affair is summarized later in this chapter, avers that

> Our universities are held in contempt anyway by a government of philistines[.] [. . .] There seems to be little we can do to reverse this. But I should have thought we could have avoided the internal contempt we bring upon ourselves when instead of repudiating the enemies of reason, truth and objectivity, we honour them.[13]

This passage presents what was, for many of those opposed to Derrida's honorary, the major issue subtending the Affair. An important filiation is perceived between governmental interference in the university, said to subordinate the institution to the logic of corporatism from without, and Derrida's work, said to do something analogous from within. This is a version of an older accusation about the complicity of 'theory' with the neoliberal professionalization of the university (one made, for example, by Terry Eagleton, whose critique of deconstruction is addressed momentarily). But it is intensified and made more specific by the fact that the Cambridge Affair took place at a moment that could have halted Thatcherism, but did not.

Readers familiar with historical objections to Derrida's work will have noticed that this is a quite different accusation from the ones that hold that it is simply inimical to *any* idea of the university or of philosophy. That more basic charge does feature prominently during the Cambridge Affair, but it is presented as though there were no friction between it, on the one hand, and the charge of neoliberalism, on the other. In my view, this overdetermination of the case against Derrida, as well as being an important trope undergirding the making of that case, also echoes a crucial gesture in Kant's *Conflict of the Faculties*, in which the philosopher relies upon a formally identical overdetermination to make his case for philosophy's policing of its borders. I address this important moment in Kant's text in chapter 2.

There is another pertinent political reading of the Cambridge Affair, which argues that the case against Derrida actually evinces the very neoliberal logic it repudiates. I make this argument at length in chapter 4, but the simple précis is that the particular sovereignty, a fusion of authority and capability prior to hegemony or ideology, in which terms the philosophy faculty is articulated in the written case against Derrida, actually corresponds exactly to contemporary Thatcherite discourse concerning higher education. What this means is that there is a genealogical link between the neoliberal reforms lamented by some of Derrida's opponents (in which Derridean philosophy was said to participate), and the Kantian idea of the university, which those reforms were perceived to threaten. This bears out Derrida's argument, made in a group of texts on the university in the 1970s and '80s, about the deconstruction at work in Kant's university model.

The second major context is that of Derrida's oeuvre – two features of it specifically. First, the Cambridge Affair develops from an initial disputation over Derrida's style, in particular its perceived nonseriousness, or 'free play', which sets it at odds with authentic philosophy. This continues to be an ambient issue in debates surrounding Derrida, but here it has definite reference points that can be traced to better understand where that accusation comes from, and what presuppositions ground it. Again, the term goes back to Kant, but not only to his aesthetic theory broadly conceived: It actually appears at a crucial moment in *The Conflict of the Faculties*, where it is the term Kant uses to clarify the qualitative distinction between the philosophy faculty and those of law, medicine, and theology. Hence, one of the principal 'nonphilosophical' characteristics of Derrida's work is actually the very attribute by which Kant's philosophy faculty is able to take shape. In chapter 2, I look closely at this transplantation of 'free play' from Kant to Derrida, and what it means for his critics.

The second aspect of Derrida's oeuvre that is at issue here is significant precisely because it is not addressed in the Cambridge Affair literature. Both sides of the debate share a rather blasé approach when it comes to ideas about community and institution, and the relationships between these. It seems taken for granted that 'belonging' to a university, qua community or institution, is a relatively straightforward matter. However, subtending terms like 'community', 'institution', and even 'belonging' is the concept of *Mitsein* (being-with) that Derrida certainly does not take for granted. Accordingly, in chapters 5 and 6 of this book, I discuss community, institution, and belonging, both in Derrida's work, and in certain major critical attempts to categorize that work; my examples are readings of Derrida by Martin Hägglund, J. Hillis Miller, and Ernesto Laclau. The point of this exercise is to try to think deconstructively about this blind spot that nevertheless makes possible the Cambridge Affair debate.

The Cambridge Affair ended abruptly. *Cambridge Minds*, a volume published in 1994 advertising the contribution of the university to the nation's well-being, does not refer to it,[14] and nothing substantial was published on the matter after the symposia. However, the questions raised during the Affair about deconstruction, philosophy, and the university merit detailed treatment.

DECONSTRUCTION AND 'THE UNIVERSITY'

In this chapter, I give readers a clear sense of the texts that comprise the Cambridge Affair. These principally were the flysheets circulated in Cambridge that offered reasons why one might vote in a particular way, and the articles that followed the award of Derrida's honorary, which offered interpretations of what was at stake in the Affair. The present volume will only make passing reference to the coverage of the Affair in the popular media, because nothing was said or written there that was not based substantially on the flysheets and articles I explicate. There would be much to consider in formal terms, as Derrida does in *Paper Machine*, about mediatic agendas and extrapolations, but I restrict myself here to what I adjudge to be particular to the Cambridge Affair – namely, the question of philosophy's disciplinary and institutional preeminence, both as virtual reference and actual performance.

If there is a rhetorical cornerstone of the Affair for those critical of Derrida's honorary, it is the belief in an enigmatic homology between 'philosophy' and 'the university', the surety of which is menaced by Derrida, who thereby becomes its symptom. But because this homology and the implied values on which it is based are articulated for the first time reactively, as a counteragent to the Derrida contagion (they react to the proposal of Derrida's honorary, to its award, or to both), then Derrida remains the condition of the homology's possibility whilst being a threat to its functionality; hence, there is a strictly symptomatic logic at work (describing the Affair, Derrida states, 'This little event is symptomatic of a number of things [Cette petite histoire est grosse de symptômes assez divers]'[15]).

Troubled unconsciously by this symptomatic quality of Derrida's work, these critics overwrite it with the related but more orthodox 'othering' trope of the parasite. The charge of parasitism has accompanied deconstruction at least since Derrida's work began to be translated in the United States and Britain, and during the Cambridge Affair it was important for Derrida's critics: Sarah Richmond branded Derrida's work 'poison for young people'; the *Observer* newspaper called Derrida a 'computer virus';[16] and Barry Smith argued that Derrida's work 'translates into the academic sphere tricks and gimmicks similar to those of the Dadaists or of the concrete poets'.[17] These charges share an argument that the 'threat' Derrida embodies is derivative rather than inceptive. That is, one needs a healthy body in order to poison it; one needs a working computer in order for a virus to corrupt it; one needs an organic 'academic sphere' in order to smuggle contraband into it. This is why the conceptual persona of the parasite recurs here – the parasite's putative secondary nature, or de-nature, means it is a trope made to follow the constitution of a fixed chronology and topology. The parasitism charge displaces the more disquieting trope of the symptom: The symptom troubles this spatial and temporal fixity because it is not secondary, but constitutive and generative. Derrida, in the only interview he gave about the Cambridge Affair, addresses this question: He wonders whether his critics considered something they knew, and recognized – his work – or whether they 'attacked' a more phantasmatic unknown:

> If it were only a question of "my" work, of the particular or isolated research of one individual, this wouldn't happen. Indeed, the violence of these denunciations derives from the fact that the work accused [le travail incriminé] is part of a whole ongoing process. What is unfolding here, like the resistance it necessarily arouses, can't be limited to a personal "oeuvre," nor to a discipline, nor even to the academic institution [ne se lasse confiner ni dans une "oeuvre" personnelle, ni dans une discipline, ni même dans l'institution académique]. Nor in particular to a generation: it's often the active involvement of students and younger teachers which makes certain of our colleagues nervous to the point that they lose their sense of moderation and of the academic rules they invoke when they attack me and my work [quand ils s'attaquent à moi].[18]

Derrida indicates three things here: First, that his work is *already* part of something; it already participates in the constitution of a 'process', and at the same time it is already constituted by this process's continuousness. Second, the resistance to this work, far from being a diagnosis of it, actually participates, wittingly or otherwise, in the same continuous process. Third, this process is not reducible to conventional ways of understanding the university, like authorship, disciplinary frontiers, and hierarchical distinctions between persons or disciplines. For Derrida, the 'violence' of some of this criticism is rooted in the fact that it knows at some level that the parasitism charge represents the intervention of a kind of censorship that represses its imbrication with its nemesis even as it is motivated, or even possibilized, by it.

Derrida argues here that 'attacks' on himself and his work have something to do with contemporary changes in the university at large. One way of seeing Derrida's point more specifically is to look at how in the Cambridge Affair (as readers will pick up from my comments on the flysheets and symposia articles, below), there develop two objections to Derrida's work that are difficult to reconcile. Derrida is, on the one hand, regarded as a seductive, poisonous, threatening figure for considered study of literature, philosophy, and the humanities in toto. However, at the same time, an interpretation emerges wherein Derrida and deconstruction are seen as acquiescent to or even emblematic of an emergent idea of the university as a purely instrumental institution devoid of concerns beyond disingenuous professionalization. Since the Affair followed more than a decade of Thatcherite incursions into the humanities founded on this instrumentalizing intent, and since the controversy about Derrida's honorary was taking place during the months leading up to the 1992 general election, it is unsurprising that some identified an isomorphism between what Stefan Collini calls 'the Thatcher government's *Kulturkampf* against universities'[19] and a perceived refusal from deconstruction to affirm or admit of the humanities any special status.

The first objection is familiar to anyone with a cursory knowledge of debates surrounding the 'Theory Wars' in Britain and the United States from the 1960s onwards, but the second (made most famously in the United States by John Guillory in his *Cultural Capital*,[20] albeit about Paul de Man) actually plays a more significant role in the Cambridge Affair. Some years prior to the Affair, Terry Eagleton insisted on the isomorphism of 'Anglophone' or 'Yale' deconstruction and the instrumentalization of the university. He argued that such deconstruction was a response to contemporary crises in criticism that instead of combating the disadvantageous working conditions in which criticism finds itself, sought cynically and in a self-abasing manner to appropriate those conditions into a methodology:

It is certainly tempting to see Anglophone deconstruction as that crisis theorized, canonized, internalized, gathered up into the academy as a new set of textual techniques or fresh injection of intellectual capital to eke out its dwindling resources. The deconstructionist disownment of authority is plainly in line with the politics of the '60s; yet it is nothing so simplistic as the view that lectures are a form of violence. For what after all could be more unanswerably authoritative than a discourse which, in the very act of pulling the carpet from under its opponents, presents them with a profile so attenuated that there is no place to hit it, which cannot be knocked down because it is always already sprawling helplessly on the floor? No more aggressive form of *kenosis* could be imagined, short of [Henry] James's later heroines.[21]

A strange hybrid emerges. Deconstruction is a countercultural practice that has 'sold out': Unable and/or unwilling to counter the ruination of the humanities, it offers a critical model that celebrates this ruination in a manner that, through its 'aggressive *kenosis*', has a certain anti-Christian aspect. But this is a cynical doomsday cult:

> The deconstructive gesture, Hillis Miller has argued, always fails, 'so that it has to be performed again and again, interminably'. This is certainly a reassuring kind of failure to run up against – one that promises to keep you in a job indefinitely, unlike those research programmes which frustratingly run out of steam just as you are about to gain promotion.[22]

Although the deconstruction Eagleton discusses 'eradicates all traces of the political from [Derrida's] work',[23] such an apprehension of it – without the dubious helpfulness of Eagleton's vague caveat – is foregrounded during the Cambridge Affair, alongside the consensus that Derrida's work is alien to the university, however that institution is understood. Nowhere is the unsteadiness of this double charge questioned in the literature, even by the *placet* side; this lacuna accords with a general absence of reference, during the Affair, to Derrida's texts on the subject of the university. This book draws from these to refute this double charge.

PRINCE PHILIP AND THE FLYSHEETS

As chancellor of the University of Cambridge (a position he held from 1976 to 2011), it fell to His Royal Highness Prince Philip to award Derrida his doctorate on June 12, 1992. Doing so, he emblematized much of the Affair's cultural significance. Alwyn Turner alleges of Philip that 'when he presented an honorary degree to the French philosopher Jacques Derrida, the father of deconstruction theory, he was heard to mutter that his own family seemed to be deconstructing'.[24] It overstates things to foreground this connection between deconstruction and familial breakdown,[25] but Philip's quip does convey an assumption about deconstruction *as* destruction, which had been shared by those opposing Derrida's honorary.[26] Similarly, a cheat sheet for Philip from Cambridge, advising him of charismatic ways of conversing with Derrida at the honorary degree ceremony, recommends the following: 'Derrida has a sense of humour, and if the Chancellor were to refer to some such phrase as "deconstruction of the Honorary Degree Ceremony" he would enjoy it'.[27] Whether Derrida did get to enjoy this witticism, or it became the remark Turner reports, these curios indicate that the Cambridge Affair played an important role in 'deconstruction' becoming a pejorative term.

Philip's broad jokes about deconstruction are consonant with much of the contemporary journalism about the Cambridge Affair. Whether because anticipation of the general election of that year monopolized 'serious' column inches, or because the Affair was perceived as intrinsically farcical,[28] newspaper coverage of the debate tended toward the flippant (the media coverage is discussed by Susannah Thomas, Cambridge's information officer at the time, in an article I address later in this chapter). The case against Derrida was more media-friendly than its counterpart, thanks to newspaper articles which parodied deconstruction or exaggerated its incomprehensibility.[29] The opposition to Derrida's honorary helped consolidate a media shorthand of 'deconstruction' that still obtains at the present time. Per Eagleton, 'The word was abroad that this purveyor of fashionable French gobbledegook was a charlatan and a nihilist, a man who believed that anything could mean anything and that there was nothing in the world but writing'.[30] Rachel Bowlby rightly argues that the Affair began to make Derrida into a 'household name' in Britain,[31] but one should stress that this happened more due to the case against Derrida than its counterpart.

The journalistic version should not obscure what was an urgent and nuanced debate. To establish what was actually at issue, it is important to reprise the Cambridge Affair in detail. This reprisal is tripartite: First, I summarize the five 'flysheets' circulated in Cambridge enjoining members to vote either for or against Derrida's honorary; second, I précis the primary literature about the Affair; and third, I analyze the Affair's construal of deconstruction.

It is worth recapping the particulars of how the Affair began. On Saturday, March 21, 1992, the proposal that Jacques Derrida be made an honorary doctor of letters at Cambridge University was formally opposed by some academic staff from Cambridge's English and philosophy departments. Howard Erskine-Hill, Ian Jack, D. H. Mellor, and Raymond Page attended the Congregation of Cambridge's Regent House that day to register the declaration *non placet*. This meant that the award of Derrida's honorary would be put to a vote

– a highly unusual procedure in the conferral of honorary degrees. The previous Cambridge honorand to have his nomination decided this way had been Quintin Hogg, Lord Hailsham, in 1963. Hailsham at the time was the Conservative Party's minister for science, and shortly after being nominated for an honorary doctorate of law at Cambridge, had spoken in the House of Lords against the widespread emigration to the United States of British scientists. Hailsham suggested that the United States, lacking a good school system, had to 'live [. . .] parasitically on the brains of other nations to supply [her] own needs'.[32] Hailsham received his honorary doctorate by a slender majority of twenty votes, and his is a useful case to compare to Derrida's because Hailsham's xenophobic comment is the kind of thing that typically would provoke a declaration *non placet*. Additionally, it should be emphasized that Hailsham's charge of 'parasite' was what threatened his incorporation into Cambridge University, whereas during the Cambridge Affair this charge, and ones cognate with it, were levelled *against* Derrida from *within* the university.

In response to the 'Derrida *non placet*' notice, a *placet* case was put together, and members of the university collaboratively authored and circulated 'flysheets', short documents supporting either the *placet* or *non placet* vote. The *non placet* campaign resorted at times to questionable tactics, principally the claim that Derrida was an apologist for Paul de Man's wartime journalism and what was called de Man's anti-Semitism.[33] However, fabulation was not the sole preserve of the *non placets*. In Prince Philip's aforementioned cheat sheet, there is this odd juxtaposition: 'Derrida is a Jew from North Africa, and proud of it. He has sometimes been smeared with allegations of anti-Semitism'.[34] A letter from David Williams (then Cambridge's vice-chancellor) to Brian McGrath (private secretary to Prince Philip), mingles fact and fiction: 'Derrida is a courageous man – he was imprisoned by the Nazis during the war and by the Communist government in Czechoslovakia later – and is of international repute in his field'. Williams's letter reassures Philip that the debate over Derrida's honorary was purely 'on matters to do with M. Derrida's intellectual contribution rather than on moral or political grounds', and yet its content indicates that this distinction did not always obtain during the dispute.[35] Whether this invented Nazi imprisonment was a simple mistake, or an overdetermined corrective to the charge of Derrida's anti-Semitism, it was certainly illustrative of a discussion that did not solely focalize 'intellectual contribution'. According to Cambridge's Statutes at the time of writing, 'Titles of degrees may be granted *honoris causa* to members of the Royal Family, to British subjects who are of conspicuous merit or have done good service to the State or to the University, and to foreigners of distinction'.[36] However, the discernment of 'distinction' is unclear and problematic.

With no face-to-face debates prior to the vote on Derrida's honorary, the flysheets circulated in support of the *placet* and *non placet* positions determined the contours of the issue. There were three flysheets on the *placet* side of the debate, and two representing the *non placet*.[37]

The first *placet* flysheet begins by outlining Derrida's 'eminence' and 'international scholarly standing', arguing that his work's incorporation of literary criticism, creative writing, and philosophy situates it 'in a genre which has had a continuous tradition in France since at least the eighteenth century'. It identifies further interdisciplinary influences of Derrida's thought, arising from his early engagements with Husserl and Heidegger. The flysheet argues that the objection to Derrida's proposed doctorate is based merely on a disagreement with 'the intellectual positions he has developed and encouraged', and that this founds the debate on a question of consensus inimical to the type of institution – the university – which would confer this honorific: 'A university is precisely an institution in which such disagreement and such plurality of view can and should be encouraged'. The flysheet concludes by opining that the *non placet* declaration was 'ill-judged', stating that 'It has done harm to this University's reputation for courtesy, and it has already attracted considerable adverse publicity'.[38]

The second flysheet is a 'top persons' flysheet, signed by eighteen Masters of Colleges.[39] At issue in this flysheet is not the particular case of Derrida: Its authors state that they present it '[w]ithout seeking to involve ourselves in the academic issues involved'. It contends that the request for a vote is 'gratuitously insulting', and contradicts Cambridge's accepted protocol concerning honorary degrees:

> By convention, nominations for Honorary Degrees have in the past been challenged on either of two grounds. The first is when something to the detriment of the recipient emerges which was not available to the Council of the Senate's nominating committee. The second is when the proposed recipient is a national politician, and when the nomination is opposed on political grounds. Neither is applicable in the case of Jacques Derrida.

The flysheet concedes that it may be the case that 'the University's procedures need revision to allow for wider consultation before an Honorary Degree is offered', but insists that on this occasion, Cambridge would become embroiled in an inappropriate controversy were it to condone 'the censorious intervention of one segment of the academic community'.[40]

The third *placet* flysheet summates Derrida's philosophy of language as derived from his reading of Husserl: 'Where Husserl held that the meaning of language depends on the self-conscious intentions and beliefs of speakers, Derrida argued that language is a social practice within which the conscious thoughts of speakers have no privileged position in the determination of meaning'. According to this flysheet, Derrida has developed this insight into a broader theory of thought, 'arguing that in this case too the content of thought is not determined by the thinker's current consciousness, but by the temporally extended rôle within the subject's life of the signs of this thought'. The flysheet argues that this thesis anchors the three central 'themes' of Derrida's work: 'the critique of the "metaphysics of presence,"' 'the commitment to an open-ended process of interpretation and re-interpretation', and '"deconstruction", an affirmation of the connectedness and interdependence of apparently opposed concepts'. *Pace* the objection that this is nihilistic, the flysheet argues that Derrida does not seek to replace 'presence' with 'absence', but instead to question ('to "deconstruct"') the binary between presence and absence, 'in order to reveal the links between thought, language, and the world'.[41]

The first *non placet* flysheet begins with a paragraph that is decisive for an understanding of the Affair:

> We most seriously oppose the Council of the Senate's proposal to award an honorary doctorate to the philosopher Jacques Derrida. While we regret any embarrassment caused by the request for a vote, we would point out that had the Council consulted the Philosophy Faculty, they would have realized how controversial the proposal is. Since the Council have no special knowledge in this matter, there can be no presumption that their proposal must be accepted just because it has been made public. Our Statutes allow for the expression of dissent on these occasions, and a vote, however it goes, will at least prevent the University endorsing without reflection doctrines which we believe undermine its intellectual foundations.

By referring to Derrida as a 'philosopher', and yet calling his proposed honorary 'controversial' from the perspective of the 'Philosophy Faculty', the flysheet implies that Derrida's honorary, although strictly a doctorate of letters, should be arbitrated as one of philosophy: The 'doctrines' ascribed to Derrida have a particular relation to philosophy. The philosophy faculty should have been consulted to supply the 'special knowledge' lacked by the Council of the Senate, and to ensure that the proposal was not unreflective. By virtue of this relation to philosophy, Derrida's work has inauspicious consequences for the 'intellectual foundations' of the university; there is, therefore, a privileged function being attributed to philosophy in relation to the university at large. I read this logic closely in chapter 3 of this book.

The flysheet denies that its objection to Derrida merely derives from disagreement with his work. Accepting that 'major new work is apt to be controversial' in any discipline, it insists that Derrida is 'controversial in a special sense', insofar as 'the major preoccupation of his voluminous work has been to deny and to dissolve those standards of evidence and argument on which all academic disciplines are based'. Next, it argues that Derrida cannot properly be considered a sceptic, 'for real sceptics apply objective criteria to challenge established orthodoxies', whereas Derrida 'appears to acknowledge no such criteria'. Nor is Derrida especially important as a philosopher of language: His contributions to this field 'do not, for example, begin to compare with those of Wittgenstein'. Derrida's insights, or at least those 'widely attributed to him', such as 'the need to examine the unacknowledged presuppositions of any discourse, to attend to philosophers' metaphors as well as to their logic, and to realize that language is not used only to convey information', are unoriginal.

The flysheet addresses more recent work 'by Derrida and his followers', in which these attitudes to language 'have been inflated into absurd but fatal falsehoods'. This has been particularly egregious in literary studies, 'in which deconstruction has been invoked to transform texts virtually beyond recognition', despite the welcome criticism of this 'fashion' from some individuals otherwise sympathetic to Derrida's work. However, the flysheet argues, it is a moot point whether Derrida himself endorses this application of his work, since his texts 'themselves assert both the irrelevance of an author's views and the impossibility of distinguishing correct from incorrect interpretations'.

The flysheet concludes with a summation of the threats posed by Derrida's 'doctrines' across 'all serious academic subjects': Notions of canon, periodization, and accuracy are compromised in literary studies; anachronism becomes acceptable in history; the significance of precedents and statutes in law is debunked; science, technology, and medicine are rendered obsolete by the denial of 'the distinctions between fact and fiction, observation and imagination, evidence and prejudice' and in the domain of politics, Derrida's work 'deprive[s] the mind of its defences against dangerously irrational ideologies and regimes'. The flysheet acknowledges that 'Derrida's bad influence has been felt more widely in the humanities than in the sciences', and argues that this influence lends credence to a caricature of the humanities, whereby the latter 'lack both the practical utility and the intellectual seriousness needed to justify proper public funding'. But Derrida's work also 'threaten[s] the very basis of all subjects', and so, 'at a most difficult time for higher education', opposition to it is of paramount importance.[42]

Much shorter than the first, the second *non placet* flysheet counters the argument of the second *placet*: that the opposition to Derrida's honorary is 'contrary to the interests of the University'. It contends that the implementation of a vote, because of the democratic nature of the same, cannot possibly be 'a discourtesy to any individual': The true discourtesy would be to acquiesce to Derrida's nomination solely to 'avoid embarrassment or adverse publicity for ourselves'. Insisting, like the first *non placet*, that objections to Derrida's nomination do not stem merely from disagreement with his 'doctrines', the flysheet amplifies the grave claims made in the opening paragraph of the first: Now, 'M. Derrida's doctrines [. . .] undermine the fundamental grounds which provide a place in the scheme of things for intellectual enquiry in any field; and so, for the very existence of universities in society'.[43]

Although not strictly a flysheet, it is appropriate to include here the most well-known[44] corroboration of the *non placet* position: Barry Smith's letter to the *Times* newspaper, countersigned by eighteen academics from around the world,[45] which was published on Saturday, May 9, a week before the Cambridge vote. This letter, entitled 'Derrida Degree a Question of Honour' and later termed by Smith a 'conscientious objection',[46] positions itself as a conduit between the academic controversy concerning Derrida's honorary and its attention in the public sphere: 'We believe that the following might shed some needed light on the public debate that has arisen over this issue'. According to Smith, those who declined to countersign his letter did so precisely in objection to its tone of censorious intervention. Roderick Chisholm, for example, argued that 'America should not serve as the world's police force' on this matter.[47]

For Smith and his countersignatories, although Derrida 'describes himself as a philosopher', his influence pertains instead to 'fields outside philosophy', such as film studies and French and English literary studies, and this justifies resistance to his honorary: 'If the works of a physicist (say) were similarly taken to be of merit primarily by those working in other disciplines, this would in itself be sufficient grounds for casting doubt upon the idea that the physicist in question was a suitable candidate for an honorary degree'. Moreover, Derrida's work is regarded by 'philosophers, and certainly [. . .] those working in leading departments of philosophy throughout the world' as inadequate to 'accepted standards of clarity and rigour'. The view from France reportedly is that Derrida is a 'cause for silent embarrassment', enshrining a caricature of contemporary French philosophy as 'little more than an object of ridicule'.

As a personage whose intellectual 'roots' are 'in the heady days of the 1960s' and whose works continually reveal this racination, Derrida 'seems to us to have come close to making a career out of what we regard as translating into the academic sphere tricks and gimmicks similar to those of the Dadaists or of the concrete poets'. At this juncture, the letter resorts to quasi-citation, referring to Derrida's 'elaborate jokes and the puns "logical phallusies" and the like', although Derrida categorically refutes this pun's occurrence in his oeuvre.[48] Although Derrida's way with jokes evinces 'considerable originality', this, again, is no reason to award him an honorary degree. Finally, Derrida's incomprehensible written style, although regarded by his supporters as correlative to the difficulty of the ideas it conveys, actually masks what are in truth 'false or trivial' assertions: 'Academic status based on what seems to us to be little more than semi-intelligible attacks upon the values of reason, truth, and scholarship is not, we submit, sufficient grounds for the awarding of an honorary degree in a distinguished university'.⁴⁹

RESPONSES TO THE CAMBRIDGE AFFAIR

After Derrida had been awarded the honorary by a majority of 336 to 204, representatives from both sides of the motion were invited to contribute to an edition of the *Cambridge Review* dedicated to the Affair. This round of articles elicited responses that appeared in another edition, four months later. Hence, the closest things to texts 'about' the Cambridge Affair are the 'Symposium' compiled in the October 1992 issue of the *Cambridge Review* entitled 'Reflections on "The Derrida Affair,"' and a collection of articles, also entitled 'Reflections on "The Derrida Affair,"' published in the same organ in February 1993.⁵⁰ This second collection will be referred to as 'The "Derrida Affair" Again', the title given to it on the cover of the February 1993 *Cambridge Review*. The June 1993 *Cambridge Review* includes a second article by Nicholas Denyer in response to an article in the second collection; I address this after my analysis of the article that prompted it. Finally, I will discuss the contributions by Howard Erskine-Hill in the December 1992 and February 1993 editions of the *Cambridge Review*, and the oration for Derrida, at the honorary degree ceremony, by Cambridge's orator, James Diggle. Several of these texts are revisited in the following chapters, but synopses of them now will clarify which aspects of the Affair were foregrounded or otherwise in these initial appraisals. I survey the articles in the Symposium in order of appearance.

Marian Jeanneret (later Marian Hobson), 'Opinio Regina Mundi?' (*placet*; 'Reflections on "The Derrida Affair"') begins by distinguishing between the conventions of voting anonymously, voting by signature, and signing a flysheet. This last has special status: 'More than an expressing of an opinion, it is a putting of one's name to something' (99). If this is the case, what does one make of the signatories' endorsement of the first *non placet* flysheet's advice that those curious about Derrida's work should consult Raymond Tallis's *Not Saussure*, 'a book which in a couple of paragraphs of limitless vulgarity presents a pitiable parody of modernist criticism beginning "Piss off, Geoffrey Hartman"'? (100). Jeanneret argues that Tallis's critique of Derrida's writings on Husserl exhibits 'no knowledge of [. . .] Husserl not derived from Derrida's own writings, so that when he attacks these latter, the phrases which imply a separate and informed reading of Husserl are specious' (100). For Jeanneret, Tallis both resorts to a vulgar parody of deconstruction, and parodies scholarship itself. This, I will show, is basically Derrida's own view of his detractors during the Affair.

Jeanneret observes that another text recommended by the *non placet* literature, John M. Ellis's *Against Deconstruction*, relies on the claim that the phrase 'free play' is Derrida's. As she notes, that phrase is an English translation of the word *jeu* inflected with a 'Kantian reference' that 'completely and mistakenly excludes the sense of play in a machine [to which Derrida is referring]' (102 n1). This significant caveat and the *non placet* ignorance thereof are discussed in the next chapter. Jeanneret argues that 'The *non-placet* flysheets attribute to Derrida "doctrines" [. . .] which not merely are never put forward in his books, but have been explicitly and roundly attacked there' (101); such tactics not only preclude substantive debate, but lend weight to the conviction that their coherence depends on such preclusion.

Nicholas Denyer, 'The Charms of Jacques Derrida' (*non placet*; 'Reflections on "The Derrida Affair"'), defends the *non placets* against the charge of insularity by maintaining that Derrida's work represents a 'fashion' in philosophy and therefore makes no intrinsic demand to be read. As evidence for the non-insularity of British philosophy, Denyer gives: the 'construction and assimilation of modern logic' as a 'great international philosophical enterprise of this century', in which British philosophy has been instrumental; and the fact that 'non-British thinkers from ten different countries should write to *The Times*, saying that Derrida's "antics" did not deserve an honorary doctorate' (103). The charge of insularity now 'easily refuted', Denyer contends that there is a 'streak in [British] culture' that only accepts something as not philosophically insular if it actively embraces specifically French philosophy, because this streak 'identifies the big wide world outside of us with the continent of Europe, and the continent of Europe with France' (103). Denyer concludes these meditations on the nature of synecdoche by suggesting that 'it may be that the fear of otherwise being or seeming philistine will predispose us to honour French philosophers regardless of their merits' (104).

Denyer now addresses 'why it was Derrida, as opposed to some other French thinker, whom this university chose to honour':

> Human beings like falsehood. They have an appetite for accepting with some part of their minds what they know to be false with another. Derrida caters for this appetite with remarks like 'la différence entre le signifié et le signifiant *n'est rien*' (his italics; *De La Grammatologie*, p. 37[51]). We all – including Derrida – know that this is false. (104)

In the interest of preparing a parody of Derrida – Denyer goes on to liken this attributed doctrine to 'the decorator, hired to put paper on your walls, [who] takes out a pencil and there inscribes the letters P, A, P, E and R' (104) – the wood has been mistaken for the trees. Here is a longer extract of the passage from which Denyer quotes:

> Dès *l'Introduction à la métaphysique*, Heidegger renonce au projet et au mot d'ontologie. La dissimulation nécessaire, originaire et irréductible du sens de l'être, son occulation dans l'éclosion même de la présence, ce retrait sans lequel il n'y aurait même pas d'histoire de l'être qui fût de part en part *histoire* et histoire de *l'être*, l'insistance de Heidegger à marquer que l'être ne se produit comme histoire que par le logos et n'est rien hors de lui, la différence entre l'être et l'étant, tout cela indique bien que, fondamentalement, rien n'échappe au mouvement du signifiant et que, en dernière instance, la différence entre le signifié et le signifiant *n'est rien*.[52]

Derrida is glossing Heidegger here, and actually challenges the latter's determination of nondifference later in the text. So it is instructive to note the irony of a discourse purporting to find falsehoods in Derrida not only proceeding via infelicity, but also using this to support a specious psychological insight about human beings '[having] an appetite for accepting with some part of their minds what they know to be false with another'. As I argue in the next chapter, a similar rebounding occurs where the phrase 'free play' is 'located' in Derrida's work – but Denyer's gesture is especially pertinent because the articles in this Symposium were intended to redeem the lack of debate taking place during the pre-vote phase of the Affair.

Denyer concludes by suggesting that Derrida attracts what he calls 'arts dons' because he offers the consolation, 'garbed in all the gorgeous pomp of theory', that 'there are no real things and we need not feel humbled by studying just words' (105). This allows arts dons to proceed safe in the knowledge that, although their own work is subjective and superficial (dealing only with language), so is the natural scientist's. This deduction is representative of the charge against deconstruction that it espouses a crass political position that reduces everything to a matter of linguistic differences, evacuating aesthetic, affective, and material concerns from discussions of art and factual concerns from discussions of science.

In 'Off Limits. Derrida in Cambridge' (*placet*; 'Reflections on "The Derrida Affair"'), Christopher Prendergast, like Jeanneret, foregrounds the question of scholarly irresponsibility: 'Since those who urged us to vote *non placet* did so on grounds of an appeal to notions of intellectual responsibility and scholarly standards (deemed to be the very foundation of the idea of a university), one must begin by remarking that those responsibilities and standards are betrayed by the very act of asking for the declaration of *non placet*' (106). Prendergast argues that the *non placet* interpretation of Derrida is incoherently formulated:

> it is never fully clear what the actual objection is: to the devil in the academy (the Great Underminer); to the Dandy (Derrida as superficial and ephemeral 'fashion'; what incidentally is the *durée* of a fashion? Derrida's work has been

actively influential for a period longer than that of many established philosophical movements); to the second-rate (Derrida's 'contributions to our understanding of language . . . do not . . . begin to compare with those of Wittgenstein'); or to the bore (nothing 'original' about Derrida; as Hegel remarked, in the infinite night all cows are black). There may well be a possible world in which all these things can be coherently believed in at once, but it is not, I think, the world I live in. (106)

Prendergast juxtaposes this incoherence with the invocation of philosophical privilege found in the first *non placet* flysheet: 'We would point out that had the Council consulted the Philosophy Faculty, they would have realised how controversial the proposal is'. For Prendergast, this complaint illuminates an idea of philosophy and of the right to philosophy fundamental to the *non placet* campaign: 'Derrida [. . .] raises interesting and entirely legitimate questions concerning what it means to philosophise and to have philosophy and philosophers as elements of our culture. For the flysheet signatories this seems, however, to add up to being a form of intellectual and cultural heresy, a veritable *trahison des clercs*' (107).

Prendergast argues that, since the philosophy faculty is comprised of members who voted *non placet* and members who voted *placet*, the notion that any 'consultation' of it would have yielded a univocal response is dubious. This observation renders the 'consultation' line of argument vulnerable to the very processes it decries in Derrida's work:

> If the matter is controversial within the [philosophy faculty], would we not then need another authority to resolve the questions over which the Faculty itself is divided? And if opinion in that higher authority were itself divided, would we not need another one and so on, thus – a richly comic moment, this – opening on to precisely that "vicious regress" held up by the signatories as evidence of the "absurdity" of Derrida's devilish "doctrines" [sic]. (107–8; Prendergast's 'sic')

The demonstration that the *non placet* campaign's critique of Derrida typically lapses into an imitation of the parodic version of Derrida presented by that critique is the principal signature of the *placet* riposte to that campaign.

Prendergast concludes by reiterating the second *placet* flysheet's central contention: To state in print 'that Derrida is unfit to receive an honorary doctorate from the University [. . .] is to do the very thing the [*non placet*] signatories tell us they are anxious to forestall: bring the University into disrepute' (108). Prendergast suggests: 'Now that good sense has prevailed and the honorary doctorate has been conferred on M. Derrida, perhaps we could invite him to *debate* with those of the signatories wishing to do so the accuracy of the characterisation of his work to which they have lent their names. [. . .] Any takers?' (108–9). This follows Derrida's invitation to Roger

Scruton, in the '*Honoris Causa*' interview, to 'take to argument'[53] – an invitation Scruton did not accept.

Brian Hebblethwaite's contribution to the Symposium, 'Derrida Non Placet' (*non placet*; 'Reflections on "The Derrida Affair"'), argues that the Affair has a moral dimension at least as pertinent as its intellectual aspect: 'One has only to read a little of Derrida's writing to become aware that one is dealing with a thoroughly decadent strand in modern philosophy'. Not only decadent, Derrida's work is also described by Hebblethwaite as 'degenerate', 'barbarous', 'idiotic', 'pernicious', 'decadent' (twice more), and 'drivel' (109–11).[54] The immorality[55] of Derrida's oeuvre has two principal manifestations: 'a fatal attraction for young, iconoclastic, minds, unwilling to ponder the heights and depths of the many very different strands in western philosophy' (110), and an implied political flippancy connected to the 'atrocious quality' of his writing:

> I fear I must, at this point, advert to Derrida's notorious defence of Paul de Man's posthumously discovered anti-semitic writings. The sheer sophistry of Derrida's defence – not only its utter silliness but its morally disreputable nature as well – can only be regarded as proof positive of what I have been saying about both the quality and the content of his work. Judgements so inane and so twisted are surely indicative of a mind not worthy of attention, let alone honour. (109)

Important here is the contention that Derrida's politics can only be 'inane' because what Hebblethwaite considers his counterintuitive style has the consequence of 'twisting' his perception in turn. The disagreeable characteristics of Derrida's style are the major grounds for Hebblethwaite's critique. Derrida's debate with John R. Searle can be reduced to a question of style: 'Let anyone read the exchange between John Searle and Derrida on the topic of intentionality; and it will at once become clear from the quality of the writing alone both what is good philosophy and what is not' (109). This is a problematic criterion because, as Hebblethwaite concedes later, if one narrowed down the field of philosophy according to this equation between good writing and good philosophy, it would become a very small one: 'It has to be acknowledged that a number of the great philosophers I have claimed to be worthy of study are also pretty obscure. Not all possess the clarity of Descartes or of Hume' (110). Why is it, then, that Hebblethwaite applauds modern Kantians and Hegelians for their lucid expositions of those 'difficult philosophers' Kant and Hegel, whilst actively discouraging the possibility of an analogous interpretive exercise concerning Derrida's work (110)?

Hebblethwaite's paradigm for philosophical legitimacy wavers increasingly the more tendentiously he attempts to establish a binary between

Derrida's work and 'truth and objective value' (109). Referring to the analogy between Derrida and Socrates made by the Cambridge orator, James Diggle, during the honorary degree ceremony itself,[56] Hebblethwaite states:

> Only one [commentator], to my knowledge, made the much more apt comparison with the Sophist, Protagoras, Socrates' arch enemy. [. . .] It was Protagoras who embraced the most extreme moral relativism in the ancient world, and Socrates' objection to his teaching was not just a philosophical one. It was a moral objection too. (We do not know enough about Protagoras to be able to judge the quality as well as the content of his philosophical teaching. But I doubt if, on any score, Protagoras would have been a suitable candidate for an honorary degree.) (109–10)

If Hebblethwaite's primary objection to Derrida is that he does not take philosophy seriously enough, that it is more intellectually and morally important than Derrida's writing allows his work to be, then one should take his analogy seriously and ask of it these questions: If philosophy is so supremely serious, so important, why does Hebblethwaite countenance its border-control being based on *not knowing*? And: If 'we do not know enough about Protagoras to be able to judge the quality as well as the content of his philosophical teaching', why does Hebblethwaite tentatively declare *non placet* in his direction, regardless? Hebblethwaite's rhetorical psychostasy here undercuts the logic of philosophical legitimacy it is deployed to support; his argument enacts the infidelity to philosophy it purports to find in Derrida.[57]

'Media, Derrida and Cambridge' ('Reflections on "The Derrida Affair"') is a neutral account of the Affair by Susannah Thomas, Cambridge's information officer. It provides a succinct overview of the pattern of media interest in the debate, and its weakly comic afterlife:

> Towards the end of June, the [newspaper] articles became more flippant and mention of Derrida was made in articles which no longer even referred to the issues involved. These included television reviews, quirky letters and I even heard mention of Derrida in 'I'm Sorry I Haven't a Clue' on BBC Radio 4, when, in a typically light-hearted game, panel members had to 'smuggle philosophers through customs' by mentioning them in a sentence – Derrida was the first to be mentioned. (113)

The quasi-comical exaggeration of Derrida that emerges from the Cambridge Affair remains the template for mentions of him in the British media at the present time. Thomas contrasts the Affair with the communication of scientific ideas in the media; she surmises that the Affair held an initial advantage because there was no section of any national newspaper reserved for philosophy, whereas science typically had its own dedicated subsection.

This meant that '[the Affair] was carried on in the news and features pages of the press which the layman might be more likely to read'. However, Thomas finds the media debate finally unsatisfactory, because 'The independent experts called to explain the issues raised by Derrida seemed to lace their philosophical comments with pointers as to the nature of Cambridge as an institution. As the University's Information Officer, it pains me to read a comment that Cambridge is "silly" when this is just one dish from the rich menu of University life'. She suggests that the institutional critique was related to the fact that it was philosophy being discussed: 'I cannot think of an instance of institutional criticism where a new scientific theory is advanced' (113).[58]

Thomas makes an important point about the Affair's direct effect on the institution it concerned:

> The idea of honorary degrees took quite a battering at some stages during this debate but I think has benefitted from it. This year has shown that it can provide an opportunity for more than a colourful and moving ceremony. I would not suggest that there should be objections each year but the occasion could act as a forum for those eminent people we honour to share their thoughts while they are here. In addition, the [*Cambridge*] *University Reporter* will in future carry a notice each year about the procedure for proposing individuals for honorary degrees. (114–15)

That the Affair could improve the transparency of the honorary degree procedure suggests that it was an institutional event, as well as an event taking place within an institution. That these two formulations name discrete types of event is important for my argument in the next chapter.

The lengthiest Symposium article is Christopher Norris's 'Of an Apoplectic Tone Recently Adopted in Philosophy' (*placet*; 'Reflections on "The Derrida Affair"'). Norris's title relates his article to a critique of philosophical tone taken up first by Kant in 'On a Newly Arisen Superior Tone in Philosophy', and then by Derrida, whose 'On a Newly Arisen Apocalyptic Tone in Philosophy' is a reading of Kant on this score.[59] For Kant, the 'superior tone' ('superior' intended pejoratively) is produced by an ecstatic 'philosophy drawn from feelings', which absconds from rational argumentation.[60] Derrida returns this question of tone to Kant's text, noting that the latter twice intimates 'the death of philosophy' in a tone that is polemical, satirical, frightened, and indignant.[61] Crucially, though, what Kant's and Derrida's texts share is a hope that philosophy will not be brought to an ultimate reconciliation with itself. It is clear why Norris, faced with calls to outlaw Derrida's work from philosophy, implements these resistances to millenarianism to contextualize his intervention in the Cambridge Affair.

Norris presents an initial caricature of Derrida: 'After all, everyone knows that, according to Derrida, philosophy is just another "kind of writing", on a par with poems, novels, literary criticism, or any sort of text you care to name' (116). He attributes this caricature to Richard Rorty, whose construal of deconstruction as radical pragmatism or 'neo-pragmatism' has long been a target of Norris's.[62] Broadly, Rorty reads Derrida, in terms both of content and form, as attacking or undermining the history of philosophy; the strategy of Derrida's iconoclastic approach is to point to the outmoded nature of 'notions like truth, right reading, argumentative rigour and so on' (116), in a quasi-literary style that gestures at all times to the provisionality and ultimate insupportability of ideas of philosophical rectitude. Although Rorty responds positively to Derrida's work for the most part,[63] Norris regards his interpretation as espousing principles undergirding the ideas about 'free play' that fuelled the *non placet* campaign, to the point that 'if [Rorty's] were anything like a fair rendition of Derrida's arguments then one could hardly blame the Cambridge Faculty of Philosophy for regarding [Derrida] as a less than worthy recipient of its highest mark of esteem' (116). Norris's critique of Rorty insists that Derrida's work does decide between 'good and bad arguments, truths and untruths, reasons for adopting some particular position',[64] and, moreover, does not debunk 'the Enlightenment project', but seeks to 'reinscribe' that project's 'critical, epistemological and ethical resources [. . .] in contexts of socio-political debate that would fully maintain philosophy's commitment to a *reasoned and responsible* critique of existing forms of institutionalized power/knowledge'.[65] Significantly, Norris's presentation of Derrida as a philosopher would distinguish Derrida's thought from a contemporary 'widespread postmodern-irrationalist drift of which [Jean] Baudrillard stands as the prime representative'.[66] Far from being an ambassador for what Hebblethwaite terms, with undeniable perissology, 'a particularly degenerate form of a decadent strand in but one tradition – the genealogical tradition – in modern philosophy', Derrida for Norris upholds the generative tenets of philosophy whilst considering how they might be put in question, or induced to question themselves.[67]

In part two of his article, Norris explains how Derrida's readings of Kant are not the iconoclasms celebrated by Rorty and condemned by the *non placets*, but rather should be understood as sharing much with an established analytic tradition of Kant scholarship – the 'minimal requirements [of] good faith, clarity, conceptual precision, the avoidance of wilful misreadings, obscurantism, logical blunders, category-mistakes, etc.' – but diverging from this tradition in placing no disproportionate emphasis on those aspects of Kant's texts that are most unproblematic based on what one already knows or takes for granted about his philosophy.[68] Norris grants that from the perspective of an understanding of Kant accrued on the path of least resistance, Derrida's presentation of Kant will appear anasemic; but he emphasizes that Derrida's approach 'amounts to [. . .] a *rigorous and principled* insistence that one read with an eye to certain "marginal" details – metaphors, footnotes, analogical devices, parenthetical remarks – which in fact play a more-than-marginal role in Kant's developing structure of argument' (119).

Norris makes a nuanced point here, because it is easy to misrepresent Derrida on this score; Eagleton does so, for example, in *Literary Theory: An Introduction*. To return to the matter of tone, Eagleton's account of Derrida's method diverges from Norris's, and ultimately is a misrepresentation, because of the tone he ascribes to it:

> Derrida's own typical habit of reading is to seize on some apparently peripheral fragment in the work – a footnote, a recurrent minor term or image, a casual allusion – and work it tenaciously through to the point where it threatens to dismantle the oppositions which govern the text as a whole. The tactic of deconstructive criticism, that is to say, is to show how texts come to embarrass their own ruling systems of logic[.]⁶⁹

This idiom of tenacious seizing and dismantling as a deconstructive 'tactic' tessellates more with Eagleton's favoured Marxist criticism than with anything Derrida has written.⁷⁰ Although Eagleton seems to be making the same point as Norris, the standardized Marxian framework he ascribes to Derrida (perhaps to correct what he sees as the 'politically evasive' character of his work⁷¹) renders his account much more in keeping with Rorty's, and the *non placet* campaign's. It is no coincidence that Eagleton files Derrida alongside Roland Barthes in the 'Post-Structuralism' chapter of *Literary Theory*, whereas Norris laments that Derrida's work entered the United States borne on 'the same mid-70s wave of Francophile cultural fashion that heralded the advent of post-structuralist works like Roland Barthes's *S/Z*' (119). Norris's claim is an historical oversimplification,⁷² but it says much about the differences between his and Eagleton's accounts.

Central to Norris's article is his emphasis on deconstruction's own resistance to (and not merely difference from) the caricature of itself through which it has become at once popular and unpopular. Specifically, Norris underscores '[Derrida's] reiterated point that deconstruction has to do with the conceptual grammar (or logical syntax) of certain elements in the text, and not – as the commonplace account would have it – with the sheer multiplicity of meanings attached to this or that isolated key-word' (120). As I have already indicated, this strategic isolation founds many of the *non placet* attempts to 'deconstruct' Derrida in turn. Norris's own means of making this point is rigorously to treat various of Derrida's more (in)famous contentions, such as his reading, in 'Plato's Pharmacy', of the *Pharmakon* in the *Phaedrus*; his location, in *Of Grammatology*, of a 'logic of supplementarity' in Rousseau's work; his early mobilization of différance, in *Voice and Phenomena*, as a means of problematizing 'Husserl's attempted synthesis of the transcendental ego as source and guarantor of meaning' (121); and, more generally, his recourse to a 'literary' (or better, 'performative') register (Norris cites *The Post Card* and *Limited Inc.*). Norris argues that the notorious appearance of any and all of these oft-bowdlerized points in Derrida's oeuvre soon dissipates if one reads them in context (120–23).

Norris concludes by schematizing the *non placet* objections to Derrida's work:

> Adorno perhaps comes closest to the mark when he remarks how obsessional are the defences mounted by an unreflecting positivism when exposed to the kind of speculative thought that refuses to take language (or 'style') for granted, and which demands – like Derrida – a vigilant awareness of the non-identity between word and concept. (124)

Norris argues that J. L. Austin, Gilbert Ryle, and Ludwig Wittgenstein could also be described in Adorno's terms, were it not for the fact that the analytic tradition that claims them for its milieu does so through an apprehension of their work that obscures its 'lively awareness of the potential within language for creating problems with any simplified – non-self-reflexive – account of meaning, reference, intentions, speech-act implicature and so forth' (124). Searle is presented as emblematic of this timid, or apprehensive, apprehension. Finally, Norris names William Empson as a precedent for Derrida, in the sense that Empson, too, was 'the victim both of Cambridge faculty intrigue and of a deep-seated prejudice against the idea that textual close-reading – of the kind so brilliantly displayed in *Seven Types of Ambiguity* – could go along with a powerful and original intelligence applied to philosophic questions' (126).[73] Although Empson in his turn was no admirer of Derrida,[74] both offer, according to Norris, 'insights [. . .] which neither the critics nor the philosophers have yet caught up with' (126).

The second collection of articles, 'The "Derrida Affair" Again', begins with Thomas Baldwin, 'Anglo-Saxon Platitudes?' (*placet*), which frustrates any impression that the two options available to voters, *placet* and *non placet*, absolutely split those who voted into 'pro-' or 'anti-Derrida' groups. Baldwin, an author of the third *placet* flysheet, shares with the *non placet* position a suspicion of the efficacy and coherence of Derrida's '"playful", deconstructive investigations' (28). Baldwin interprets this 'strategy' of Derrida's as issuing from a suspicion of empiricism, where empiricism is taken to mean an a priori understanding of human experience derived from observation and experiment, and hence one that is based on a general scientific model.

The aspect of Derrida's style to which Baldwin objects is his notional attempt to write outside of the presuppositions and methodologies dictated by such a model: Baldwin admits to being 'persuaded by [Willard Van Orman]

Quine that philosophical reflection has to take place within an understanding of the world and ourselves that is supplied by the sciences, not from an external point of view that can only be indirectly indicated by playful deconstruction' (28). Quine countersigned Smith's letter to the *Times* supporting the *non placet* campaign, and for Baldwin to endorse him here indicates an even-handed attitude to the debate. Despite his acknowledged debts to Quine, Baldwin argues that the charges of 'Meaning-scepticism and radical indeterminacy' levelled at Derrida in the *non placet* literature are actually 'the less-or-more serious teasers of analytic philosophers, in particular of Quine', and thus 'It is altogether a bit rich for Derrida to be abused by Hebblethwaite for subscribing to a doctrine he has explicitly disavowed, when that very doctrine has in fact been championed by one of Derrida's critics' (29). Baldwin's article evinces a *placet* position predicated not on a wholesale acceptance of Derrida's ideas, but on a wish to take them into account (or hold them to account) philosophically. For Baldwin, 'philosophers do not need to agree with those whose writings they respect' (29).

For the sake of clarity, I include at this juncture Nicholas Denyer's second article, 'Anglo-Saxon Platitudes' (*non placet*) from the June 1993 *Cambridge Review*,[75] because it is a response to Baldwin. Here, Denyer develops his remarks, from 'The Charms of Jacques Derrida', concerning what he regards as Derrida's conflation of sense and reference (in his preferred Fregean terms, *Sinn* and *Bedeutung*). Per Denyer, there is a clear distinction between the sense of an expression (its signification), and its reference (its truth-value), so that, whilst 'the phrase "believes that hunting tigers cannot possibly be dangerous" has at least two senses (believes that tigers cannot possibly be dangerous when they are hunting; believes that it cannot possibly be dangerous to hunt tigers) [. . .] we may doubt that it is true of even one person' (89).

Denyer imputes to Derrida an ignorance of this framework, using three examples. First, from *De la grammatologie*:

> The first concerns Derrida's use of 'signifier'. He glosses 'le signifié' as 'sens ou chose, noème ou réalité'; this implies that what is signified by the word 'paper' is the thing or reality paper, even though what is signified by that word could also be called a 'sense' or an 'object of thought'. (89)

Noting the confusion introduced by Denyer apparently conflating 'signifier' and 'le signifié' ('signifier' actually translates as 'le signifiant'), it is more important that Denyer misses what is an account *by* Derrida *of* a particular account of signification which would not make the distinctions Denyer identifies; it is not Derrida's own position:

> L'évidence rassurante dans laquelle a dû s'organiser et doit vivre encore la tradition occidentale serait donc celle-ci: l'ordre du signifié n'est jamais

contemporain, est au mieux l'envers ou le parallèle subtilement décalé – le temps d'un souffle – de l'ordre du signifiant. Et le signe doit être l'unité d'une hétérogénéité, puisque le signifié (sens ou chose, noème ou réalité) n'est pas en soi un signifiant, une *trace*: en tout cas n'est pas constitué dans son sens par son rapport à la trace possible. L'essence formelle du signifié est la *présence*, et le privilège de sa proximité au logos comme *phonè* est le privilège de la présence.[76]

Derrida is suggesting that the conflations lamented by Denyer are actually an effect of the occidental discourse on signification he is describing and its need to make of the sign 'l'unité d'une hétérogénéité'. Derrida is writing in a quasi-citational mode, whose indicators are missed by the haste in which Denyer critiques him. Ironically, Denyer creates two senses here from a passage which seems to be unambiguous, *believing* a particular sense of the passage (that it signifies Derrida's own view), and hence unsettling his own prior formulation whereby signification and belief are kept separate.

Denyer's second example, also from *De la grammatologie*, pertains to Derrida's reading of Lévi-Strauss:

> A second example concerns Derrida's use of 'concept'. The example is complicated by the use of 'répondre à', presumably as the converse of 'signifier'. Derrida reasons: 'À l'expression de <<société sans écriture>> ne répondrait donc aucune réalité ni aucun concept'. [. . .] For our purposes [. . .] the important point [. . .] is the equation between there being nothing of which the phrase 'society without writing' is true, and there being no sense expressed by that phrase. Such an equation is blatantly false[.] (90)

That Denyer overlooks the conditional tense in which Derrida's argument is phrased means he also overlooks the structure of this argument more generally. It suffices to restore Denyer's citation to its immediate syntagmatic context:

> Si l'on cesse d'entendre l'écriture en son sens étroit de notation linéaire et phonétique, on doit pouvoir dire que toute société capable de produire, c'est-à-dire d'oblitérer ses noms propres et de jouer de la différence classificatoire, pratique l'écriture en général. À l'expression de <<société sans écriture>> ne répondrait donc aucune réalité ni aucun concept. Cette expression relève de l'onirisme ethnocentrique, abusant du concept vulgaire, c'est-à-dire ethnocentrique, de l'écriture.[77]

Attention should here be paid to the movement between conditional and present tense in Derrida's argument. *If* one stops understanding writing in its strict, linear-phonetic sense, *then* no reality or concept would correspond to the expression 'society without writing'. To the present-tense occidental construal of writing which permits the designation of other forms of inscription as illiterate, Derrida opposes, in the conditional, what he might later have termed an 'unconditional' understanding of writing. This hypothetical understanding would have the ideational effect of cancelling the concept of a 'society without writing' because it would question not only the material existence of such a society but the logic by which the possibility of such a society might be construed. Derrida is thinking about what could happen if one ceased understanding writing in precisely the sense which, for Denyer, must endure. He is not unaware that he is doing so.

For Denyer's third example, he considers Derrida's 'melodramatic remarks about *pharmakon*'. Again, it is a question of sense: properly speaking, *pharmakon* is not a word with several different senses, but, 'as we might expect from a word that has given us "pharmacy", *pharmakon* is true of drugs generally, both those that kill and those that cure' (90). It is debatable whether 'pharmacy' (as it is 'given [to] us') inherits with equanimity both narcotic functions (pharmacies would be very different places if it did); moreover, to reduce the operations of 'Plato's Pharmacy' to the word *pharmakon* is to reify these and ignore the dissemination between the term and those cognate with it from which Derrida's argument is derived. Again, Denyer hypostatizes for convenience: To the consilience recommended by Baldwin, he opposes a rigidity possible only through selective periphrasis of Derrida's work.

This kind of asymmetry is also perceived by Nicholas Lash in his piece, 'Occasions of Contempt' (*placet*; 'The "Derrida Affair" Again'). Lash's article predominantly addresses what Lash views as the disproportionate and overdetermined reaction to Derrida from Brian Hebblethwaite, Lash's 'friend and colleague' (30). As Lash observes, despite Hebblethwaite's arguably jingoistic attack on Derrida's style ('[Hebblethwaite] prefers boiled beef and carrots, a diet of "plain" speech, to all this fancy foreign muck'), there is very little of clarity in Hebblethwaite's 'unsubstantiated allegations of inanity, twisted sophistry, absurdity, unreadability, falsehood, triviality and general balefulness', which proceed in a 'rhetoric [which] freewheels, [and] makes no engagement with anything that Derrida has actually written' (30–31). To demonstrate, Lash considers two texts mentioned by Hebblethwaite: George Steiner's *Real Presences*, which Hebblethwaite cites as a straightforward disputation of deconstruction, and Graham Ward's article, 'Why Is Derrida Important for Theology?',[78] which Hebblethwaite regards as aberrant work by an otherwise excellent theologian.

Lash observes that Steiner's text, although hostile to a jargonistic tendency he perceives in deconstruction, not only concedes but actually praises its position in a lineage of philosophy ('from Heidegger and Sartre to deconstructionism') characterized as an 'almost obsessional form of questions recurring at the very *edge* of philosophical investigation, questions (to indicate a very ancient figure) concerning what might lie "beyond" philosophy's "beginning" and its "end"'. For Lash, there is, *pace* Hebblethwaite's construal of the text, a 'recognition' in *Real Presences* of 'the gravity of the challenge which [deconstruction's] diagnosis makes disturbingly explicit' (30–31).

Concerning Ward's article, Lash addresses Hebblethwaite's charge that it contains nothing but 'one or two clear theological points aided in no way at all by references to Derrida's impenetrable jargon' (31; Lash quotes from 'Derrida Non Placet', 111). Lash discerns in the article 'four "values for theology" of Derrida's work – two negative, two positive', summarizing these thusly:

> Negatively, Derrida's philosophy, as read by Ward, demands of theological statements the recognition "that they are not, nor ever can be, unequivocal statements of truth" and that "there is no revelation which is not already a text, not already a representation, not already interpreted". Positively, his work "enables theologians to clarify the relationship between metaphysics and theology", and, with its intimations of a promise, a non-stateable "Yes" beyond the beginning and the end of our philosophy, Derridean *"différance* continually sharpens the presence of the Word and gives weight to the unerasable nature of the theological." (31; Lash quotes from 'Why Is Derrida Important for Theology?', 265–68)

Lash interprets the debate in terms of Plato's *Politeia*:

> By implication, moreover, it seems likely that [on Hebblethwaite's account] not only Derrida and the larger part of French philosophy are to be excluded from the city, but, behind them, entire tribes headed by Heidegger and Nietzsche are to be kept standing, shivering, in the fens. For all the lip-service paid to the desirability of "deep" and "serious" reflection on *'different* versions of the world' [in Hebblethwaite's article], it seems as though criteria of tolerable difference (of intellectual style and strategy, for example) are, in fact, being drawn with disturbingly proconsular constriction and assurance. (31)

Lash reaches the same conclusion that I did above regarding Hebblethwaite's equally 'proconsular' devaluation of Protagoras: that there is an inexplicable discrepancy between how seriously he enjoins one to treat philosophy, and how flippantly he delineates its borders.

Lash concludes his article by admitting to being 'moderately grateful for the fact that, as one French observer put it, "Cambridge didn't try to conceal the spectacle of conflict"' (32). Although Lash does not attribute this quotation, it comes from Derrida's *'Honoris Causa'* interview, and is worth citing in full because here Derrida is most vehement about the stakes of the Affair:

> Cambridge didn't try to conceal the spectacle of conflict, nor the gestures of rejection and censorship which shook its august body, and finally at the end of a debate and a vote which were as democratic as could be, chose not to close its doors to what is coming [à ce qui vient[79]].[80]

Derrida here describes the Affair in a register that, later, would characterize his writings on the nexus of alterity, ethics, and event. Conceiving of his work as an *arrivant* in this way, Derrida underscores the role of the university in the possibility of such a nexus.

Christopher Prendergast's second article about the Affair, 'On Yawns and the Effortless Superiority of a Cambridge Man' (*placet*; 'The "Derrida Affair" Again'), begins by echoing his point (made in 'Off Limits') that, for all the criticism of Derrida's work during the Affair (particularly from Denyer and Hebblethwaite), there was a marked unwillingness to translate this into debate with Derrida himself. Prendergast skips Hebblethwaite's piece (which 'speaks of "drivel" in a more or less continuous stream of the same and of the "degenerate" in a manner that itself degenerates so fast that not even Oswald Spengler could keep up with it'), in favour of a stringent analysis of Denyer's first article, 'The Charms of Jacques Derrida'.

Disputing Denyer's reading of the phrase 'la différence entre le signifié et le signifiant *n'est rien*' in *De la grammatologie* (which I read from a different perspective in my discussion of that article), Prendergast takes Denyer to understand it as 'il n'y a aucune différence entre le signifié et le signifiant', which would pay attention neither to Derrida's italics, nor to the 'unusualness of the formulation and thus to the fact that there is some work of interpretation to be done here'. Prendergast delicately argues that Derrida's formulation has a compact performative force that Denyer's glossing of it lacks – specifically, that it maintains the Saussurean distinction between signifier and signified in terms of their roles in the constitution of the sign, before cancelling this distinction in order to avoid the tendency to prioritization (typically of the signified) that it (the distinction) invites, and to insist instead on the mutual constitution of signifier and signified. Put simply, it is not that there is no difference between signifier and signified, but that this difference should not be taken to index an ontological disparity or hierarchy; hence, the difference '*n'est rien*' (32–33).

At the centre of Prendergast's article is a discussion of Denyer's latent lexicon and tropology of sexual frustration. Prendergast observes a curious turn by Denyer to 'talk of "romance" and "Venus"':

> Here one must of course oneself quote (*in extenso*): "Like everybody else, arts dons know that romance can blossom. But, unlike some other people, arts dons get little pleasure from seeing this in the mystifying guise 'With Venus in the cusp of Libra, there is a possibility that romance might blossom this weekend'. That, I take it, is because arts dons are not so inclined to dwell upon the possibility of romance. There are however other truisms which confront arts dons every day." Well, Denyer can "take it" any way he likes, and, where "blossoming" is concerned, once more must speak for himself. Indeed, and as we shall shortly see, he does precisely that, in terms that render his somewhat dispiritingly flaccid relation to romance and Venus entirely intelligible. (34)

Prendergast relates this passage to Denyer's subsequent discussion of the 'Emperor's New Clothes' effect of Derrida's work: 'Part of the charm Derrida has for arts dons is, I therefore suggest, that he dresses up such truisms as these. Something that when naked is rather drab, and that nevertheless keeps coming to mind, has a satisfyingly important air when garbed in all the gorgeous pomp of theory'.

Highlighting the terms 'dresses up', 'garbed', 'gorgeous pomp', and 'naked', Prendergast suggests that the economy of Denyer's article sets up an opposition. On the one hand, there is Derrida (dressing his philosophy in the alluring and seductive garb of metaphor; a double dressing-up, because '"Dress" has also been a metaphor, in writing about rhetoric from Antiquity onwards, for metaphor itself'), Venus (whom this erotic register has not really left behind), and the harlot ('The clothing that figurative language puts on nature is dangerously alluring and seductive; and from there it is but a step to the commonplace association of rhetoric with the harlot'). On the other hand, there is 'Denyer, spokesman for the banality of truisms, on the side of the naked'. However, by the lights of Denyer's own argument, 'the naked turns out to be "drab" (uninteresting)', and Prendergast can show that Denyer cannot avoid rehearsing the same quasi-erotic fascination with metaphorical play he condemns as the appeal of Derrida's work to others (35). Even as Denyer proceeds to a 'common sense' discussion of the difference between the word 'cat' and his own 'small tortoise-shell female' – a difference that Derrida not only would not dispute, but would insist upon in philosophically unprecedented ways in *The Animal That Therefore I Am*[81] – he risks a slippage that clothes his own discourse in the metaphorical garb it ostensibly repudiates:

> In the very paragraph in which [Denyer] speaks of his cat, he also speaks of "poison" (Derrida's reading of Plato's *pharmakon*). Do we smell a rat here (Denyer, a Classicist, says *pharmakon* is to be found "somewhere" in Plato)? Or something a bit fishy perhaps? Maybe everything got really tangled at this point; what with cats and poisons (not to mention Venus as mermaid) all swirling around, could it be that *poisson* was also swimming about "somewhere" in the textual bowl? (35)

If Denyer invokes his cat in order to make a 'common sense' point against what Prendergast terms 'textual dispersal', he actually demonstrates the opposite. Unable to denude his argument, he actually '[gets] his metaphorical knickers in a twist', and 'getting your knickers in a twist is evidently bad news for both seekers of truth and seekers of romance, as well as being a very powerful constraint on securing a satisfactory outcome to striptease. At an even more basic level, it is also not good for locomotion' (35). The spectacle of 'Denyer crashing to the ground, sprawling around in his defence of the truistic nature of truisms' exemplifies 'the unpredictable outcomes of writing' to the extent that 'Denyer's piece remains a far more eloquent defence of Derrida than any of the pro-Derrida pieces published in the special issue of the [*Cambridge*] *Review*' (36).

Howard Erskine-Hill's 'Viewpoint' (*non placet*), from the December 1992 *Cambridge Review*,[82] is a short memoir of the Affair. Erskine-Hill states that the controversy was inevitable: 'It is hard to believe that anyone who was in the University during the so-called "MacCabe Affair" of 1980–1981 which received a great deal of publicity, could expect the proposal of Derrida to go through without protest'. Confessing to the 'terror' aroused in him by deconstruction – '[Derrida's] cult rejects the idea of objectivity in principle [. . .] It is society's adherence in principle to the ideals of objectivity and truth which is the ordinary individual's intellectual defence against coercion. Derrida opens straight out into *1984*' – Erskine-Hill recalls that it was 'at high table in Pembroke [College] when somebody mentioned Derrida's name as having been included [on the list of proposed honorary graduands that year]'. In the ensuing conversation, a colleague suggested Erskine-Hill declare his opposition, and around the same time, 'I heard from my old friend Alastair Fowler, Emeritus Professor of English at Edinburgh, who asked: "What is Cambridge doing, giving a doctorate to Derrida? A dark day for British intellectual life."' This was the first 'seed' of Erskine-Hill's opposition, but, he states, 'I never contemplated being a lone protester or single campaigner against what the University proposed to do'. Fortunately, Erskine-Hill found a kindred spirit in D. H. Mellor, again in the intellectual crucible of Pembroke's dining hall. They concurred that it was a mistake that the Council of the Senate did not consult the philosophy faculty before his nomination, forming a mutually beneficial alliance: 'I and those who sympathised with me in my Faculty could secure a condemnation of Derrida from the people most competent to judge him. Hugh Mellor, Professor of Philosophy in a distinguished but small Faculty, had the hope of recruiting support from the larger Faculty of English'. In other words, the English faculty would make up the numbers in order to ratify the philosophy faculty's expertise (173–74).

Pertinently, Erskine-Hill states that the *non placet* campaign never expected victory. Instead, it aimed 'to deny anyone the possibility of claiming that Derrida now represented an orthodoxy in Cambridge'. To this end, on Saturday, March 21, Erskine-Hill and Mellor were joined at the Senate House by Ian Jack and Raymond Page (with an unnamed fifth supporter lest one of the other four be absent), uttering the declaration *non placet* at an MA graduation ceremony.[83] Despite Erskine-Hill's initial assumption that the declaration's effects would only be felt in Cambridge, he became subject to considerable attention from the national press, although was reluctant to engage with this until he and Mellor had drafted their *non placet* flysheet (the first of the two). Once they had drafted it, they submitted it to a legal colleague 'to be vetted for libel' (174), and were mainly satisfied with the final version: Erskine-Hill only regrets that they did not include a reference to David Lehman's *Signs of the Times* – specifically to its discussion of 'Derrida's attempt to use deconstruction to exonerate Paul de Man from the anti-semitism of his wartime articles in *Le Soir*' (175) – and that the 'plain' style of the flysheet might have been regarded as indexing a correlatively simplistic argument.

Erskine-Hill acknowledges Smith's letter to the *Times* as codifying 'international opposition to what Cambridge was proposing to do, on the part of those best qualified to judge', and states that 'the Non-Placet side had very warm support from Parisien philosophers who for understandable reasons did not wish to sign a letter in *The Times*' (175–76). Commending the sobriety of the *non placet* campaign,[84] he criticizes its *placet* counterpart for having been moved to dogmatism 'by fashion and influence', stating that, if influence were a sufficient criterion for the award of an honorary, then 'Dr J. P. Goebbels would have been acceptable in the 1930s, or in the 1950s T. D. Lysenko' (176).

Finally, Erskine-Hill recalls the day of the vote itself: 'On coming out of the entrance of Pembroke to go to the Senate House I fell in immediately with Gillian and John Beer. It was an encounter not quite without embarrassment though we had had good relations throughout the campaign' (176). Previously, Erskine-Hill had requested Gillian Beer's signature for his flysheet, only to discover her prominent role in the *placet* campaign (175). Arriving at the Senate House, Erskine-Hill saw large numbers on the *non placet* side of the room and 'wondered briefly and for the last time whether we might not snatch victory out of the jaws of defeat'. A late increase on the *placet* side scuttled his hope, but he had the last laugh: 'we had succeeded, against heavy odds, in mounting a most substantial protest, supported by some of the greatest names in Cambridge in all fields. I have to confess that the moment when this support was apparent, when I saw people coming to our side whom I had not even expected to vote, was one of pure pleasure' (176). Had the *non placet* campaign moved more rapidly, he concludes, 'I think we could have won the final vote' (177).

THE ORATOR

James Diggle was Cambridge's orator between 1982 and 1993, and was the person to 'present' Derrida as a doctor *honoris causa* of Cambridge. It is relevant, given the content of Diggle's oration, to précis how he understands the office of orator. In Diggle's history of the office at Cambridge and Oxford, he makes two crucial points. First, the orator remains a genuinely 'public' figure, because she 'acts on behalf of the whole University, not on behalf of [herself or] himself or of any one College'; the founding statute of the office stipulates that the orator shall 'faithfully compose letters in the name of the University against any persons whatsoever, even though they be his own friends, and in defence of any persons, though his own enemies'.[85] Second, the modern requirement that the orator provide an English translation of her Latin entails the subordination of literalism to the approximation of sense:

> An English version can be, and should be, more than a crib. A good Latin style is very different from a good English style, and declamatory Latin (if it is to have the rhythms and the rhetorical mannerisms of Cicero) is quite unlike readable English. Furthermore, it is desirable to diverge in the English from the Latin, where a point can be made appropriately in one language but not in the other, or where a similar effect (such as humour) can be gained simultaneously in both languages, but by different means.[86]

Diggle indicates two oratorical principles: that of a certain ambassadorial impartiality beyond any intra-institutional factionalism, and that of striving to create the same effect (humour is his example) in both the Latin and its translation. Applied to the Affair, this permits the expectations that Diggle's oration would not indicate a bias toward either the *placet* or *non placet* positions, and that anything Diggle said of Derrida in Latin would also be said in English.

Neither expectation is borne out by the oration itself, 'Iacobvm Derrida'. It begins with the phrase, 'Annos abhinc triginta famae fundamenta iecit hospes hic noster' ('Our honorand laid the foundations of his fame thirty years ago').[87] It is noteworthy that the recognizably philosophical trope of ground-laying, or *Grundlage*, here is collocated with no achievement other than 'fame'. Moreover, Diggle describes Derrida as 'hospes' (translated as 'honorand'), a word whose composition ('hostis' plus 'potis') retains an ambivalence. 'Hostis', denoting at once the guest, stranger and enemy, blends with the root of 'potis' ('pot') denoting mastery and ownership, and so 'hospes' would signify both 'guest-master', as it does for Émile Benveniste, and also the master-stranger and master-enemy.[88] Perhaps Diggle uses this term fairly to acknowledge the Affair (he states at the end of his oration that Derrida 'does not shun controversy'[89]), although one might ask why he does not render the ambivalence of this term in his translation, according to his own stipulations. The way in which Diggle describes the relative roles of the Latin oration and its English translation is pertinent here: 'The Orator must provide an English translation for the audience to read while he is orating'.[90] I infer that this ascribes to the Latin text a private, institutional plane of content not necessarily available to the 'audience' for whom the translation is made available.

This can be substantiated with reference to Diggle's boast that he 'deconstructed' Derrida in his oration 'for those who could see it', and that it was only another Cambridge classicist, Rupert Thompson, who perceived this.[91]

Doubtless there are many who gratefully would learn from Diggle how to 'deconstruct' Derrida, but in the absence of his elaboration I conjecture one example. Referring to the 'more playfully entitled' of Derrida's works – '*Otobiographies* and *The Postcard from Socrates to Freud and Beyond*' – which in the Latin he describes as 'ridibundam' ('laughing'), Diggle cites from Horace's *Satires*: 'sed *deridentem dicere uerum quid uetat*?' This phrase is not given in the English translation; it translates as 'what is to prevent one from telling truth as he laughs?',[92] and 'ridentem' also carries a sense of mockery. However, Diggle has modified Horace's first participle from 'ridentem' to '*deridentem*', inflecting laughter or mockery with Derrida's name, and vice versa. Although the English translation states that this 'playfulness' is but one aspect of Derrida's work, the Latin literally renders 'Derrida' synonymous with laughter and mockery. Hence, before what on Diggle's terms would mark the 'public' availability of the oration – its translation into English – there is a sort of private joke, which reveals as ersatz the apparent equanimity of the address's translation. This countermands the two principles of oration I took from Diggle's essay on the office, and is hardly an edifying spectacle, despite Diggle's assertion that it was done to 'salve [his] conscience'.[93] If this is what Diggle calls a 'deconstruction', then his oration crystallizes certain aspects of deconstruction as it is perceived in the *non placet* literature: cabbalism, duplicity, elitism, mockery, trickery, and moral relativism.

The slipperiness of James Diggle's oration is a good point on which to conclude this opening chapter, because as a text the oration both 'officially' marks the end of the Cambridge Affair, and, read closely, does nothing of the kind. This utterance is doubly performative – rubberstamping Derrida's honorary doctorate whilst archiving a sceptical attitude towards it, 'for those who could see it'. At the moment of the Affair's 'closure' the debate is kept open, in the kind of gesture that, put simply, is the starting point for deconstruction in general. The chapters that follow all take an interest in the Affair as an unfinished business.

NOTES

1. 'The Villanova Roundtable: A Conversation with Jacques Derrida', *Deconstruction in a Nutshell: a Conversation with Jacques Derrida*, ed. John D. Caputo (New York: Fordham University Press, 1997), 16.

2. Ruth Morse and Stefan Collini, 'Reflections on "The Derrida Affair,"' *The Cambridge Review*, Vol. 113, No. 2318 (October 1992), 99.

3. Simon Morgan Wortham, *Counter-Institutions: Jacques Derrida and the Question of the University* (New York: Fordham University Press, 2006), 4.

4. See John D. Caputo, 'Deconstruction in a Nutshell: The Very Idea(!)', *Deconstruction in a Nutshell*, 38–40; Caputo, *The Prayers and Tears of Jacques Derrida:*

Religion without Religion (Bloomington and Indianapolis: Indiana University Press, 1997), 282; Jeff Collins and Bill Mayblin, *Introducing Derrida: A Graphic Guide* (London: Icon, 2011), 5–11; Simon Critchley, 'Derrida: the reader', *Derrida's Legacies: Literature and Philosophy*, eds. Simon Glendinning and Robert Eaglestone (London and New York: Routledge, 2008), 6–7; Critchley, 'Derrida's Influence on Philosophy . . . And On My Work', *German Law Journal*, Vol. 6, No. 1 (2005), 28; Penelope Deutscher, *How to Read Derrida* (New York and London: W. W. Norton & Company, 2005; repr. 2006), xi; Simon Glendinning, *Derrida: A Very Short Introduction* (Oxford: Oxford University Press, 2011), 8–14; James Holden, 'Biographical Note', *life.after.theory*, eds. Michael Payne and John Schad (London and New York: Continuum, 2003; repr. 2004), 1–2; David Mikics, *Who Was Jacques Derrida?: An Intellectual Biography* (New Haven and London: Yale University Press, 2009), 225–26; Benoît Peeters, *Derrida: A Biography*, 446–48; Jason Powell, *Jacques Derrida: A Biography* (London and New York: Continuum, 2006), 3, 187; Herman Rapaport, *The Theory Mess: Deconstruction in Eclipse* (New York and Chichester: Columbia University Press, 2001), 39–43; James K. A. Smith, *Jacques Derrida: Live Theory* (New York and London: Continuum, 2005), 4–6; Marko Zlomislic, *Jacques Derrida's Aporetic Ethics* (Lanham, MD and Plymouth: Lexington Books, 2007), xxvii–xxix. Most surprising within this trend is Simon Morgan Wortham's *Counter-Institutions*. Here, in an introduction to Derrida's 'deeply complex and highly ambivalent relationship to orthodox academia' (1), Wortham refers only to Derrida's 'significant number of honorary doctorates from universities in the United States, Britain, Italy, and other countries in Europe and beyond, including the one awarded him by Cambridge University in 1992, after the well-known fiasco involving a letter of opposition written by academic colleagues dismissive of Derrida's work' (3).

5. For example, by 1991 Conor Cruise O'Brien could, with his dates slightly wrong, describe the controversy at Cambridge over Colin MacCabe's tenure there as pertaining to deconstruction: 'In a famous case in Cambridge (England) eight years ago, deconstruction underwent a setback' (O'Brien, 'Devaluing the University', *Times*, March 5 1991). O'Brien's article figures the 'Theory Wars' as concerning the imperialist expansion of deconstruction.

6. Jacques Derrida, *'Honoris Causa*: "This is *also* extremely funny"', trans. Marian Hobson and Christopher Johnson, Derrida, *Points. . . : Interviews, 1974–1994*, ed. Elisabeth Weber, trans. Peggy Kamuf et al. (Stanford: Stanford University Press, 1995), 408.

7. See Barbara Johnson, *Freedom and Interpretation: The Oxford Amnesty Lectures 1992*, ed. Johnson (New York: Basic Books, 1993), 5n: 'During the spring of 1992 a group of Cambridge dons opposed the awarding of an honorary degree to Derrida (the first such objection in thirty years). It would seem that the tension between the British and French intellectual traditions is still alive and well'. An article by Ray Monk for the *Independent*, 'Is Jacques a Cambridge Chap?' (*Independent*, May 15, 1992) argues that 'In the last 50 years Britain has become extremely insular and philosophically adrift', citing the opposition to Derrida in Cambridge as evidence for this. The article, and especially its presentation of Gilbert Ryle as personifying this British 'insularity', prompted criticism from, among others, D. H. Mellor and Jenny

Teichman, both of whom signed flysheets opposing Derrida's doctorate (see the 'Letters' pages of the *Independent*, May 18 and 20, 1992). Monk then apologised for his depiction of Ryle ('Letters', *Independent*, May 22, 1992).

8. 'Derrida *honoris causa Universitatis silesiensis*, 11 Dec 1997', Irvine, Box 120, Folder 10 (my translation). For Derrida's visit to Katowice, see Richard Terdiman, 'Given memory: on mnemonic coercion, reproduction and invention', *Memory Cultures: Memory, Subjectivity, and Recognition* eds. Susannah Radstone and Katharine Hodgkin (New Brunswick: Transaction, 2005; repr. 2009), 191.

9. Derrida, 'Allocution proférée à l'Université de Coimbra', *Derrida à Coimbra/Derrida em Coimbra*, coord. Fernanda Bernardo (Viseu: Palimage Editores, 2005), 41.

10. For Kant, only as a scholar can one make full and free ('public') use of one's reason, whereas the 'private use of reason', such as in civic office, necessarily is 'very narrowly restricted' by obeisance to government direction. In all Kant's examples – the officer, the citizen, the clergyman, and even the present monarch, Frederick the Great (by virtue of a certain public use of reason on his part, which permits that of his subjects) – the private and public uses of reason coexist in a single subject. See Kant, 'An answer to the question: What is enlightenment?', Kant, *Practical Philosophy*, ed. and trans. Mary J. Gregor (Cambridge: Cambridge University Press, 1996), 17–22.

11. See Kant, *Zum ewigen Frieden, Kant's gesammelte Schriften Bande VIII*, ed. The Royal Prussian Academy of Sciences (Berlin: Georg Reimer, 1912), 369. See also Kant, 'Toward Perpetual Peace: A Philosophical Sketch', *Toward Perpetual Peace and Other Writings on Politics, Peace, and History*, trans. David L. Colclasure, ed. Pauline Kleingeld (New Haven and London: Yale University Press, 2006), 93.

12. See Derrida, 'Mochlos ou le conflit des facultés', Derrida, *Du droit à la philosophie* (Paris: Galilée, 1990), 400–1: Derrida argues that the need for the university's effective autonomy to be state-sanctioned – 'autorisée (*berechtigt*) par une instance non universitaire, ici par l'État' – renders that autonomy heteronomous, 'une représentation d'autonomie', in two senses of representation: a delegation of autonomy by the state to the university, and the university's performance or even mimicking of autonomy. Furthermore, the philosophy faculty, facing what Kant calls the 'illegal conflicts' whereby the public seeks truth in the 'demagogues' of the higher faculties of law, medicine, and theology, is powerless to redress this imbalance (necessarily having no executive power) and requires government intervention; without this intervention, the government 'voue à la mort la faculté de philosophie' (431). See also Derrida, 'Mochlos, or The Conflict of the Faculties', trans. Richard Rand and Amy Wygant, Derrida, *Eyes of the University: Right to Philosophy 2*, trans. Jan Plug et al (Stanford: Stanford University Press, 2002), 85–86, 107.

13. Brian Hebblethwaite, 'Derrida Non Placet', *The Cambridge Review*, Vol. 113, No. 2318 (October 1992), 111.

14. See *Cambridge Minds*, ed. Richard Mason (Cambridge: Cambridge University Press, 1994; repr. 1998). This collection was based on lectures given to the Cambridge University International Summer School in July 1993.

15. '*Honoris Causa*', 417–18/Johnson MS.

16. 'Honoris Causa', 405–6.

17. See Barry Smith et al., 'Derrida Degree a Question of Honour', *Times* (Saturday May 9, 1992); reprinted in *Points*, 420.

18. 'Honoris Causa', 409/Johnson MS.

19. Collini, *What Are Universities For?* (London: Penguin, 2012), 22. See also Collini, *English Pasts: Essays in History and Culture* (Oxford: Oxford University Press, 1999; repr. 2003), 319.

20. For an excellent reading of Guillory's critique, see Marc Redfield, *Theory at Yale: The Strange Case of Deconstruction in America* (New York: Fordham University Press, 2016), 125–57.

21. Eagleton, *The Function of Criticism: From* The Spectator *to Post-Structuralism* (London: Verso, 1984), 102–3.

22. *Function*, 105.

23. *Function*, 101.

24. Alwyn W. Turner, *A Classless Society: Britain in the 1990s* (London: Aurum Press, 2013), 357. Terry Eagleton relates a version of this anecdote in his review of Benoît Peeters's biography of Derrida, and Peeters relates a third version in that book itself. See Eagleton, '*Derrida: A Biography* by Benoît Peeters – review', http://www.theguardian.com/books/2012/nov/14/derrida-biography-benoit-peeters-review (accessed October 10, 2014); Peeters, *Derrida: A Biography*, trans. Andrew Brown (Cambridge and Malden, MA: Polity, 2013), 447.

25. Others have not been so hesitant: See Roger Scruton, 'The Idea of a University', *The American Spectator*, Vol. 43, No. 7 (September 2010), 50–52. For my critique of Scruton on this theme, see Gildea, 'Roger Scruton's Daughters', *Influence and Inheritance in Feminist English Studies*, eds. Emily J. Hogg and Clara Jones (Basingstoke and New York: Palgrave Macmillan, 2015), 80–94.

26. For example, John M. Ellis's book, *Against Deconstruction* (Princeton and Guildford: Princeton University Press, 1989), cited in one of the flysheets opposing the award of Derrida's honorary, observes 'two major strands in deconstructive criticism', of which 'the one that derives more directly from Derrida's view of the nature of signification – the limitless, infinite, indeterminate play of signifiers – is less important than the other, which derives from Derrida's temperament, habits of thought, and style' (67). In what frequently is a sober critique of deconstruction, Ellis cannot resist clarifying that this second, more important deconstruction is the outcome of '[Derrida's] temperamental addiction to provocative statements' (67), which becomes, later in the book, '[deconstruction's] temperamental addiction to challenging and contradicting authority' (113).

27. Cambridge Degr. H. 2A (part 2).

28. Brian Hebblethwaite, lamenting the 'baleful' academic influence of deconstruction, refers to '[deconstruction's] effect on English departments in the United States – and here in places, pilloried to perfection by David Lodge in the course of his novel, *Nice Work*' ('Derrida Non Placet', 110). Peeters's Derrida biography in turn regards the *non placet* campaign as evocative of 'the novels of David Lodge' (*Derrida*, 447), whereas Jean Lacoste, writing in *Quinzaine Littéraire* (August 1, 1992), describes the Affair instead in terms of the work of P. G. Wodehouse (Irvine, Box 144, Folder 4).

29. See John Casey, 'Much ado about the man who believes in nothing' (*Daily Mail*, May 16, 1992), and William Leith, 'Now you read it, now you don't' (*Independent on Sunday*, May 17, 1992); the latter prefers an exercise in 'deconstructing a £5 note' to any discussion of Derrida's work.

30. '*Derrida: A Biography* by Benoît Peeters – review'.

31. See Rachel Bowlby, 'Domestication', *Deconstruction: A Reader*, ed. Martin McQuillan (Edinburgh: Edinburgh University Press, 2000), 305.

32. Geoffrey Lewis, *Lord Hailsham: A Life* (London: Pimlico, 1998), 187.

33. 'Derrida Non Placet', 109.

34. Cambridge Degr. H. 2A (part 2).

35. Cambridge Degr. H. 2A (part 1).

36. *Statutes and Ordinances of the University of Cambridge: And Passages from Acts of Parliament Relating to the University* (Cambridge: Cambridge University Press, 2014), 5 (Statute A §2).

37. I refer to these flysheets in this book (for example, 'first *placet* flysheet') according to the order in which they were reprinted in the *Cambridge Reporter*, Vol. 122, No. 29 (Wednesday, May 20, 1992), 685–88. I am grateful to Stefan Collini, Marian Hobson, and Christopher Johnson for their generous and informative responses to my questions concerning the circumstances of the flysheets' circulation.

38. 'First *placet* flysheet', *Reporter*, Vol. 122, No. 29, 685.

39. See 'Derrida day of reckoning', *Times Higher Educational Supplement*, No. 1019 (Friday, May 15 1992), 2.

40. 'Second *placet* flysheet', *Reporter*, Vol. 122, No. 29, 686.

41. 'Third *placet* flysheet', *Reporter*, Vol. 122, No. 29, 686.

42. 'First *non placet* flysheet', *Reporter*, Vol. 122, No. 29, 687.

43. 'Second *non placet* flysheet', *Reporter*, Vol. 122, No. 29, 688.

44. See 'Derrida Degree a Question of Honour', 419–21.

45. These were: Hans Albert, David Armstrong, Ruth Barcan Marcus, Keith Campbell, Richard Glauser, Rudolf Haller, Massimo Mugnai, Kevin Mulligan, Lorenzo Peña, Willard Van Orman Quine, Wolfgang Röd, Edmund Ruggaldier, Karl Schuhmann, Daniel Schulthess, Peter Simons, René Thom, Dallas Willard, and Jan Wolenski.

46. See Jeffrey Sims, 'Prefatory Remarks', 'Revisiting the Derrida Affair with Barry Smith', *Sophia*, Vol. 38, No. 2 (September/October 1999), 142.

47. 'Revisiting', 151.

48. See '*Honoris Causa*', 404.

49. Smith later specified the kind of attack he had in mind: 'People won't die, of course [from Derrida's influence]; but there is something like a spiritual death, as when a psychopath throws acid at a Rembrandt painting. [. . .] Many minds have been corroded by Derridian acid' ('Revisiting', 155–59).

50. The Symposium's editorial introduction recognizes that 'The sequence of events meant that there was curiously little opportunity for real debate: a "*non placet*" was voiced; fly-sheets were circulated and, eventually, published; a vote was taken' ('Reflections on "The Derrida Affair"', 99).

51. As Christopher Prendergast notes, 'The remark is in fact to be found on p. 36, but never mind'. (Prendergast, 'On Yawns and the Effortless Superiority of a Cambridge Man', *The Cambridge Review*, Vol. 114, No. 2320 [February 1993], 33.)

52. Derrida, *De la grammatologie* (Paris: Les Éditions de Minuit, 1967), 36. Gayatri Chakravorty Spivak's translation reads:

> From *The Introduction to Metaphysics* onward, Heidegger renounces the project of and the word ontology. The necessary, originary, and irreducible dissimulation of the meaning of being, its occultation within the very blossoming forth of presence, that retreat without which there would be no history of being which was completely history and history of being, Heidegger's insistence on noting that being is produced as history only through the logos, and is nothing outside of it, the difference between being and the entity—all this clearly indicates that fundamentally nothing escapes the movement of the signifier and that, in the last instance, the difference between signified and signifier is nothing. Derrida, *Of Grammatology, Corrected Edition*, trans. Spivak (Baltimore and London: The Johns Hopkins University Press, 1974; repr. 1997), 22–23.

53. '*Honoris Causa*', 406.
54. 'Derrida Non Placet', 111.
55. See also Hebblethwaite, 'A critique of Don Cupitt's Christian Buddhism', Hebblethwaite, *Ethics and Religion in a Pluralistic Age* (Edinburgh: T&T Clark, 1997), 120: Hebblethwaite refers to 'a post-modernist Derridean deconstruction of all essences, including the human self and its inherited cultures and life-ways'.
56. See James Diggle, 'Iacobvm Derrida'/'Jacques Derrida', Diggle, *Cambridge Orations, 1982–1993: A Selection* (Cambridge: Cambridge University Press, 1994), 87: '[Derrida] does not shun controversy, for controversy ensures debate, and in true debate nothing remains unexamined. As Socrates said, that which is unexamined is without meaning'.
57. For Protagoras and Derrida, see Jean-Michel Rabaté, *The Future of Theory* (Oxford: Blackwell, 2002), 101–9.
58. 'Media', 113.
59. These texts are published together in *Raising the Tone of Philosophy: Late Essays by Immanuel Kant, Transformative Critique by Jacques Derrida*, ed. Peter Fenves (Baltimore and London: The Johns Hopkins University Press, 1993).
60. Kant, 'On a Newly Arisen Superior Tone in Philosophy', trans. Peter Fenves, 58.
61. Derrida, 'On a Newly Arisen Apocalyptic Tone in Philosophy', trans. John P. Leavey, 124.
62. See Norris, *Uncritical Theory: Postmodernism, Intellectuals and the Gulf War* (London: Lawrence & Wishart, 1992), especially 32–51 and 126–58; Norris, 'Philosophy as *Not* Just a "Kind of Writing": Derrida and the claim of reason', *Redrawing the Lines: analytic philosophy, deconstruction, and literary theory*, ed. Reed Way Dasenbrock (Minneapolis: University of Minnesota Press, 1989), 189–203; Norris, 'Deconstruction, Ontology, and Philosophy of Science: Derrida on Aristotle', *Questioning Derrida: with his replies on philosophy*, ed. Michel Meyer (Aldershot: Ashgate, 2001), 39–65. According to Norris ('Deconstruction, Ontology, and Philosophy of Science', 61, n4), the specific texts by Rorty that the former's critique engages are 'Philosophy as a Kind of Writing: an essay on Derrida', Rorty, *Consequences of Pragmatism* (Brighton: Harvester Press, 1982), 90–109, and 'Deconstruction and Circumvention', Rorty, *Essays on Heidegger and Others* (Cambridge: Cambridge

University Press, 1991). For Rorty's response, see Rorty, 'Two Meanings of "Logocentrism": a reply to Norris', *Redrawing the Lines*, 204–16.

63. Rorty is less sympathetic to Derrida where he perceives him upholding, or at least conceding the inescapability of, transcendental philosophical argument, which Rorty glosses as the 'discovery of conditions of possibility (of consciousness, or language, or Dasein, or whatever)' whose procedure necessarily exempts the language in which this discovery is made from any suspicion of contingency. According to Rorty, this exemption founds the myth that the transcendental cannot be broken with; but if one recasts the transcendental as a 'gimmick' or neologism invented by Kant as a means of clearing a space for his philosophy so that it is neither Newtonian nor Rousseauian, this mystique disappears. See Rorty, 'Is Derrida a Quasi-Transcendental Philosopher? (Review of Geoffrey Bennington and Jacques Derrida, *Jacques Derrida*)', *Contemporary Literature*, Vol. 36, No. 1 (Spring 1995), 178–85. For the relations between Rorty and Derrida on this topic, see Caputo, *More Radical Hermeneutics: On Not Knowing Who We Are* (Bloomington and Indianapolis: Indiana University Press, 2000), 84–124.

64. *Uncritical Theory*, 127.

65. *Uncritical Theory*, 33–34.

66. *Uncritical Theory*, 33.

67. The text by Derrida with whose title Norris's title engages corroborates exactly Norris's presentation of Derrida vis-à-vis the 'Enlightenment'. See also Fenves, 'Introduction: The Topicality of Tone', *Raising the Tone of Philosophy*, especially 27–33.

68. For Éamonn Dunne, 'If reading is predestined, directed, goal-oriented, and prejudicial, then it is not reading'. See Dunne, *Reading Theory Now: An ABC of Good Reading with J. Hillis Miller* (New York and London: Bloomsbury, 2013), xxiii.

69. Eagleton, *Literary Theory: An Introduction (Second Edition)* (Oxford: Blackwell, 1996), 116.

70. For another criticism of Eagleton's formulation of deconstruction in *Literary Theory*, see Willy Maley, '*À Propos* of Marx, Attribute to Derrida: A Note on a Note in *Margins of Philosophy*', *Deconstruction Reading Politics*, ed. Martin McQuillan (Basingstoke and New York: Palgrave Macmillan, 2008), 178–79. Maley argues that Eagleton's interpretation of deconstruction is incoherent in two respects: First, it argues that Derrida's 'own work' is discernible despite there being no discernible border between that work and the work of Derrida's (American) 'acolytes'; second, it somehow arrives at the conclusion that the bowdlerization of deconstruction as a reading strategy which 'denies the existence of anything but discourse' (*Literary Theory*, 148; '*À Propos* of Marx', 179) is somehow the consequence of Derrida's own work, even though Derrida, in Eagleton's interpretation, is 'in practice oblivious to language as "discourse"' (*Literary Theory*, 148; '*À Propos* of Marx', 178).

71. *Literary Theory*, 128.

72. See Mark Currie, *The Invention of Deconstruction* (Basingstoke: Palgrave Macmillan, 2013), 28–35. Currie indicates that this 'view [. . .] of American [New] criticism as a calm consensus disrupted in the 1960s by wild ideas from continental Europe' (34) retroactively ascribes both to the New Criticism and to French 'theory' a homogeneity and serenity they in fact lacked.

73. Norris is referring to Empson's expulsion from Cambridge, and the removal of his Charles Kingsley Bye-Fellowship in 1929, following a scandal precipitated by the discovery of a quantity of condoms in Empson's rooms. Whether Empson's expulsion was abetted by his critical methodology is open to debate. For an account of the episode, see John Haffenden, *William Empson, Volume I: Among the Mandarins* (Oxford: Oxford University Press, 2005), 242–73.

74. In a 1971 letter to Norris, Empson writes, 'I feel very bad not to have answered you for so long, and not to have read those horrible Frenchmen you posted to me. I did go through the first one, in translation, Jacques Nerrida [sic], and nosed about in several others, but they seem to me so very disgusting, in a simple moral or social way, that I cannot stomach them'. John Haffenden, 'Introduction', William Empson, *Argufying: Essays on Literature and Culture*, ed. Haffenden (London: Chatto and Windus, 1987), 52.

75. Denyer, 'Anglo-Saxon Platitudes', *The Cambridge Review*, Vol. 114, No. 2321 (June 1993).

76. *De la grammatologie*, 31:

> The reassuring evidence within which Western tradition had to organize itself and must continue to live would therefore be as follows: the order of the signified is never contemporary, is at best the subtly discrepant inverse or parallel—discrepant by the time of a breath—from the order of the signifier. And the sign must be the unity of a heterogeneity, since the signified (sense or thing, noeme or reality) is not in itself a signifier, a *trace*: in any case is not constituted in its sense by its relationship with a possible trace. The formal essence of the signified is *presence*, and the privilege of its proximity to the logos as *phonè* is the privilege of presence. *Of Grammatology*, 18.

77. *De la grammatologie*, 161:

> If writing is no longer understood in the narrow sense of linear and phonetic notation, it should be possible to say that all societies capable of producing, that is to say of obliterating, their proper names, and of bringing classificatory difference into play, practice writing in general. No reality or concept would therefore correspond to the expression "society without writing." This expression is dependent on ethnocentric oneirism, upon the vulgar, that is to say ethnocentric, misconception of writing. *Of Grammatology*, 109.

78. Graham Ward, 'Why is Derrida Important for Theology?', *Theology*, Vol. 95 (1992), 263–70.

79. I thank Christopher Johnson for the unpublished French text of the '*Honoris Causa*' interview, hereafter 'Johnson MS'.

80. '*Honoris Causa*', 418.

81. For the ethical question posed by Derrida concerning the relation of 'my' cat to cats in general, see Derek Attridge, 'The Impossibility of Ethics: On Mount Moriah', Attridge, *Reading and Responsibility: Deconstruction's Traces* (Edinburgh: Edinburgh University Press, 2010), 56–77.

82. Howard Erskine-Hill, 'Viewpoint', *The Cambridge Review*, Vol. 113, No. 2319 (December 1992).

83. Erskine-Hill recalls that because he 'had not absolutely counted on my support until the last moment', Mellor did not inform the vice-chancellor of the impending

non placet declaration until the day it was uttered. The Cambridge archive contains a draft letter confirming this from the vice-chancellor (David Williams) to Mellor, which reads:

> Thank you for telephoning me shortly before the Congregation last Saturday. The Graces were published in February and it would have been helpful if whatever doubts you have had been communicated to me earlier. Be that as it may, could I ask you to let me have as soon as possible (preferably before I go to the USA on University business on 1 April) a statement of the grounds for the non placet? I do not wish to rely on press reports and will need to answer questions from, among others no doubt, the nominee himself. Cambridge Degr. H. 2A (part 1).

84. Erskine-Hill tacitly admits that this phlegmatism was not always the case in a letter to the *Cambridge Review* (Vol. 114, No. 2320 [February 1993], 36), in which he retracts the following sentence in 'Viewpoint': 'Later, Dr Conor Cruise O'Brien wrote to express his regret that "that charlatan was home and dry"' (177). Erskine-Hill had requested that this sentence be omitted from the published article, but did so too late.

85. James Diggle, 'Introduction', Diggle, *Cambridge Orations*, x–xi.

86. 'Introduction', xv.

87. Diggle, 'Iacobvm Derrida'/'Jacques Derrida', 86–87.

88. For Derrida's reading of these multiple senses of 'hostis', see Derrida, 'Hostipitality', trans. Barry Stocker and Forbes Morlock, *Angelaki*, Vol. 5, No. 3 (December 2000), 13–16. See also Derrida, *Rogues: Two Essays on Reason*, trans. Pascale-Anne Brault and Michael Naas (Stanford: Stanford University Press, 2005), 63. Jacques Rancière reads in Derrida's treatment of 'hospes' a figure of 'the other that cannot come to the place of the same, the other whose part cannot be played by another'. See Rancière, 'The Aesthetic Dimension: Aesthetics, Politics, Knowledge', *Critical Inquiry* 36 (Autumn 2009), 13–14.

89. 'Jacques Derrida', 87.

90. 'Introduction', xv.

91. James Diggle, by email (March 19, 2015). Reproduced with permission:

> The composition was entirely my own. Nobody suggested what I should write, or was required to approve it. The sources I used were testimonials submitted by his proposers (which weren't very helpful), and such information as I could find from books or from writings in the press. I did contact one of his proposers, asking for advice, but received no reply. [. . .]
>
> I enjoyed writing the speech. If you read it very carefully, comparing the Latin with the English, you will see that I deconstructed [Derrida]. Only one person, to my knowledge, saw how (Rupert Thompson). I'm not going to give it away – read the two speeches side by side, and you'll see it. [. . .]
>
> I voted with the Yes party. It was my job to support him, and then to praise him. Which I did, salving my conscience by deconstructing him, for those who could see it.

92. Horace, *Satires*, I. i. 24, Horace, *Satires, Epistles, and Ars Poetics*, trans. H. Rushton Fairclough (London: William Heinemann, 1947), 7.

93. See Diggle, 'email'.

Part 2

Chapter 2

Some Kantian Stereotypes
(The Conflict of) *The Conflict of the Faculties*

> There is a great deal worth objecting to in Kant's *Conflict of the Faculties*. —NOVALIS[1]

Having summarized the *placet* and *non placet* arguments regarding Derrida's honorary doctorate, I now want to consider how both the opposition between *placet* and *non placet*, and the internal coherence of the two positions, become troubled by nothing other than the question of the vote in the *placet* and *non placet* arguments.

The conferral of an honorary degree typically takes place without any public or institutional turbulence. This is a question above all of democracy and diplomacy. It is likely that not all university members support a given nomination for an honorary, but objections do not tend to be formally expressed. One could say that the process of conferral relates to a democracy before democratic legislation or codification, in the name of an approach to *Wissenschaft* animated by a sort of necessary condition of commensurability that is not orthodoxy. There is also the possibility that people don't care enough about honorary degrees to make a fuss. Accordingly, Bill Readings describes the modern research university as 'a space in which it is possible to think the notion of community otherwise, without recourse to notions of unity, consensus, and communication'[2]; Stefan Collini views it as 'a protected space in which various forms of useful preparation for life are undertaken in a setting and manner which encourages the students to understand the contingency of any particular packet of knowledge and its interrelations with other, different forms of knowledge'[3]; and Thomas Docherty argues that we must continually affirm the university as making possible 'a search for the *limits* of knowledge, [. . .] typified by a drive towards unknowability'.[4] Hence, the university 'community' may be irreducible to (ideas of) consensus, dogma, and *doxa*, and able to critique these naturalized paradigms of community.

The award of an honorary could be said to develop a university community's dimensions and topology. It is an invitation to belong, which should be seen as withdrawing from ideas of straightforward resemblance. Derrida acknowledged this element of singularity when he received an honorary doctorate from the University of Coimbra in 2003: 'One should always give thanks for a unique gift, for example for the honour of a doctorate *Honoris Causa* which is unlike anything else and which one therefore receives, whatever one's age, with the happiness of a child'.[5] Here, Derrida mentions the Cambridge Affair as an event that taught him that the stakes of an honorary degree are sometimes those of 'the tradition, the politics and the future of the university'.[6]

According to Derrida's understanding of the honorary, there is a *chance* provided by this invitation to belong, which may allow the belonging proffered to be more than collusion or factionalism. But this chance always wavers on the threshold of an idea of institutional self-identity that seeks to extend the invitation to those who *already* belong, or at least already chime with the philosophical presuppositions of the institution in question. This tension pervades the Cambridge Affair down to its ostensibly most straightforward aspect: the actual vote on whether Derrida's honorary be awarded. In this chapter, I am interested in how the injunction to vote, differently understood by participants in the Affair, actually indexes considerable anxiety regarding questions of philosophical belonging and propriety.

Tellingly, the *placet* and *non placet* flysheets relate to one another in surprising ways regarding the role played by the call to vote on Derrida's nomination. The first *placet* flysheet argues that 'The voicing of a *non placet* to M. Derrida's nomination was ill-judged. It has done harm to this University's reputation for courtesy, and it has already attracted considerable adverse publicity'.[7] The second *placet* (the 'top persons' flysheet) views Derrida's involvement as incidental to a larger question of decorum:

> It may be that the University's procedures need revision to allow for wider consultation before an Honorary Degree is offered. To accept on this occasion the censorious intervention of one segment of the academic community would, however, involve the University as a whole in an academic controversy which should be conducted in a different forum.[8]

The claim here is that the politicking caused by the declaration *non placet* generates the controversy of the Affair. This wish to defer controversy will be shared by the first *non placet* flysheet, but it is instructive first that this flysheet recommends a *placet* vote as a vote against the injunction to vote per se, before being a vote against the injunction to vote *non placet*.

The first *non placet* flysheet contains the most pertinent sentence of the entire Affair: 'While we regret any embarrassment caused by the request for a vote, we would point out that had the Council consulted the Philosophy Faculty, they would have realized how controversial the proposal is'.[9] I covered in the previous chapter Christopher Norris's objection to the supposition that controversy is improper to philosophy, and I devote the next chapter to this crucial theme. Here, I emphasize what this flysheet considers the object of controversy, and its proposed means of avoiding similar controversies in future. While the second *placet* flysheet argues that the declaration *non placet* is the cause of any controversy, the first *non placet* flysheet opines that the source of the controversy is the grace proposing Derrida's honorary in the first place. The declaration *non placet* and consequent vote, for the authors of this flysheet, are the unhappy but necessary means of highlighting the controversy that was not made apparent to the Council of the Senate when the honorary was proposed:

> We most seriously oppose the Council of the Senate's proposal to award an honorary doctorate to the philosopher Jacques Derrida. While we regret any embarrassment caused by the request for a vote, we would point out that had the Council consulted the Philosophy Faculty, they would have realized how controversial the proposal is. Since the Council have no special knowledge in this matter, there can be no presumption that their proposal must be accepted just because it has been made public. Our Statutes allow for the expression of dissent on these occasions, and a vote, however it goes, will at least prevent the University endorsing without reflection doctrines which we believe undermine its intellectual foundations.[10]

It is worth contrasting this understanding of the vote with that articulated by the final reprinted flysheet (the second *non placet*):

> The view has been put forward that, at this stage, opposition to an honorary degree for M. Jacques Derrida is a discourtesy; and also that it has now become contrary to the interests of the University to oppose the award of an honorary degree.
>
> We have reviewed these opinions carefully, and consider them to be mistaken. It cannot possibly be a discourtesy to any individual to utilize the long-established democratic procedures of the University; nor can it possibly be contrary to the University's interests to take its decisions in accordance with those procedures. It would indeed be discourteous to let it appear that the offer of an honorary degree was, in the very least, to avoid embarrassment or adverse publicity for ourselves.
>
> Those objecting to the proposal do not merely disagree with M. Derrida's doctrines. Understood fully, those doctrines undermine the fundamental grounds which provide a place in the scheme of things for intellectual enquiry in any field; and so, for the very existence of universities in society.[11]

Against the second *placet* flysheet's argument that the *non placet* vote is indecorous, the second *non placet* flysheet's appeal to 'fundamental grounds' seems to align it with the first *non placet*'s argument that Derrida's work espouses 'doctrines' that 'undermine [Cambridge's] intellectual foundations'. However, I will now attend closely to the different ways in which the 'democratic procedure' of the vote is understood by the two *non placet* flysheets, and how this affects the integrity presupposed by the shared appeal to 'fundamental grounds' and 'intellectual foundations'.

There is no appeal to 'courtesy' in the approach encouraged by the first *non placet* flysheet, which casts voting as a last-ditch resistance, forcing a rational reflexivity upon Derrida's nomination, and upon any future nominations. This jars with the second *non placet*, which avows that '[it cannot] possibly be contrary to the University's interests to take its decisions in accordance with those procedures [the injunction to vote]'. Here, voting is invested with a sense of the a priori, with which the university's decisions should aspire to accord, whereas in the first *non placet* it appears to have a capacity to mutate the university's ideology. In the first *non placet*, the vote operates as a kind of disruption, changing what would otherwise have been a smooth process of incorporation into the Cambridge Affair. The appeal to a vote ruptures the history of *Honoris Causae* at Cambridge, the history of Derrida in Britain, the question of what and who regulates honorary degrees, and thus the question of the archive – who and what belongs, and why? And how much does the contested archive of democracy allow one to belong? And to how much of itself does democracy allow one to belong? Or is something of democracy lost in its articulation of itself? In *Glas*, Derrida considers the process of cicatrizing, which at once heals, via the formation of a scar, and scars unwounded flesh.[12] Analogously, the *non placet* flysheets' attempt to foreclose an institutional body seeks both to make whole and to disrupt the sought-for wholeness. Between the disparate understandings of the injunction to vote articulated by those flysheets, this is what is at issue.

These disparate understandings of the vote's function both express a Kantian heritage, and in particular they indicate an internalization of Kant's late text, *The Conflict of the Faculties*. This text, and the unique space it seeks to preserve for philosophy, is recognizable in the literature of the Affair to the point of overdetermination, and yet never mentioned. Indeed, the text is discussed, in general, surprisingly rarely. Richard Rand suggests that the lack of attention to this text gives rise to a situation where 'It is as if, to borrow a Kantian distinction, "historical" knowledge has been forsaken for an (assumed) acquisition of "rational knowledge."'[13] I would add that to vocalize a text that privileges philosophy more or less nonstop, but never to cite it, could be said to translate in a certain way the idea of the right to philosophy.

As I will argue, however, the disjunction between these two flysheets where the vote is concerned actually autoimmunizes their Kantian *Corpus Juris* from itself, splicing this text that codifies more than any other the 'devenir-faculté de la raison' that takes place, according to Derrida, between Leibniz's formulation of the Principle of Sufficient Reason and Kant's three Critiques.[14] I develop my argument with a necessary detour into a text by Charles Taylor, which opposes Kant and Derrida in relation to philosophical propriety.

THE ETHICS OF AUTHENTICITY

In *The Ethics of Authenticity*, published a year before the Affair, Charles Taylor situates Derrida in a genealogy that introduces an unethical mutation of anthropocentrism into philosophy, placing him in a history of 'a movement of "high" culture, towards a kind of nihilism, a negation of all horizons of significance, which has been proceeding now for a century and a half'. Intensifying with Nietzsche and encompassing Baudelaire and 'some strands of modernism', this movement 'has emerged among writers who are often referred to today as postmodern, such as Jacques Derrida or the late Michel Foucault'.[15] For Taylor, 'The impact of these thinkers is paradoxical', in that Derrida, Foucault et al. claim to challenge, and expose the artificiality of, our 'ordinary categories' of authenticity and even 'the very notion of the self', but all this amounts to is a recentring of the self whereby it is disabused of any ethical responsibility:

> But, in fact, the Nietzschean critique of all "values" as created cannot but exalt and entrench anthropocentrism. In the end, it leaves the agent, even with all his or her doubts about the category of the "self," with a sense of untrammelled power and freedom before a world that imposes no standards, ready to enjoy "free play," or to indulge in an aesthetics of the self. As this "higher" theory filters down into the popular culture of authenticity – we can see this, for instance, among students, who are at the juncture of the two cultures – it further strengthens the self-centred modes, gives them a certain patina[16] of deeper philosophical justification.[17]

In an earlier text, *Sources of the Self* (which was specifically recommended by *non placet* signatory Brian Hebblethwaite as an *exposé* of Derrida's fraudulence), Taylor does so without even inverted commas around the term 'free play': 'The Derridian insight into the illusions of the philosophies of "presence" opens the way to an endless free play, unconstrained by a sense of allegiance to anything beyond this freedom'.[18] This orthodoxy in the reception of Derrida is problematic. But it has been influential, and invoked in support as well as detraction of his work.[19] Against this, one can suggest more recent scholarship that suggests that even the notion that Derrida's work at some point shed any resemblance to Taylor's formulation and 'became' ethical is now viewed as a narrative oversimplification (this is also the view espoused by Derrida himself[20]). Less adequately explored is the claim that deconstruction participates in a certain pedagogical irresponsibility – the insinuation that Derrida is responsible for excess or self-indulgence across the institutional body.[21]

This is most apparent in the lascivious taint given to the notion of 'free play' as a 'postmodern' echo of Nietzschean misbehaviour. Christopher Johnson highlights a tendency in the Anglophone reception of Derrida to invoke 'free play' as a positively – or negatively – inflected terminus of the phrase's value for textual interpretation.[22] He notes that this translation of the French *jeu* 'probably stems initially from "polysemic" glosses of "Le système [sic], le signe et le jeu dans le discours des sciences humaines", the paper [Derrida] read at Johns Hopkins University in 1966, and later published as a chapter of *L'écriture et la différance* (1967)'.[23] Furthermore, interpreting *jeu* as 'free play', as Taylor does in his book,[24] does not recognize that *jeu* in Derrida refers, broadly, to the sense in which *jeu* needs to be considered as *et le jeu* – a kind of remainder within the relations through which a given structure is erected, which can be seen to trouble that structure – but *only* through its crucial syntagmatic involvement with *la structure* and *le signe*. Murray Krieger, avowedly no Derridean, also reads *jeu* as sounding a cautionary note – as an 'almost-but-not-quite-free play' that countenances a self-reflexive element to critical practice, limiting the interpretive recklessness he sees elsewhere in deconstruction.[25] But if you replace these important qualifications with 'free play' understood as a creed whereby unaccountability and irresponsibility serve themselves, you will end up with Taylor's formulation where it represents a libertine flight from questions of ethics – and indeed Krieger elsewhere refers to 'Structure, Sign and Play in the Discourse of the Human Sciences' as Derrida's 'blockbuster essay on "Free Play,"'[26] describing 'free play' as characterized by 'randomness'.[27]

The matter of 'free play', therefore, is a question of translation, but also citation, periphrasis, and memes. Across Derrida's oeuvre there is an imperative to attend responsibly to these questions of material textual dissemination, which have a particular relevance to academic and mediatic discourses (and intensifications in their places of overlap, such as the Cambridge Affair). To cite just one text among many, the seriously playful 'Living On • Border Lines' (1979) shows Derrida responding to his institutionalization as the figurehead of 'American deconstruction' with an elaborate injunction to take care with textual transformation.

'Living On • Border Lines', like the translated 'Structure, Sign and Play in the Discourse of the Human Sciences', should be understood materially as pivotal to the internationalizations and institutionalizations of deconstruction, specifically in the sense that, as part of the collection *Deconstruction and Criticism*, it most clearly represents Derrida's affiliation with the 'Yale School'.[28] However, it also arrives at a moment that Vivienne Orchard rightly notes is too often relegated to a shorthand for Derrida's political applicability[29] – his active membership of the Groupe de recherches sur l'enseignement philosophique (GREPH), which he cofounded in 1974.

GREPH's remit was to establish philosophy as a discipline – and as disciplinary critique (and auto-critique) – at as early a point in curricula as other subjects in French schools. GREPH focused on reforms proposed by René Haby (then Minister of Education) in 1975 that sought to defer philosophical instruction until as late as possible in students' education, as an optional subject in the 'Terminale' year (the final year of secondary education in the lycée, which immediately precedes the baccalauréat diploma). As Derrida states, 'The particularity of Greph consisted in demanding not only that philosophy continue to be taught, and not as an option, in the Terminale, but that it be given the right accorded to every other discipline, that is, a progressive and "long" teaching from the "youngest" classes on'.[30] According to Derrida, the Haby Reforms' proposed deferral of philosophy is especially reactionary because it delays philosophical critique (which must always involve critique *of* philosophy) until an educational stage that comes after potentially innumerable political, ideological, and epistemological techniques of thought (philosophies, although not named, conceived, or taught as such) have been communicated to students across already available disciplines, with no opportunity for analysis of their rhetorical, performative, and legislative dimensions. For Derrida, the Haby Reforms therefore represent a continuation of a suspicion and suppression of philosophy that intensified in France after 1968,[31] and GREPH's critique is largely directed against their desire to abolish, along with the name 'philosophy', philosophy's constitutive critique and auto-critique, whilst introducing, unannounced and uncritically, certain presuppositions and orthodoxies. GREPH institutionalizes the critique of this wish to translate, cite, and paraphrase aspects of philosophy, and of a philosophy *of* philosophy.

'Living On • Border Lines' should be read in historical and thematic relation to Derrida's ongoing interest in the pedagogical responsibility for philosophy. In part, it is a dramatized commentary on aspects of a text (here 'Living On') that do not survive anthologization. With apparent aleatory, 'Border Lines' considers: the unenviable nature of the task of translating Derrida's text for the anthology[32]; memoranda pertaining both to matters intratextual – 'Direct the entire reading of *L'arrêt de mort* toward the end'[33]

– and paratextual – 'Dedicate "Living On" to my friend Jacques Ehrmann'[34]; and the relevance (or not) of an apparently unrelated textual order: 'Read yesterday, among some graffiti: "do not read me."'[35]

Simultaneously, however, 'Border Lines' is aware of its public visibility, cross-referencing other Derrida texts for the supposed reader and pretending to conspire with that reader against the third-party translator, who will prepare his text for anthologization in *Deconstruction and Criticism*, nine years before it appeared in French in *Parages*[36]: 'My desire to take charge of the Translator's Note myself'.[37] The joke here is that the joke itself only works because of the translator's success with the text. Author, reader and translator experience a contorted and shifting temporality, as Derrida foregrounds a certain experience of space and time: that of the university.

The first injunction of 'Border Lines' reads: '*10 November 1977*. Dedicate "Living On" to my friend Jacques Ehrmann. Recall that it was in response to his invitation, and to see him, that I first came to Yale'.[38] This dedication appears nowhere in 'Living On', if 'Living On' is understood as the text 'proper', distinct from its footnote commentary, 'Border Lines'. The footnoted instruction is the dedication: the injunction to dedicate only survives in the apparently 'secondary' text. Here, Derrida is not simply engaging in a 'free play' that would dissolve the text into 'indeterminacy' or 'ineffability'. Instead, he illustrates through the mutual contamination of 'Living On' and 'Border Lines' the responsibility of commentary, referencing, citation – how they are important and should be read, as opposed to being taken *as read*. The continuing injunction to dedicate is the dedication. Nothing is less idly playful in Derrida's work than inscriptions of friendship and dedication, and by announcing these themes in what is ostensibly a footnote, Derrida questions the supposed neutrality and transparent iterability which often govern, in academic discourse, conventions of notation, citation, and translation.

Derrida's dedication is irreducible to an easily bracketed con-text: the instruction to dedicate finds no referent (a dedication 'proper') in 'Living On', and yet is indispensable to the occasion for the text, for two reasons. First, as Derrida acknowledges, Jacques Ehrmann was responsible for Derrida's first invitation to Yale; and second, Ehrmann is crucial to understanding the relation between 'Living On • Border Lines' and *Deconstruction and Criticism*. It must be in tribute to Ehrmann, author of *La Mort de la littérature*, that Derrida's text largely forgoes the focus on Percy Bysshe Shelley's *The Triumph of Life*, which was the remit of *Deconstruction and Criticism* – 'a very artificial rule (especially for me, evidently!)', Derrida reflects in *Parages*[39] – in favour of Maurice Blanchot's texts *L'Arrêt de mort* and *La Folie du jour*.[40] Moreover, *La Mort de la littérature* (originally published anonymously) presents a selection of texts considered unauthored that typically are understood as foreign to literary studies (television listings, recipes, newspaper adverts, timetables), submitting them, and the idea of them, to an analysis[41] that focuses on a conventional wisdom that would strictly separate anonymous, instrumental 'langue ordinaire' from the determinately authored 'objet poétique'.[42]

Derrida's refusal to treat his footnote as simply instrumental and 'secondary' thus finds common cause with Ehrmann's text. The dedication, therefore, conveys a resistance to merely instrumentalist reading – the taking *as read* – which, Derrida recalls, had been his own preoccupation since at least the 1960s, when he taught alongside Louis Althusser at the École normale supérieure: 'I constantly felt, not like raising objections, but like saying: "You have to slow down. What is an object? What is a scientific object?"'[43] Derrida's response to what he perceived as Althusser's hasty acceptance of the transparency, iterability, legibility, and legislation of the idea of a scientific object is recapitulated in 'Living On • Border Lines', in relation to an apparatus of notation, citation, translation, periphrasis, archivization, hierarchization, reproduction, and transmission by which academic discourse maintains the life of texts, authors, and itself. The text cannot be read quickly, and its form or forms means that it cannot be taken as read.

Derrida's treatment of the idea of 'living on' argues this point:

> But who's talking about living [de vivre]?
> In other words on living [sur vivre]?
> This time, "in other words" does not put the same thing into other words, does not clarify an ambiguous expression, does not function like an "i.e." It amasses the powers of indecision and adds to the foregoing utterance its capacity for skidding. Under the pretext of commenting upon a terribly indeterminate, shifting statement, a statement difficult to pin down, it gives a reading or version of it that is all the less satisfactory, controllable, unequivocal, for being more "powerful" than what it comments upon or translates. The supposed "commentary" of the "i.e." or "in other words" has furnished only a textual supplement that calls in turn for an overdetermining "in other words," and so on and so forth.[44]

The act of periphrasis, translation, notation, annotation introduces and acts as the problematic condition of textual living on (*survivre*). To 'make sense' of what is in words, to prolong the survival of that quiddity and to survive it, is to construct words in a manner that is never disinterested.

Reading is indissociable from commentary in that it privileges, often unconsciously, one weighting of what is read that is fundamentally the same as the prioritizing of a certain meaning that, ultimately, makes commentary possible. This weighting is a question of emphasis, of making an often-unacknowledged decision concerning how to treat the space of words, and components of words (morphemes) in relation to each other – a *syntactic bypass*. With this phrase I try to describe a caution, even an ethics, whose operation in Derrida's work on a grander scale is lucidly explained by Rodolphe Gasché. For Gasché, deconstruction 'begins by taking up broached but discontinued implications – discontinued because they would have contradicted the intentions of philosophy'. Crucially, these discontinuations are rarely avowed as such in the given text Derrida is reading; they are often the forgotten remainder when one idea is translated or paraphrased into another.[45] To an extent, this is necessary practice both for everyday intelligibility and philosophical coherence; but, as Derrida now shows, slowing down over syntagmatic correspondences hints at a relation of non-contemporaneity, spatial and temporal, between terms:

> For example, several pairs of quotation marks may enclose one or two words: "living on" ["*survivre*"], "on" living ["*sur*" vivre], "on" "living," on "living," producing each time a different semantic and syntactic effect; I still have not exhausted the list, nor have I brought the hyphen into play. Translating (almost, in other words) the Latin *de*, the French *de* or the English "of," "on" immediately comes to contaminate what it translates with meanings that it imports in turn, those other meanings that rework "living on" or "surviving" (*super, hyper*, "over," *über*, and even "above" and "beyond"). It would be superficial to attribute this contamination to contingency, contiguity, or contagion. At least, chance makes *sense* here [l'aléa fait-il sens], and that's what interests me.
>
> Be alert to these invisible quotation marks, even within a word: *survivre*, living on. Following the triumphal procession of an "on," they trail more than one language behind them.
>
> Forever unable to saturate a context, what reading will ever master the "on" of "living on"? For we have not exhausted its ambiguity: each of the meanings we have listed above can be divided further [. . .] and the triumph *of* life can also triumph *over* life and reverse the procession of the genitive. I shall demonstrate shortly that this is not wordplay [*de jeux de mots*], not on your life.[46]

By 'chance makes sense here', Derrida refers to a recalcitrant element in the processing of language (the procession in a text from one mark to the next) that is crucial to its intelligibility. This element is glimpsed in the question: Why does there seem to be an appropriate path through the textual process, and what traces does it leave behind, pick up, and trail through the text? These are not questions that one should hope to be answered definitively, as that hope would already have appropriated them to the order of that syntactic bypass of which they offer a critique. The statement of an answer and the making intelligible, that is, may preserve a text, but doing this itself only cleaves to one translation of 'survivre', one idea of the idea of living on.

Instead, Derrida suggests, through his treatment of 'sur( )vivre', the opening up of a workable space of différance, where the non-contemporaneity of a text with itself is not something to be bypassed, or resolved, but dwelt on through a methodological deceleration. Survival is not based on the 'triumph' of a major term, but on patient attention to the conditions of this triumph: 'The unity of the word is not to be fetishized or substantialized'.[47] When in 'No Apocalypse, Not Now' Derrida states, 'In the beginning there will have been speed',[48] ('Au commencement, il y aura eu la vitesse'[49]), he points to a naturalized myth of existence, and gives for consideration another question of syntax. First, he opposes qualitative and quantitative experiences of speed – 'Are we having today *another* experience of speed? Is our relation to time and to motion becoming qualitatively different? Or, on the contrary, can we not speak of an extraordinary, although qualitatively homogeneous, acceleration of the same experience?' – before challenging his own formulation, slowing down his introduction: 'And on what temporality are we relying when we put the question that way?'[50] Derrida elaborates his suspicion of his own formula, questioning a logic that would oppose the qualitative and the quantitative:

> So my first formulation remained simplistic. It opposed quantity and quality, *as if* a quantitative transformation, once certain thresholds of acceleration had been crossed [une fois franchis certains seuils d'accélération], could not induce qualitative mutations [des mutations qualitatives] within the general machinery of a culture, with all its techniques for handling, recording, and storing information [avec toutes ses techniques d'information, d'inscription et d'archivation], *as if every invention* were not the invention of a process of acceleration or, at the very least, a new experience of speed.[51]

What Derrida maintains here, by this deceleration, is the possibility that speeding up *at all* can induce qualitative 'mutation': There exist no criteria for delimiting between movement and mutation, nor between the quantitative and the qualitative. Derrida's interest in the history of reckoning with oppositions does not privilege the ones that announce themselves as big metaphysical questions, but disseminates into all methods of reading that would bypass a certain syntax, and seek to reduce spaces to homogeneity. The humanities, Derrida suggests, can question this original bypass ('In the beginning there will have been speed'), deploying their own 'incompetence' to critique the instrumentalism of a scientific military competence that would ably bring about apocalypse, the ultimate spatially homogenizing event. Reluctant to circumscribe the humanities too strictly, Derrida offers this account: 'We are specialists in discourse and in texts, all sorts of texts [Nous sommes des spécialistes du discours et du texte, de toutes sortes de textes]'.[52]

Derrida's oeuvre coheres through this heterogeneous interest in syntax, which frustrates ideas of an ethical 'turn' in his work as much as it does the attempt to reduce to 'free play' the type of reading engendered by this interest. The germination of this specific idea, I have suggested, is perceptible even prior to any of his publications, when he was an *agrégé répétiteur* at the ENS under Althusser, and is a question of real importance for the identity of a university and its community, which can be thought in terms of this syntagmatic différance.

'FREE PLAY'

'Border Lines', staged as an elliptical, diaristic footnote to 'Living On', dwells on the question of how a visiting professor at Yale such as Derrida might interact with the grammar of a university, given a certain mutual politics of translation and visitation:

> If *questions of method* [. . .] – if the question of teaching (not only the teaching of literature and the humanities) runs throughout this book, if my participation is possible only with supplementary interpretation by the translators (active, interested, inscribed in a politico-institutional field of drives, and so forth), if we are not to pass over all these stakes and interests (what happens in this respect in the universities of the Western world, in the United States, at Yale, from department to department? How is one to step in? What is the key here for decoding? What am I doing here? What are they making me do? How are the boundaries of all these fields, titles, corpora, and so forth, laid out? Here I can only locate the necessity of all these questions), then we must pause to consider translation [on devra s'arrêter sur la traduction[53]].[54]

The introduction of the pause to consider translation is a rhetorical gesture that corresponds to the same logic as the deceleration Derrida would recommend to Althusser (or the Pentagon!). The significance both of the university and of Derrida's own work explicitly become fused by these questions of syntax and translation, which must not be passed over.

In an interview for *Le Figaro Magazine* twenty years after the publication of 'Living On • Border Lines', Derrida objects to a question about the putative 'cult' in the United States around his work:

> Forgive me for putting it like this to you, but this reference to the United States has become a cliché in relation to me, and I always wonder what it is that motivates this keenness to pack me off to the United States or confine me there. [. . .] This "deconstruction" interests people in places quite some way from the United States, and in many countries, European and non-European, it is often better received and understood, and not attacked so much.[55]

Derrida objects to certain presupposed national and institutional paradigms (North American, European) in his work's reception, questioning the idea that there must be a single place of original or authoritative dissemination. This critique of perceptions of and through university institutions echoes his discussion of translation in 'Border Lines':

> If there is something that arrests translation [S'il y a un arrêt de la traduction], this limit is not due to some essential indissociability of meaning and language, of signified and signifier, as they say. It is a *matter of economy* (economy, of course, remains to be *thought*) and retains an essential relationship with time, space, counting words, signs, *marks* [plutôt des marques]. The unity of the word is not to be fetishized or substantialized. For example, with more words or parts of words the translator will triumph more easily over *arrêt* in the expression *arrêt de mort*. Not without something left over, of course [non sans reste, bien sûr], but more or less easily, strictly, closely, tightly. Beware of the "new mode of expression [nouvel idiome]" of the "totally new language" and the like.[56]

'Marque' also means 'brand name' and 'licence' (such as those that would cover the objects analyzed by Jacques Ehrmann), legislative inscriptions that rely on ideas of measurable exchange. But there is always an accompanying immeasurable remainder, which no amount of translation will account for.

Even successful translation *must triumph* – this paradoxical expression suggests that translation always testifies to the triumph of a dominant translation of 'survivre' whose trace is the syntactic bypass, at once entirely necessary and entirely fundamentalist. Derrida is not arguing for an irreducibly 'original' text whose inherent purity resists translation, and that would accord with the logic of a triumphantly exclusive university space (and that of a 'totally new language'), since this is as much based on an idea of straightforward economic equivalence as is a fantasy of complete translatability (both are based on self-equivalence: The 'original' text hypothesis posits a given text as equivalent to itself; the absolute translation hypothesis posits translation as equivalent to itself). Instead, Derrida suggests that the very possibility of translational success dramatizes a predicament attendant on reading at large – the dominant translation of 'survivre' in whose name all reading takes place – that does not distinguish between original and translation, or between translation understood as interlinguistic (between languages of communities) and as explicatory (the 'i.e.', 'as if', or 'quasi-'), that is, between translations of translation. This dominant translation is operative in the university: Derrida's decelerated reading of *survivre* suggests that the syntax of the university space needs to be paused over, even if one always risks arresting it.

In 'Where a Teaching Body Begins and How It Ends', a text that precedes 'Living On • Border Lines' by two years, Derrida considers this syntax in relation to his role as representative of the 'teaching body' ('le corps enseignant'):

So, here I am the teaching body.

I – but who? – represent a teaching body, here, in my place, which is not indifferent.

In what way is this a glorious body?

My body is glorious. It gathers all the light. First of all, that of the spotlight above me. Then it is radiant and attracts all eyes. But it is also glorious in that it is no longer simply a body. It is sublimated in the representation of at least one other body, the teaching body of which it should be at once a part and the whole, a member letting the gathering together of the body be seen; a body that in turn produces itself by erasing itself as the barely visible, entirely transparent, representation of both the philosophical and the socio-political corpus, the contract between these bodies never being brought to the foreground.

Benefit is derived, always, from this glorious erasure, from the glory of this erasure. It remains to be known by what, by whom, in view of what. Accounting for it is always more difficult than one believes, given the erratic character of a certain remainder [un certain reste]. The same goes for all the supplementary benefits derived from the very articulation of these calculations, for example, here, today, by he who says: "I – but who? – represent a teaching body."[57]

As in 'Living On • Border Lines', the aneconomic *reste* calls into question what takes place in the translation of 'I' between 'my body' and 'the teaching body'. Derrida revisits this 'un certain'/uncertain *reste* in 'Living On • Border Lines' to question a syntactic bypass that would too hastily yoke together morphemes, texts, the voices in an anthology (*Deconstruction and Criticism*), and the constituents of an institutional 'context' in which the readings of these are practised, which they presuppose, and which presupposes them. One cannot responsibly dissociate Derrida's *jeu* from its syntax, which renders it indissociable from institutional critique; moreover, doing so would actually engage in the most irresponsible 'free play'. 'Living On • Border Lines' refuses to render these questions – of anthologization, institutionalization, translation, and always of ipseity – apart from the literary critiques of Shelley, which will not do without Blanchot, which will not do without Ehrmann, and so on.[58]

Derrida insists upon this point often, and it is not foregrounded enough in the reception of his work ('the contract between these bodies never being brought to the foreground'). He elaborates this stance in New Zealand in August 1999, suggesting that the 'deconstruction of the concept of unconditional sovereignty' – a concept that 'is the heritage of a barely secularised theology'[59] – needs to be thought in the university: 'It would be necessary to dissociate a certain unconditional independence of thought, of deconstruction, of justice, of the Humanities, of the university, and so forth from any phantasm of sovereign mastery'.[60] 'Living On • Border Lines' is a little thorn in the side of this sovereignty, a thinking of syntax that suggests a figure of reading that thinks this dissociation. It takes issue above all with the idea of the equivocating 'as', which can equally be a word of straightforward economy, comparison, measure – of syntactic bypass – and simultaneously plays its part in the irreducible 'as if', precondition of literature that should never be left behind or bypassed.[61]

When Charles Taylor stigmatically isolates *jeu*, therefore, he actually exemplifies the irresponsible 'free play' against which he inveighs. Bypassing the question of the term's connective, syntactical role in Derrida's oeuvre, and translating it as a slogan of irresponsible autonomy, is actually an act of this kind of autonomy. However, Taylor is right to identify 'free play' as an idea in the history of philosophy: It is there, just not where he finds it. Instead, we might look to someone he seeks to immunize from the terms of his critique of authenticity:

> Self determining freedom has been an idea of immense power in our political life. In Rousseau's work it takes political form, in the notion of a social contract state founded on the general will, which precisely because it is the form of our common freedom can brook no opposition in the name of freedom. This idea has been one of the intellectual sources of modern totalitarianism, starting, one might argue, with the Jacobins. And although Kant reinterpreted this notion of freedom in purely moral terms, as autonomy, it returns to the political sphere with a vengeance with Hegel and Marx.[62]

Here, Kant is presented as a fire blanket, a philosophical protector and a protector of philosophy from political violence. Elsewhere in *The Ethics of Authenticity*, Kant is left contemplating beauty, whilst Nietzsche, Artaud, Bataille and other 'apostles of evil' of whom 'Derrida, Foucault, and their followers' are themselves disciples,[63] pit authenticity against morality in a 'deviant' and 'parallel' development:

> For Kant, [. . .] beauty involves a sense of satisfaction, but one that is distinct from the fulfilment of any desire, or even from the satisfaction accruing to moral excellence. It is a satisfaction for itself, as it were. Beauty gives its own intrinsic fulfilment. Its goal is internal.
> But authenticity too comes to be understood in parallel fashion, as its own goal.[64]

Kant is a blameless and fixed point of reference, and a prominent motif in Taylor's reading of history is the deviation from the Kantian path.[65] Self-determining freedom and the reconfiguration of morality as oppressive, avatars of 'free play', comprise a deviation from Kant's work that leaves the latter's integrity intact.

Chapter 2

The trouble with this narrative is that what Taylor understands by 'free play' (an ethically abdicative egocentric whimsy, a dangerous *paidia*) not only is not opposed to Kantian thought, but actually draws from it. As Marian Jeanneret points out, '*Jeu* translated as "free play" in its Kantian reference and implication of spontaneity completely and mistakenly excludes the sense of play in a machine'.[66] Derrida himself underscores this point in the 'Discussion' that followed 'La Structure, la signe et le jeu' when it was given in the Johns Hopkins Humanities Center in 1966, at the international symposium 'Les Langages Critiques et les Sciences de l'Homme'. Responding to Jean Hyppolite's request for him to 'define a structure', Derrida elaborates the space that structuration cannot help but leave open for *jeu*:

> How to define structure? Structure should be centered. But this center can be either thought, as it was classically, like a creator or being or a fixed and natural place; or also as deficiency, let's say; or something which makes possible "free play," in the sense in which one speaks of the "jeu dans la machine," of the "jeu des pièces," and which receives – and this is what we call history – a series of determinations, of signifiers, which have no signifieds finally, which cannot become signifiers except as they begin from this deficiency.[67]

I cite this from a collection called *The Structuralist Controversy* – the same text that Taylor uses in *The Ethics of Authenticity* for his discussion of Derrida. Tellingly, Taylor does not mention this clarification and its link to a politics of historical critique; moreover, in an endnote discussing 'free play' in Derrida, Taylor cites 'Structure, Sign and Play in the Discourse of the Human Sciences', omitting from his reference its status as translation,[68] and not remarking on the translators' note to that text's title, which indexes the problems of translation's links to hierarchization and the shaping of textual survival: 'The text which follows is a translation of the revised version of M. Derrida's communication ['La Structure, le signe et le jeu']. The word "jeu" is variously translated here as "play," "interplay," "game," and "stake," besides the *normative translation* "free play."'[69]

If an idea of 'free play' (as distinct from *jeu*) occurs in Derrida's work, it must be understood materially and historically, as a striving to be freed from *jeu* in one's hermeneutic horizons, which Derrida identifies as twinned with – but irreducible to – the affirmation of *jeu*:

> There are thus two interpretations of interpretation, of structure, of sign, of freeplay [jeu]. The one seeks to decipher, dreams of deciphering, a truth or an origin which is free from freeplay [échappant au jeu] and from the order of the sign, and lives like an exile the necessity of interpretation. The other, which is no longer turned toward the origin, affirms freeplay [jeu] and tries to pass beyond man and humanism, the name man being the name of that being who, throughout the

history of metaphysics or of ontotheology – in other words, through the history of all of his history – has dreamed of full presence, the reassuring foundation, the origin and the end of the game.[70]

Quoting from this passage, Taylor omits the first interpretation of interpretation, presenting the second as though it is the only one, as though it has no flipside. This exemplifies a popular reading of this text, noted by Samuel Weber.[71] However, the first interpretation of interpretation is, literally, crucial here (it forms a chiasmus with the second), because it posits *jeu* not as a resource for some liberated subjectivity, but as constitutively marked by systematicity: According to this formulation, the desire to fix meaning represents the real 'free play' (the desire to be free from, to escape *jeu*), that is understood as the imperative to ignore the responsibility called for by *jeu* – the responsibility to acknowledge the utter pervasion of the order of the sign in anthropocentric thought, to slow down, to pause to consider it.[72]

Taylor rushes past the bifurcated structure of Derrida's injunction, so that he can posit Kant's theory of beauty as '[involving] a sense of satisfaction, but one that is distinct from the fulfilment of any desire',[73] which historically is perverted by the self-interestedness of Nietzsche – whose critiques of Kant included a rejection of the idea that experience of the beautiful could be disinterested.[74] However, I would argue that Taylor's discussion of Kant and beauty is based upon Kantian 'free play' without naming it, and that this in turn is based on the dream of freedom from *jeu* (Derrida's first 'interpretation of interpretation'), which he also does not name. Taylor splits and recombines Derrida and Kant in order to make an argument that would definitively oppose them to one another.

For Kant, the 'free play' of mental powers is fundamental to the aesthetic experience, whose resultant pleasure is indissociable from the feeling of free life itself.[75] (This link between 'free play' and 'free life' is easier to understand if one bears in mind that, for Kant, this aesthetic experience is found in nature rather than in art.) The typical Kantian process whereby cognitive satisfaction is achieved in the subsumption of the given object of intuition under a determinate concept is altered in the 'free play' crucial to the different-ness of the Kantian aesthetic. The aesthetic experience does not satisfy through the cognitive categorization of things into their proper place (subsumption under a determinate concept), but instead through confirming the disinterested, de-empiricized, and thus free-playing purposiveness of the cognitive faculties (the harmony between our faculties and the particular objects to which they relate), which in turn confirms this purpose at large – and hence a common aesthetic sensibility, given Kant's stipulation that judgements must be shown to have a universal, legislative validity in order to function at all.[76] Having satisfied itself – through aesthetic experience – of a harmonious constitution, this harmony in turn grounds the perception of the unity of objects. This severally validating experience is what Taylor refers to when he discusses Kant's theory of beauty as satisfaction freed from (empirically motivated) desire; Kant calls it 'free play'.

Everything Taylor claims about Derridean 'free play' is actually an inheritance and inflection of this Kantian self-validation. Taylor's duplicity in his handling of Kant, on the one hand, and a putative genealogy linking Derrida and Nietzsche, on the other, tends toward the Kantian designation of 'free play' unelaborated in Taylor's text, more than it does to its invented Derridean counterpart – and certainly more than it engages with the nuanced *jeu* of Derrida's lexicon. What are the consequences of this duplicity, and how does it inform an understanding of the Cambridge Affair?

GRAFTING PHILOSOPHY

Taylor accuses Derrida of participating in a philosophical movement that establishes irresponsible 'free play' as part of its system, based largely on an interpretation of *jeu* that is influential in much Anglophone reception of Derrida's work,[77] and in Taylor's case structures a reading in which his own invented 'free play' is constitutively apparent. The philosophical movement in which, for Taylor, this translation confirms Derrida's participation can be traced to Nietzsche and represents a deviation from the immunization of philosophy that Taylor reads in Kant. However, Taylor can only construct this prosecution by another translation of 'free play' – from Kant to Derrida. This second, counter-transferential translation implants in Derrida a demonic double of Kant's aesthetic pleasure, bifurcating both Derridean *jeu* and Kantian 'free play' and using these corrupt files to make a case for Kant (and) against Derrida. Avital Ronell is a user of the term *tropium* to articulate an experience shared by literature and recreational drug use: 'an injection of a foreign body' to express one's 'inner experience'.[78] We might wonder what is at stake when the foreign body is injected into another.

In a sense, it is inevitable that this manoeuvre can only be performed through a hermeneutic capriciousness that itself corresponds to the doubly translated Anglo-Kantian chimera of 'free play' that Taylor portrays as intrinsic to Derrida's system. Taylor's presentation of Derrida as a mutation of Kant channels into the former – as ethically irresponsible 'free play' – a crucial aspect of the latter's thought, via a duplicitous selection process that actually generates the irresponsibility it plants on Derrida and then finds. The mutations and deviations that Taylor's philosophical-historical narrative purports to describe only take place in this narrative. To doctor the records in this manner, to falsify the evidence: Why this strange juridical process of transference?

The answer is clear: Without a certain Kantianism, there is no case against Derrida. But the uniformity of Kantianism is far from certain. When, in part I of *The Conflict of the Faculties*, Kant discusses the conflict between the philosophy faculty and the theology faculty, a fissure opens in his argument:

> [The] philosophy faculty does theologians no harm if it uses their statutes to corroborate its own teachings by showing that they are consistent with these statutes; one would rather expect the theology faculty to feel honored by this. But if the two faculties still find themselves in thoroughgoing conflict about interpreting the Bible, I can suggest only this compromise [Vergleich]: *If biblical theologians will stop using reason for their purposes, philosophical theologians will stop using the Bible to confirm their propositions.* But I seriously doubt that biblical theologians would agree to this settlement [Vertrag].[79]

What deal does Kant try to broker here? This text, hastily printed in 1797 upon the death of King Frederick Wilhelm II (who had forbidden Kant from publishing on questions of religion), shows Kant both asserting the philosophy faculty's right to use the resources available to theological scholarship, and simultaneously suggesting that it will refrain from doing so if its own *raison d'être*, reason, is not co-opted by the theology faculty. Susan Meld Shell argues that the second gesture shows Kant to have become inclined to quiescence about religious matters thanks to either the spectacle of the French Revolution, his experience of censorship by Frederick Wilhelm II, or both.[80] No doubt these factor in Kant's hesitancy, but they do not account for this catastrophic figure of ceasefire, truce, or hostage exchange, which nullifies the lower/higher faculty distinction that animates the *Conflict* at large. *Vergleich*, which can signify comparability (and specifically comparative analysis) and *Vertrag*, which often refers specifically to a legal contract (and as such is involved in the discourse of the higher faculty of law), problematize, by reducing the conflict of the faculties to a dynamic of mutual recognizability, the asymmetry of the facultative exchange that is the crux of the *Conflict*.

Kant proposes giving the Bible back to the theology faculty in exchange for the philosophy faculty's exclusive use of reason, whereas earlier in the text he describes the distinction between the lower faculty (philosophy) and the higher faculties (law, medicine, theology) as being predicated, precisely, on the impossibility of such an exchange for his facultative schema:

> So the biblical theologian (as a member of a higher faculty) draws his teachings not from reason but from the *Bible*; the professor of law gets his, not from natural law, but from the *law of the land*; and the professor of medicine does not draw his *method of therapy as practiced on the public* from the physiology of the human body but from *medical regulations*. As soon as one of these faculties presumes to mix with its teachings something it treats as derived from reason, it offends against the authority of the government that issues orders through it

and encroaches on the territory of the philosophy faculty, which mercilessly strips from it all the shining plumes that were protected by the government and deals with it on a footing of equality and freedom. The higher faculties must, therefore, take great care not to enter into a misalliance with the lower faculty, but must keep it at a respectful distance, so that the dignity of their statutes will not be damaged by the free play of reason [die freien Vernünfteleien].[81]

Without the untranslatable, aneconomic privilege of this 'free play' (which allows the philosophy faculty to subtend the others), the *Conflict* loses the form specific to it. How do we read this uncertain mediation between economy and aneconomy, symmetry and asymmetry? What is the place proper to the philosophy faculty?

The deal Kant would broker with the theology faculty would render the 'free play of reason' to its proper place – the philosophy faculty – and thus restore it to its aneconomy, on which is founded the asymmetrical relationship between the lower faculty and higher faculties. But this deal must sacrifice, provisionally, precisely that aneconomy, because in its articulation of propriety and possession (perhaps in its articulation altogether), expropriation has already taken place. The attempt to regulate that which escapes economy is self-defeating, because propriety and property are always bound up in a circular economics of exchange, measurability, and translation. For Derrida, only gifts have a chance to remain aneconomic, but only up to the point that the gift is conceptualized as such, when it would enter into an economics of exchange. It is always, and singularly each time, a case of 'the gift, *if there is any*'.[82] By contrast, in the *Conflict*, Kant's 'free play' of reason can only announce itself as aneconomic through recourse to figures of exchange and translatability.

If 'free play' in the *Conflict* is anxious, and jealous of its own expropriation, then is it such a surprise that it returns, demonized, in a narrative of post-Kantian philosophy that seeks to immunize Kant from such expropriations, which, for Taylor, would represent a fall toward Derridean 'free play'? What is rather less expected, however, is that this uncertainty between economy and aneconomy is recapitulated in the *non placet* flysheets' injunctions to vote against Derrida's honorary.

(THE CONFLICT OF) *THE CONFLICT OF THE FACULTIES*

We saw at the beginning of the chapter that the disparity between these injunctions is between the recourse to a vote regarded as according with the (aneconomic) a priori precondition of the university (second *non placet* flysheet), and the recourse to a vote understood as that which does not accord, which introduces a rupture in exchange with which any future proposed awards of honoraries would be thought (first *non placet* flysheet). Brian Hebblethwaite, signatory of both of these flysheets, recommends consulting Taylor in order to learn why one ought to vote against Derrida, in the name of what is proper to philosophy. The problem is that Taylor's thesis – that Derridean 'free play' takes self-understanding away from its Kantian unimpeachability – plants evidence on Derrida that it takes from Kant, constructing their oppositionality (and Kant's unimpeachability) through a reading that frees itself from any responsibility to Derrida's texts, even as it accuses him of philosophical irresponsibility, of being a contraband philosopher.[83] However, by signing *non placet* twice, Hebblethwaite actually highlights an inconsistency in the self-understanding of philosophy as it is inherited from Kant, and the *Conflict*. To finish, I will explain this assertion, and how it threatens the philosophical border control to whose uncertainty the falsification of evidence testifies.[84]

Both *non placets* conceive of the function of the vote differently, but this difference actually shows the *Conflict* to be a pluranimous text. The two flysheets signed by Hebblethwaite represent two interpretations of this text that, taken together in their shared recommendation to vote *non placet*, actually leave the philosophy faculty – in the name of whose Kantian insuperability they speak – positioned uncertainly between conservation and revolution. The idea in the first *non placet*, that 'a vote, however it goes, will at least prevent the University endorsing without reflection doctrines which we believe undermine its intellectual foundations', *seems* to appeal to the same sense of conservatism as the second *non placet*'s appeal to 'accordance' with 'the long-established democratic procedures of the University'. However, the former is, according to the *Conflict*, revolutionary: Concerning the French Revolution, Kant predicts its achievement to be a certain mnemonic rupture, a 'force' that will ensure the eventual success of the reason with which it accords:

> Now I claim to be able to predict to the human race – even without prophetic insight – according to the aspects and omens of our day, the attainment of this goal [a republican constitution]. That is, I predict its progress toward the better which, from now on, turns out to be no longer completely retrogressive. For such a phenomenon in human history is *not to be forgotten*, because it has revealed a tendency and faculty in human nature for improvement such that no politician, affecting wisdom, might have conjured out of the course of all things hitherto existing, and one which nature and freedom alone, united in the human race in conformity with inner principles of right, could have promised. But so far as time is concerned, it can promise this only indefinitely and as a contingent event.
>
> But even if the end viewed in connection with this event should not now be attained, even if the revolution or reform of a national constitution should finally miscarry, or, after some time had elapsed, everything should relapse into its

former rut (as politicians now predict), that philosophical prophecy still would lose nothing of its force. For that event is too important, too much interwoven with the interest of humanity, and its influence too widely propagated in all areas of the world to not be recalled on any favourable occasion by the nations which would then be roused to a repetition of new efforts of this kind; because then, in an affair so important for humanity, the intended constitution, at a certain time, must finally attain that constancy which instruction by repeated experience suffices to establish in the minds of all men.[85]

Kant's reasoning, which confirms to him that 'the human race has always been in progress toward the better and will continue to be so henceforth',[86] governs the first *non placet* flysheet's justification for a vote – that it will institute an unforgettable rupture in the award of honoraries. This is argued, by Kant, in the name of a democracy to come, which could not help but seek to move beyond 'the long-established democratic procedures of the University' whose insuperable integrity as a Kantian Regulative Idea are precisely the second *non placet* flysheet's justification for a vote: 'It cannot *possibly* be a discourtesy to any individual to utilize the long-established democratic procedures of the University; nor can it *possibly* be contrary to the University's interests to take its decisions in accordance with those procedures' (my emphasis). Triangulating the *non placet* flysheets with Kant's *Conflict* (codex of the philosophy faculty's right to philosophy, which speaks through both flysheets) indicates that there is a crucial relationship of non-contemporaneity between the distinct democracies the two flysheets understand.

Enjoining their readers to vote in the same way, the *non placet* flysheets articulate a decisive homological relation – but even as they issue this injunction, a reading of the time and the place proper to democracy in each shows a relation haunted by the very différance whose most dedicated thinker they seek to keep out of their university. Ten people signed both of the *non placet* flysheets, and only one of the second *non placet* signatories did not sign the first. All *non placet* flysheet signatories voted *non placet*. And yet what do these *non placet* flysheets authorize one to vote for, in the last analysis, other than the trepidation of the philosophy faculty and its sometimes obscene methods of border control?

NOTES

1. Novalis, *Notes for a Romantic Encyclopaedia*: Das Allgemeine Brouillon, ed. and trans. David W. Wood (Albany: SUNY Press, 2007), 144.
2. Readings, *The University in Ruins* (Cambridge, MA: Harvard University Press, 1996; repr. 1999), 20.
3. Collini, *What Are Universities For?* (London: Penguin, 2012), 56.

4. Docherty, *The English Question, or Academic Freedoms* (Eastbourne and Portland, OR: Sussex Academic Press, 2008), 141.

5. 'On doit toujours remercier pour une chose irremplaçable, par exemple pour l'honneur d'un doctorat *Honoris Causa* qui ne ressemble jamais à aucun autre et qu'on reçoit alors, à tout âge, comme un enfant comblé'. Derrida, 'Allocution proférée a l'Université de Coimbra', *Derrida à Coimbra/Derrida em Coimbra*, coord. Fernanda Bernardo (Viseu: Palimage Editores, 2005), 39 (my translation).

6. 'Allocution', 41 (my translation).

7. *Reporter*, Vol. 122, No. 29, 685.

8. *Reporter*, Vol. 122, No. 29, 686.

9. *Reporter*, Vol. 122, No. 29, 687.

10. *Reporter*, Vol. 122, No. 29, 687.

11. *Reporter*, Vol. 122, No. 29, 688.

12. Derrida, *Glas*, trans. John P. Leavey and Richard Rand (Lincoln, NE and London: University of Nebraska Press, 1986), 258.

13. *Logomachia: The Conflict of the Faculties*, ed. Richard Rand (Lincoln, NE and London: University of Nebraska Press, 1992), viii.

14. Derrida, 'Chaire vacante: censure, maîtrise et magistralité', *Du droit à la philosophie*, 359.

15. Charles Taylor, *The Ethics of Authenticity* (Cambridge, MA and London: Harvard University Press, 1991; repr. 2003), 60. See also Taylor, *Sources of the Self: The Making of the Modern Identity* (Cambridge: Cambridge University Press, 1989), 499: 'certain contemporary "post-modern" writers, influenced by Nietzsche, like Jacques Derrida and Michel Foucault'.

16. See also Raymond Tallis's contention that 'The continuing dissemination of postmodern Theory and its increasingly powerful grip on the humanities almost beggars belief: there can be few liberal arts students who do not encounter Theory in their courses and for many of them, such as those studying literature, it lies like an incubus over the entire curriculum' (Tallis, 'Sokal and Bricmont: Is this the beginning of the end of the dark ages in the humanities?' *PN Review*, Vol. 25, No. 6 [June 1999], 36).

17. *Authenticity*, 60–61.

18. *Sources of the Self*, 488.

19. J. Hillis Miller's short essay '*Jeu*' is an example of this tendency. Arguing that *jeu* is a byword for 'a limitless play of signs' in a world with 'no paternal presence setting the rules of the game', this nowhere suggests the heterogeneity of the relations between signs. At worst, it presupposes a rarefied institutional context in which we might 'play a game of *jeu*', rather than offering a sense, which I elaborate below, in which *jeu* might challenge that presupposition. (J. Hillis Miller, '*Jeu*', in *Reading Derrida's Of Grammatology*, eds. Sean Gaston and Ian Maclachlan [London and New York: Continuum, 2011], 43–47).

20. In *Rogues*, Derrida rejects this consensus: 'there never was in the 1980s or 1990s, as has sometimes been claimed, a *political turn* or *ethical turn* in "deconstruction," at least not as I experience it. The thinking of the political has always been a thinking of différance and the thinking of différance always a thinking *of* the political, of the contour and limits of the political, especially around the enigma of the autoimmune *double bind* of the democratic' (Derrida, *Rogues: Two Essays on Reason*, trans.

Pascale-Anne Brault and Michael Naas [Stanford: Stanford University Press, 2005], 39). For the mutual involvements of deconstruction and democracy before *Rogues*, see Alex Thomson, *Deconstruction and Democracy: Derrida's* Politics of Friendship (London and New York: Continuum, 2005), 11–54.

21. This view is echoed by Barry Smith, author of the letter to the *Times* during the Affair. In an interview about the Affair, Smith insinuates an amorality endemic to 'deconstruction': 'It may be fun for clever people to deconstruct the opposition between honesty and dishonesty, between originality and plagiarism, between sanity and insanity, between good literature and trash, and between truth and castration. But it is less fun to see the effects of such intellectual shananigans [sic] in the wider society'. (Jeffrey Sims, 'Revisiting the Derrida Affair with Barry Smith', *Sophia*, Vol. 38, No. 2 [September/October 1999], 147.) Another critic of Derrida, John R. Searle, identifies 'free play' as one of the appeals of deconstruction to American 'literary theorists', aligning it with a certain educational irresponsibility: '[The] lives of [literary theorists] are made much easier than they had previously supposed, because now they don't have to worry about an author's intentions, about precisely what a text means, or about distinctions within a text between the metaphorical and the literal, or about the distinction between texts and the world because everything is just a free play of signifiers' (Searle, 'The World Turned Upside Down', *The New York Review of Books* [October 1983]; reprinted in *Working Through Derrida*, ed. Gary Brent Madison [Evanston, IL: Northwestern University Press, 1993], 183).

22. Christopher Johnson, *System and Writing in the Philosophy of Jacques Derrida* (Cambridge and New York: Cambridge University Press, 1993), 8.

23. *System and Writing*, 203, n17.

24. *Authenticity*, 130, n37.

25. Murray Krieger, *Arts on the Level: The Fall of the Elite Object* (Knoxville: University of Tennessee Press, 1981), 46.

26. Krieger, *Words about Words about Words: Theory, Criticism, and the Literary Text* (Baltimore and London: The Johns Hopkins University Press, 1988), 74.

27. Krieger, *Theory of Criticism: A Tradition and Its System* (Baltimore and London: The Johns Hopkins University Press, 1976), 172.

28. Derrida, 'Living On • Border Lines', trans. James Hulbert, Harold Bloom et al., *Deconstruction and Criticism* (New York: Continuum, 1979). In an introduction to the later French text, published in *Parages*, Derrida discusses *Deconstruction and Criticism*'s remit as a Yale School showcase – a proposal that its writers accepted as a *gageure*, or (impossible) task/wager. See Derrida, *Parages* (Paris: Galilée, 1986), 118.

Deconstruction and Criticism still represents the most overt anthologization and systematization of deconstruction:

- (i) More or less, it articulates a milieu ('Romantic poetry', particularly Percy Bysshe Shelley – only referred to as 'Shelley'. See Barbara Johnson, *A World of Difference* (Baltimore and London: The Johns Hopkins University Press, 1987), 32–33.
- (ii) It expresses an institutional hegemony (Derrida was at the time visiting professor of humanities at Yale, and Harold Bloom, Paul de Man, Geoffrey Hartman, and J. Hillis Miller, the other contributors, were all professors there).

(iii) Especially in Miller's essay, 'The Critic as Host', the volume engages with the question of whether deconstruction 'belongs' to literary studies. Specifically, Miller's text is part of a discussion with M. H. Abrams and Wayne C. Booth, which took place in the journals *Diacritics* and *Critical Inquiry*, in which Abrams objects that there is something fundamentally *not normal* about 'substitut[ing] the rules of the deconstructive enterprise for our ordinary skill and tact at language'. Miller's response attempts to recoup Abrams's and Booth's view that the deconstructive 'mode' is 'parasitical' on 'the obvious or univocal reading' from its negative inflection, specifically from their detractive treatment of an idea of the 'parasitic'. See Abrams, 'Rationality and Imagination in Cultural History', *Critical Inquiry*, Vol. 2, No. 3 (Spring 1976), and Abrams, 'The Deconstructive Angel', *Contemporary Literary Criticism: Modernism Through Poststructuralism*, ed. Robert Con Davis (New York and London: Longman, 1986). More generally, Hartman's 'Preface' to *Deconstruction and Criticism* articulates a homology between the contributors which presupposes deconstruction as thetic and as such allows for a homolysis of sorts: 'Derrida, de Man, and Miller are certainly boa-deconstructors, merciless and consequent, though each enjoys his own style of disclosing again and again the "abysm" of words. But Bloom and Hartman are barely deconstructionists. They *even write against it on occasion*' (ix; my italics).

(iv) Broadly, one can posit a recognizable methodology that privileges etymological displacement (especially in Bloom, 'The Breaking of Form' and 'The Critic as Host') and the fragmentary (especially in de Man, 'Shelley Disfigured' and Hartman, 'Words, Wish, Worth: Wordsworth'). Derrida's text, in the middle of the book, is interested in syntax and synsemantics, as I suggest here: This can be read as a speed bump to those who would too soon make the connection between anthology and univocity.

29. See Vivienne Orchard, 'The "GREPH" movement: philosophical and historical perspectives' (unpublished doctoral thesis: Queen Mary, University of London, 2002), and Orchard, *Jacques Derrida and the Institution of French Philosophy* (London: Legenda, 2011).

30. Derrida, 'The Crisis in the Teaching of Philosophy', trans. Jan Plug, Derrida, *Who's Afraid of Philosophy?: Right to Philosophy 1*, trans. Jan Plug et al (Stanford: Stanford University Press, 2002), 111.

31. 'When philosophical education was stifled from the lycée on, an ideology and, in the end, implicit but very particular philosophical contents that had insinuated themselves, necessarily, through other teachings were allowed to take hold without critique. [...] And thus also a certain implicit philosophy, for the front here does not form between philosophy and nonphilosophy, but between specific philosophical practices and contents. The Haby Reform does not represent an antiphilosophy, but rather certain forces linked to a certain philosophical configuration, which, in a historico-political situation, have an interest in favoring this or that institutional structure' ('The Crisis', 110–11).

32. 'Border Lines', 76–78, 96–100, 169–74, *passim*.

33. 'Border Lines', 131.

34. 'Border Lines', 75.
35. 'Border Lines', 145.
36. See Benoît Peeters, *Derrida* (Paris: Flammarion, 2010), 687, n30.
37. 'Border Lines', 77.
38. 'Border Lines', 75.
39. 'une règle très artificielle (elle l'était surtout pour moi, bien évidemment)'. *Parages*, 118 (my translation).
40. See *Derrida* (Peeters), 368, and Sarah Wood, *Derrida's* Writing and Difference*: A Reader's Guide* (London and New York: Continuum, 2009), 167.
41. 'Qui donc a *fait* ces "textes"? [...] Qu'est-ce que ça veut dire: "faire" un texte? Ou, se faisant écho, ces deux questions: Qui a fait un "texte"? Comment se fait un "texte"? Ou encore, formulées autrement, De qui, et de quoi, un "texte" est-il fait?' [Jacques Ehrmann], *'Textes' suivi de* La Mort de la littérature (Paris: L'Herne, 1971), 113–14.
42. *'Textes'*, 114. Furthermore, the signature 'J. D'. that ends the 1971 lecture 'Signature événement contexte' (whose translation in *Glyph* in 1977 – as 'Signature Event Context' – and the debate with John R. Searle it prompted constitutes another pertinent moment in Derrida's international institutionalization), resembles Ehrmann's 'J. E'. with which *La Mort de la littérature* (also 1971) concludes. 'Border Lines' recalls the paratextual coming-together of the two signatures:

> [Ehrmann] had the good fortune to sign J. E. when he wrote his initials. This permitted him to inscribe my copy of his book *"Textes" suivi de "La mort de la littérature,"* published anonymously, as follows: "To J. D. in friendly remembrance of this '10 November' on which J. E. called you." J. E. are also the last letters of these "texts," their final paraph in his untranslatable signature. 'Border Lines', 75–76.

See Derrida, 'Signature événement context', Derrida, *Marges de la philosophie* (Paris: Les Éditions de Minuit, 1972), 393. For the Searle debate, see *Limited Inc.* (Evanston, IL: Northwestern University Press, 1988), and *Derrida* (Peeters), 404.
43. Derrida, 'Politics and Friendship: An Interview with Jacques Derrida', *The Althusserian Legacy*, eds. E. Ann Kaplan and Michael Sprinker (London and New York: Verso, 1993), 188.
44. 'Living On', 75/'Survivre', 119.
45. Gasché, *The Tain of the Mirror: Derrida and the Philosophy of Reflection* (Cambridge, MA and London: Harvard University Press, 1986; repr. 1997), 136.
46. 'Living On', 76–77/'Survivre', 121.
47. 'Border Lines', 170.
48. Derrida, 'No Apocalypse, Not Now (full speed ahead, seven missiles, seven missives)', trans. Catherine Porter and Philip Lewis, Derrida, *Psyche: Inventions of the Other, Volume 1*, eds. Peggy Kamuf, Elizabeth Rottenberg (Stanford: Stanford University Press, 2007), 387.
49. Derrida, 'No apocalypse, not now (à toute vitesse, sept missiles, sept missives)', Derrida, *Psyché: Inventions de l'autre* (Paris: Galilée, 1987), 363.
50. 'No Apocalypse, Not Now', 388.
51. 'No Apocalypse, Not Now', 388/'No apocalypse, not now', 364.
52. 'No Apocalypse, Not Now', 391/'No apocalypse, not now', 368.

53. 'Survivre', 145.
54. 'Border Lines', 96–100.
55. Derrida, '"What Does It Mean to Be a French Philosopher Today?"' (Interview with Franz-Olivier Giesbert), Derrida, *Paper Machine*, trans. Rachel Bowlby (Stanford: Stanford University Press, 2005), 114.
56. 'Border Lines', 169–71/'Survivre', 213–14.
57. Derrida, 'Where a Teaching Body Begins and How It Ends', trans. Jan Plug, Derrida, *Who's Afraid of Philosophy?*, 90/'Où commence et comment finit un corps enseignant', Derrida, *Du droit à la philosophie*, 143.
58. Sean Gaston suggests that Derrida's writing on the specifically Kantian university between 1975 and 1990 (the texts collected in *Du Droit à la philosophie*) 'is mediated by his reading of Kafka in "Préjugés: devant la loi"'. This offers another inextricable syntagm. See Gaston, *Derrida and Disinterest* (London and New York: Continuum, 2005), 57–58. For 'Préjugés', see Derrida, *La faculté de juger* (Paris: Les Éditions de Minuit, 1985); the English translation, by Avital Ronell with Christine Roulston, is in Derrida, *Acts of Literature* ed. Derek Attridge (London: Routledge, 1992).
59. Derrida, 'The Future of the Profession or the Unconditional University (Thanks to the "Humanities", What *Could Take Place* Tomorrow)', trans. Peggy Kamuf, *Derrida Downunder*, eds. Laurence Simmons and Heather Worth (Palmerston North: Dunmore Press, 2001), 237. For a commentary on this text, see Michael A. Peters, 'The University and the Future of the Humanities', Michael A. Peters and Gert Biesta, *Derrida, Deconstruction, and the Politics of Pedagogy* (New York: Peter Lang, 2009), 115–20.
60. 'The Future of the Profession', 246.
61. 'The Future of the Profession', 245.
62. *Authenticity*, 27–28.
63. *Authenticity*, 66.
64. *Authenticity*, 64.
65. Brian Hebblethwaite, who recommended the reading of Taylor as an exposé of Derrida's 'decadence', phrases the narrative this way: 'Philosophical idealism has tended rather to assert the dependence of the world on *our* minds. This is the dominant characteristic of those post-Kantian strands in western philosophy, which, losing confidence in the objectivity of God and His creation, have tended greatly to exaggerate the contribution of the human mind to the constitution of how things are' (Hebblethwaite, '"True" and "False" in Christology', *The Philosophical Frontiers of Christian Theology: Essays Presented to D. M. MacKinnon*, eds. Brian Hebblethwaite and Stewart Sutherland [Cambridge: Cambridge University Press, 1982], 229). There is not space here to analyze the theological reception of Derrida in Britain that preceded the Affair, but it is a rich topic.
66. Marian Jeanneret, 'Opinio Regina Mundi?', *The Cambridge Review*, Vol. 113, No. 2318, 102, n1.
67. Derrida, 'Structure, Sign, and Play in the Discourse of the Human Sciences', trans. Richard Macksey and Eugenio Donato, *The Structuralist Controversy: The Languages of Criticism and the Sciences of Man*, eds. Macksey and Donato (Baltimore and London: The Johns Hopkins University Press, 1972; repr. 1977), 268.

68. *Authenticity*, 130, n37. Quoting Taylor's reference in full exemplifies how supposedly 'neutral' or 'apolitical' paratextual features can be suffused with latent agendas:

> The connection between Derrida's anti-humanism and a radical, untrammelled sense of freedom emerges in passages like the one alluded to here, where he describes his mode of thinking as one that "affirms free play and tries to pass beyond man and humanism, the name man being the name of that being, who throughout the history of metaphysics or of ontotheology – in other words, through the history of all of his history – has dreamed of full presence, the reassuring foundation, the origin and end of the game." Derrida, "Structure, Sign and Play in the Discourse of the Human Sciences," in Richard Macksey and Eugenio Donato, eds., *The Structuralist Controversy* (Baltimore: The Johns Hopkins University Press, 1972), 264–65.

Taylor cites translations elsewhere in his notes; he also quotes Rousseau in French and Herder in German. There is a suspension of this practice where Derrida is concerned.

69. *The Structuralist Controversy*, 247, n1 (my italics).

70. *The Structuralist Controversy*, 264–65/Derrida, 'La Structure, le signe et le jeu dans le discours des sciences humaines', in Derrida, *L'Écriture et la différence* (Paris: Éditions du Seuil, 1967), 427.

71. See Samuel Weber, *Institution and Interpretation. Expanded Edition* (Stanford: Stanford University Press, 2001), 3–4.

72. The question of the *seriousness* of this text returns in Derrida's 1990 address, 'For the Love of Lacan', in which he criticizes Jacques Lacan for his perceived flippant treatment of it:

> René Girard reported to me that after my lecture in Baltimore, when he was seeking to elicit from Lacan his own (generous) assessment, Lacan supposedly replied: "Yes, yes, it's good, but the difference between him and me is that he does not deal with people who are suffering," meaning by that: people in analysis. What did he know about that? Very careless. To be able to say such a thing, so imperturbably, and know such a thing, he could not have been referring either to suffering (alas, I too deal with people who suffer – all of you, for example) or to transference, that is, to love, which has never needed the analytic situation to claim its victims. Derrida, 'For the Love of Lacan', Derrida, *Resistances of Psychoanalysis*, trans. Peggy Kamuf, Pascale-Anne Brault, Michael Naas (Stanford: Stanford University Press, 1998), 67.

73. *Authenticity*, 64.

74. See Derrida, *The Death Penalty, Volume I*, eds. Geoffrey Bennington, Marc Crépon, Thomas Dutoit, trans. Peggy Kamuf (Chicago and London: University of Chicago Press, 2014), 141. For an overview of Nietzsche's critiques of Kantian aesthetics, see Matthew Rampley, *Nietzsche, Aesthetics and Modernity* (Cambridge: Cambridge University Press, 2000), 166–89.

75. See Paul Guyer, 'Free Play and True Well-Being: Herder's Critique of Kant's Aesthetics', *The Journal of Aesthetics and Art Criticism*, Vol. 65, No. 4 (Autumn 2007), 364, *passim*.

76. See Guyer, 'Gerard and Kant: Influence and Opposition', *The Journal of Scottish Philosophy*, Vol. 9, No. 1 (2011), 62: 'Kant's proposal is that the subjective but universally valid pleasure in beauty is due to the *free play* of the cognitive powers of imagination and understanding stimulated by the representation of an object, and that such a state is "noticeably pleasurable" precisely because its satisfaction of the general goal of cognition takes place without the use of a determinate concept'. See also Ruth Ronen, *Aesthetics of Anxiety* (Albany: SUNY Press, 2009), 17: 'Pleasure is what accompanies a given presentation restricted by no determinate concept, that is, given to the free play of the faculties'.

77. 'Opinio Regina Mundi?', 102, n1.

78. Avital Ronell, *Crack Wars: Literature Addiction Mania* (Urbana and Chicago: University of Illinois Press, 1992; repr. 2004), 29.

79. Immanuel Kant, *The Conflict of the Faculties*, trans. Mary J. Gregor/*Der Streit der Fakultäten* (Lincoln, NE and London: University of Nebraska Press, 1979; repr. 1992), 79/78.

80. See Susan Meld Shell, *Kant and the Limits of Autonomy* (Cambridge, MA and London: Harvard University Press, 2009), 249–52.

81. *Conflict*, 35/34.

82. Derrida, 'Given Time: The Time of the King', trans. Peggy Kamuf, *Critical Inquiry*, 18 (Winter 1992), 166–67.

83. In *The Metaphysics of Morals*, Kant suggests a homology between contraband and the figure of the child born outside of wedlock. It is partly based on this homology that Kant argues for the exceptionality of maternal homicide as a homicide but not a murder: because it is a sort of 'contraband merchandise', the 'annihilation' of the child outside of wedlock can take place 'below the radar', in the same manner that such contraband existed in society. This is the first excerpt of Kant that Derrida cites in his seminar series on the death penalty. In the genealogy of modern philosophy propounded by Taylor and countersigned by Hebblethwaite, there recurs this troubling (and again, obliquely Kantian) coalescence of the figures of the drug and of the 'illegitimate' offspring (see *The Death Penalty I*, 123–28).

84. Jeffrey Mehlman notes in passing a similar police-like aspect to Searle's disagreement with Derrida: 'Now, it happened that of those prepared to hear me out on the Berkeley campus the philosopher John Searle was among the most eager. Might I have made a proselyte? In my enthusiasm, I had failed to note that the charmingly conscientious Searle had the philosophical temperament of a cop. The set of cross-purposes was not without its comic aspect. Whereas I thought I was conducting a conversion, he thought he had found a police informant who would feed him enough hard information to put a philosophical malefactor away for a good long time'. Jeffrey Mehlman, *Adventures in the French Trade: Fragments Toward a Life* (Stanford: Stanford University Press, 2010), 74.

85. *Conflict*, 159.

86. *Conflict*, 159. For this section of the *Conflict*, see *Kant and the Limits of Autonomy*, 285–92. Derrida acknowledges the originality embodied for Kant by the French Revolution in 'History of the Lie: Prolegomena', Derrida, *Without Alibi*, ed. and trans. Peggy Kamuf (Stanford: Stanford University Press, 2002), 47–48.

Chapter 3

The Place of Philosophy

If you don't integrate the possibility of fiction in the most serious statement [. . .] then you don't understand everyday language itself.[1] —Derrida

Philosophy constantly retells its past in new mythic forms, and its relation to that past is often mythophilic whether or not the past it creates for itself is a past to which it would return or a past that it requires in order to legitimate its contemporary understanding of itself.[2] —Jeff Malpas

In an interview about the Cambridge Affair, Derrida was asked about the accusation that his work was not philosophical: 'Some of your critics have wished to deny that what you write can really be classified as "philosophy"'.[3] Derrida's interviewers (Stefan Collini, Marian Jeanneret, and Christopher Johnson) suggest that this accusation relies on an essentialist, exclusive idea of philosophy: 'Can you comment on the role of this kind of intellectual essentialism in general, and particularly in what seems to you at stake in promoting an exclusive definition of "philosophy"'?[4] In its reference to 'an exclusive definition', their question implies an impossible figure: Can something be defined exclusively, in a nondifferential manner?

Derrida's response implies that impossible figuration is integral to the discipline of philosophy:

> The question of knowing what can be called "philosophy" has always been *the very question* of philosophy, its heart, its origin, its life-principle [La question de savoir ce qui peut être appelé "philosophie" a toujours été la *question même* de la philosophie. Son cœur, son origine, son principe de vie]. Since this gesture, which is originally and constitutively a philosophical gesture, is both repeated and examined in everything I write, since my work would have no sense outside

its explicit, recurrent, and systematic references to Plato, Aristotle, Descartes, Kant, Hegel, Nietzsche, Husserl, Heidegger, and several other authors (whether in the canon or not), references made over a period of thirty years, the motives of those who want to deny that my work is "philosophy" must be sought elsewhere. That is their problem, not mine. Most often, I think these inquisitors confuse philosophy with what they have been taught to *reproduce* in the tradition and style of a particular institution [dans la tradition et le style d'une institution déterminée], within a more or less well-protected – or rather, less and less well-protected [plus ou moins bien protégée, de moins et moins bien protégée] – social and professional environment.[5]

Derrida makes three important points. First, legitimation of philosophy is 'originally and constitutively a philosophical gesture' – philosophy is *not* defined differentially, and this impossible definition and its reiterations comprise the place of philosophy. Second, this gesture is not inherently conservative – Derrida avows its operation in his own work – but can become conservative if inflected in a certain manner. Third, this conservative inflection is associated by Derrida with specific, contemporary threats to the 'less and less well-protected' environment in which philosophy is practised. This chapter addresses the significance of Derrida's first two points in terms of the Cambridge Affair, and the following one discusses Derrida's third point in terms of the Affair's immediate historical and political context.

THE CAMBRIDGE AFFAIR IN THE HISTORY OF PHILOSOPHY

My analysis is guided by Martin Hägglund's account of Socrates's distinction between philosophy and literature in Plato's *Republic*. Here, 'Socrates' main charge against Homer is that his poetry leaves us in the grip of the desire for mortal life', whereas philosophy ought to be concerned with a 'desire toward the immutable presence of the eternal. [. . .] The task of philosophy is to convert the desire for the mortal into a desire for the immortal that can never be lost'. Hägglund regards this as the original expression of a logic of desire that persists throughout philosophy's history. In this history, desire ostensibly is oriented toward 'a state of absolute fullness to which no object can ever be adequate'; hence, all desire seeks to transcend the condition of temporality, because temporality causes mortality. Quoting Socrates in Plato's *Symposium*, Hägglund writes: 'Socrates argues that temporal objects do not answer to what we really desire. The proper destination of desire is rather an eternity that "neither comes into being nor passes away" and thus transcends temporal finitude'.

Hägglund suggests, however, that although the formulation of desire in the *Symposium* founds 'the conception of desire as a desire for immortality', another reading of this formulation is possible, which is 'incompatible with a metaphysical logic of lack'. Analyzing Socrates's rehearsal of a speech by Diotima of Mantinea, which begins with the assertion that 'Mortal nature (*physis*) does all it can to live forever and be immortal', Hägglund argues that this desire is both striven for and made impossible by material, temporal means. Diotima/Socrates names reproduction begetting subsequent generations of person, but observes straightaway that the principle of reproduction also applies to every moment of a person's life. For all that we refer to a given person as the same 'from childhood to old age', actually this is not the case: 'Every day he is becoming a new man, while the old man is ceasing to exist'. This continual becoming, asserts Diotima/Socrates, applies to psychological states as much as it does to physical ones. The nature of mortality (its distinction from divinity) is therefore that it 'cannot [. . .] always be the same in every respect; it can only leave behind new life to fill the vacancy that is left behind in its species by obsolescence'.

Following Diotima/Socrates's argument, Hägglund concludes that this 'obsolescence' refers not only to the temporal limitations of a given generation, but also of life itself. 'Obsolescence' designates each successive moment in a given life; it describes the inexistence of the present as such. For Hägglund, 'A temporal being is constantly ceasing to be and can only perpetuate itself by leaving traces of the past for the future. [. . .] If something survives it is never present in itself; it is already marked by the destruction of a past that is no longer while remaining for a future that is not yet'. If Diotima/Socrates describes the measures by which mortals pursue their desire for immortality, then these measures entail 'temporalizing the notion of immortality'. Hägglund argues that if the desire for immortality comprises the logic of desire in the history of philosophy, then we must consider the conclusions about that logic that are drawn from his demonstration that this desire is not only materially impossible, but actually generated by its material impossibility.[6]

Hägglund's reading of Socrates's citation of Diotima challenges the passage from poetry to philosophy discussed by Socrates in the *Republic*, in what is an argument for, and from, the legitimacy of philosophy. Hägglund does not return to this homology (mortality and immortality; poetry and philosophy), but his demonstration of the material structure that founds and frustrates the desire for immortality is indispensable for the following discussion of the desire for philosophy and its articulation in the Cambridge Affair – which, as we shall see, desires above all an immortal place for philosophy.

Much of this chapter revolves around a statement in the first 'Derrida *non placet*' flysheet, which is perhaps the most significant thing written in the whole debate:

> had the Council [of the Senate] consulted the Philosophy Faculty, they would have realized how controversial the proposal [to award Derrida's Honorary Doctorate] is.[7]

The sovereignty afforded the philosophy faculty here is crucial to understanding the asymmetry between the *placet* and *non placet* positions, despite their important likenesses. As texts exhorting their implied reader to vote a certain way, the *placet* and *non placet* flysheets correspond to the ancient genre of 'philosophical protreptic'. The exhortative protreptic text is designed to alter the behaviour of its audience; more strictly, a protreptic text encourages its audience to embark upon a certain course of study. Philosophical protreptic, therefore, designates texts of that nature specifically associated with philosophy.[8] The flysheets are all exhortations to philosophy; furthermore, they retain the conflation of the exhortation to philosophy and the exhortation to virtue and to the care of the soul characteristic of fourth-century BCE protreptic.[9] The reappearance of this conflation – widely considered abandoned since Aristotelian ethics distinguished knowledge from virtue[10] – in the flysheets indicates what is at issue here. The Affair, from both *placet* and *non placet* perspectives, quickly becomes a question of philosophical authenticity in its broadest historical extension.

The asymmetry I mentioned, however, lies in the statement quoted above, which presents itself as the sovereign articulation of philosophical law through a reduction of a Socratic dialogue to its barest coordinates, screening from its audience the element of pedagogy essential to its philosophical status. That is, the consultation and realization, and passage from one to the other, are only given in their exteriority; philosophical interiority is withheld from the audience, as an unattainable privilege. This withholding is indispensable to the philosophical sovereignty the statement conveys, even as it threatens its own philosophical sovereignty through the bypassing of pedagogy. This is a double bind: a kind of philosophical autoimmunity.

This autoimmune, impossible interiority is engendered by the statement's portrayal of the philosophy faculty as constituted by legislative *consensus*; accordingly, I argue in this chapter that the legislation of the interior place 'proper' to philosophy, a concern that marks philosophy as a discipline, is not a gesture which is the same each time. I argue that the model of legislative philosophical sovereignty propounded in this *non placet* statement actually *founders* on the historical-philosophical trope of interiority on which it understands itself to be *founded*.

I want to say a few more things about this statement, and especially its grammar. But before doing so, it is worth noting that the singular mind accredited to the 'philosophy faculty' here is patently unfeasible. Could any faculty in the modern university confidently annex to its own collective such an unwavering self-identity? Could one imagine a philosophy faculty, caught up and intervening in the field's analytic/Continental Divide, say, being able to presuppose as one of its fundamental attributes a fixed, unified 'consultation', especially when such a consultation would pertain to a philosopher whose appropriateness to philosophy is a question that strikes at the heart of that Divide? Such a legislative single-mindedness clearly is a fantasy, yet it is precisely such a fantasy that constitutes the grounds and key principle of this *non placet* statement. If it is so fantastical, why is this statement so decisive for the Affair?

According to a fragment of Kant,

> There are two fields in which pure reason tries to acquire a possession, mathematics and philosophy. – In the first case, no one has ever claimed an ability to decide over it on the basis of authority, but this claim can do no harm, since mathematics is merely an instrument, whereas philosophy alone can determine the final purpose of human reason and with mere concepts of reason de-.[11]

Kant suggests that 'decid[ing] over' (*entscheiden*) philosophy is as integral to its uniqueness among 'fields' (*felden*[12]) as the work produced in that field, because philosophy, rather than being an instrument, constitutes the authentic position according to which the efficacy of instrumental disciplines can be determined.[13] This fragment does not separate the legislative decision distinguishing philosophy from everything else (and distinguishing authentic from inauthentic philosophy), from the practice of philosophizing. These two aspects of philosophy are key to what follows. I will call the former 'metaphilosophy' and the latter 'philosophy'.

Is the decision over philosophy in fact integral to the discipline's avowed singularity? Novalis states, 'The true philosophical system must contain the pure history of philosophy. The former applied to the specialized chronicle of the development of philosophy among man – yields the history of human philosophy',[14] but already his adjectivalization of truth – its evaluation of the philosophical – suggests that philosophy's monumental nature (what Rodolphe Gasché calls its 'eternal aspiration toward self-foundation'[15] and Jean-Luc Nancy 'the self-engendering which defines the philosophical as such [l'auto-engendrement qui définit proprement le philosophique]'[16]) requires a metaphilosophical care, which is spatio-temporally finite – the 'timing of the moment of judgment', which, according to Peter Sloterdijk, 'penetrate[s] philosophical consciousness'.[17] Only by this metaphilosophical element – the implicit determination of what constitutes 'the true philosophical system' – can the history of philosophy be determined in its 'purity'. Novalis later defines philosophy as 'an art of self-division and self-union – an *art of self-specification* and *self-generation* [eine Selbstscheidungs und Verbindungskunst – eine *Selbstspeficiations* und *Generationskunst*]',[18] intimating an artisanal, even curatorial intervention in philosophy's aspiration toward self-foundation.

In his 1805 series of lectures at Erlangen, 'On the Nature of the Scholar',[19] Johann Gottlieb Fichte demonstrates the notion that philosophy is constituted by its own legislation. In the sixth lecture, 'Of Academical Freedom', Fichte argues that one can conceive of academic freedom according to the two perspectives from which every object might be considered, the historical and the philosophical: 'As every object might be looked upon from a double point of view, – partly historical, partly philosophical, – so may the subject of our present inquiry [academic freedom]' (185).

Historically, academic freedom arises from a 'contempt' expressed by the founders of the first modern universities for the heavy-handed pedagogy of the 'lower preparatory schools', characterized by 'supervision on the part of the teacher over the morality, industry, or scientific progress of the Student'. These founders, 'scholars of distinguished talent and energy', lived by and were solely interested in their own 'scientific pursuits', and their distinction partly stemmed from their elevation above the supervisory role of schoolteachers. Accordingly, a different dynamic between scholar and student arose, with the student becoming the mere 'hearer' of the oracular pronouncements of the scholar (186–87).

Fichte states that the student would have had three available responses to this situation of indifference on the part of their teacher: to feel honour and entitlement; to become careless of their own moral and scientific development; or to address this indifference by exercising, 'because of this want of foreign superintendence [fremder Aussicht], [. . .] a stricter surveillance [strengere Aussicht] over themselves' in these matters (187–88/117–18). He dismisses the first two as unreasonable – the first because it would misunderstand the teachers' 'disregard and contempt' for their students; the second because he 'cannot believe it' (187–88). More reasonable, Fichte suggests, is the third response, 'if out of this freedom from outward constraint had arisen a clearer perception of [the students'] duty to urge themselves onward so much the more powerfully, to watch over themselves so much the more incessantly, and to look upon their Academic Freedom as liberty to do all that is right and becoming *by their own free determination* [Entschlusse]' (188/118).

Fichte posits something like a superego[20] here: 'Free determination' in genuine scholarship becomes inflected by a self-discipline that compensates for the absence of an external pedagogical *Aussicht*, animated by the memory of that absence's grounding in scholarly self-interest. Fichte makes clear that 'the Academic Freedom of the Student, taken historically, according to its actual introduction into the world, exhibits in its origin, in its progress, and in what of it still exists, an unjust and indecent contempt for the whole class of Students, as a most insignificant class [eine ungebührliche Geringschätzung des ganzen Standes der Studirenden, al seines höchst unbedeutenden Standes]' (188/118). This means that the historical self-determination of the modern university student – and the scholar they may become – is characterized by a disposition toward justice: It is a legislation that supersedes, whilst continuing to incorporate, the unjustly self-interested attitude to which it responds. For Fichte, moral and ethical (and 'work-ethical') legislation henceforth become essential to the historical development of the modern university and its disciplines, and are most closely affiliated with the self-interested and self-reflexive aspects of those disciplines. This is how 'actually existing Academic Freedom' (188) comes about.

The 'philosophical' dimension of academic freedom pertains to 'how the actually existing [i.e., 'historical'] Academic Freedom will be accepted by the Student who understands and honours his vocation' (188). Academic freedom, philosophically, is the reasonable means by which the self-legislating disposition brought about by the historical development of academic freedom might be attained. Fichte approaches this question through three 'sentences' (*Sätze*), outlining his conceptions of the law, of citizenship's constitution by the law, and finally of the unique relation to the law enjoyed by the scholar.

First, Fichte argues that the 'outward' behaviour of the citizen is everywhere regulated by the limitations of the law, and the more 'perfect' a given legal system is, the tighter will this regulation be: The law should 'approximate to' a comprehensive regulation of its citizens. The ideal law installs 'conscience' at the passage between '*inward* freedom and morality' and outward behaviour, ensuring that the inward temptation to countermand the law 'is counterbalanced in the conscience of the Citizen by the firm conviction, that should he give way to the temptation, he must by consequence suffer a certain amount of evil' (189). Fichte acknowledges that 'the just man' will behave justly even in the absence of law, but states that an inward tendency to justice is impossible to demonstrate externally, and indeed might be fabricated. Therefore, there is no outward distinction to be made between the authentically just man, and the one who only behaves justly because of the 'threatenings [Drohung] of the law'; motive is 'not outwardly apparent' (189/122). Fichte's second 'sentence' confirms that citizenship – in view of which the scholar and the 'unlearned person' are identical – is understood as the constitution of the subject under 'external legislation'. The principle of this legislation remains the same even if one takes the specific example of the civic role of the scholar and the obligations of this role to the state. Again, one cannot discern whether the scholar, in his societal determination, acts from 'inward integrity' or from 'fear of punishment' (189–90).

Having made these provisions, Fichte delivers his third 'sentence', which indicates 'the relations [or affairs: Verhältnisse] of the Scholar with which external legislation [Gesetzgebung] cannot interfere', and for which there is no external juridical model or precedent (190/123). This is the scholar's relation to the Divine Idea (*die göttliche Idee*). The Divine Idea is Fichte's term for the universal foundation of all particular, natural appearances (138). The scholar's vocation is to become a sort of host for the Divine Idea, giving it the freedom to live, to love itself (*lebt und sich liebt*) (142–43/15), and to assume a 'definite form within him' (158). The 'person' of the scholar has no intrinsic purpose, or even selfhood, beyond this responsibility for hosting the Divine Idea. The scholarly love of the Idea, and his quest for knowledge of it, are actually the appearance of the Idea's love for itself (158–59).

This relation to the Divine Idea, peculiar to the scholar, distinguishes him from other citizens. It has the character of a law because it is the scholar's responsibility to interpose between the purity of the Divine Idea and a world which is not yet ready for it: 'In the Divine Idea he carries in himself the form [Gestalt] of the future Age which one day must clothe itself with reality; and he must show an example and lay down a law [Gesetz] to coming generations, for which he will seek in vain in either present or in past times' (190/123–24). This self-legislation will make possible the reconciliation of the Divine Idea with some future reality, and this self-legislation alone escapes the purview of the legislative forms to which citizens are subject. The fulfilment of this self-legislative duty is the exclusive right, duty, and privilege of the scholar: 'The Scholar must be a law [Gesetz] unto himself and hold himself to its fulfilment' (190/123).

The 'philosophical' dimension of academic freedom is therefore the act of legislation that makes possible the Divine Idea in a world whose existing precepts the Idea would challenge. Absolute philosophical responsibility is indissociable from a juridical decision, and is a commitment to jurisdiction even, or especially, where it may seem impossible. The decision of philosophy does not come after any philosophical content, but actually constitutes the exemplary philosophical act – if philosophy is understood, with Fichte, as grounded in the principle of academic freedom. What Sloterdijk calls the 'endogenous' nature of Fichtean thought – how it exemplifies philosophy's avowed lack of obligation to anything but itself[21] – is possible through this mutual imbrication of metaphilosophical legislation and philosophical content. The influence of Fichte's claim can be seen in the work of *non placet* philosopher D. H. Mellor: 'Philosophy is really no more of a spectator sport than mathematics is – by which I mean that it's not like poetry, for example, which you needn't be a poet to judge, whereas you do need to be a philosopher to judge philosophy, just as you need to be a mathematician to judge mathematics'.[22]

I am interested in how this mutual ground of legislation and content, particular to philosophy, explains crucial formal properties of the 'Derrida *non placet*' case. To make this argument coherently, it is necessary to indicate how the self-understanding of philosophy as a discipline is informed by this mutual ground, and that the figure or image of philosophy it constructs is always characterized by a certain impossibility, itself also particular to philosophy. This argument also lays much of the groundwork for the following chapter, where I show how this philosophical impossibility is simultaneously appealed to, and denied, during the Affair, due to specific demands upon philosophy brought about by academic institutional circumstances throughout the 1980s.

IMPOSSIBLE GRAMMAR

> A question about the place does not stand outside of place; it is properly *concerned* with place.[23] – Derrida

Let us return to our *non placet* statement and look more closely at it. '[H]ad the Council consulted the Philosophy Faculty, they would have realized how controversial the proposal is'. This statement makes the case that the philosophy faculty's hypothetical response to its hypothetical consultation would have been an absolutely comprehensive, impartial, and omni-temporal one ('how controversial the proposal *is*'), leading to the Council of the Senate's realization of the dimensions and scope of the Derrida proposal's controversy ('*how* controversial the proposal is'). This statement presupposes an exclusive coalescence of *possibility* and *certainty*: One, and only one, possible and certain hypothesis is encoded in its 'would have'. In *Politics of Friendship*, Derrida explains this logic:

> For a possible that would only be possible (non-impossible), a possible surely and certainly possible, accessible in advance, would be a poor possible, a futureless possible, a possible already *set aside* [*mis de côté*], so to speak, life-assured. This would be a programme or a causality, a development, a process without an event. [. . .] What would a future be if the decision were able to be programmed, and the risk (*l'aléa*), the uncertainty, the unstable certainty, the inassurance of the "perhaps", were not suspended on it at the opening of what comes, flush with the event, within it and with an open heart?[24]

The connection between this a priori certain possible and a sort of 'setting aside' is crucial, and it arises in the *non placet* statement. To explain how, four main problems must be worked through.

Here is the first problem. The statement seems straightforward enough: Cambridge's Council of the Senate, upon receipt of the proposal that Derrida be awarded an honorary doctorate of letters, should have notified the philosophy faculty, and asked for its reaction. This reaction would have been one of sufficient consternation to make the council aware that the proposal was controversial. There would have been enough opposition to the proposal from within the philosophy faculty to make the council aware that support for the proposal was not unanimous.

However, this reading does not account for the confident annexing of the *degree* of controversy to the judgement of the philosophy faculty. Why is no other faculty given the opportunity to respond to the proposal before it is made official? The honorary proposed for Derrida is an honorary doctorate of *letters*, not of philosophy; does the philosophy faculty therefore wish to have a say concerning all honorary doctorates of letters? Indeed, does it wish to oversee the award of all doctorates of letters, or even any award conferred by Cambridge where the recipient is involved in the group of disciplines one terms the 'humanities'? Does the philosophy faculty wish for its judgement to supersede that of any other faculty related to the humanities? Can one ignore this extreme possibility, if the philosophy faculty here has appointed itself the exclusive locus of the *controversiality* of the Derrida proposal?

Here is the second problem. Does our statement presuppose that controversy is undesirable, and should be foreclosed where possible? Does it presuppose a risk attendant on controversy, and does that risk constitute a *crisis*, a pivotal point between recovery and death?

The crisis our statement names is the 'controversy' of the Derrida proposal, which risks causing an undesirable division in the self-identity of the university, and in fact has already begun to do so. This double temporality is important. On the one hand, the controversy constitutes a 'narrative' crisis, in that it is seen to be a point of *peripeteia*, and our statement suggests that this type of crisis – 'controversy' – is best avoided where philosophy is concerned. On the other hand, the idea that *peripeteia* can be avoided is paradoxical, because an instance of *peripeteia* only takes place as the unexpected – that which, beyond not having been expected, *could not have been expected*.[25] Our statement is therefore a performative contradiction: It *recommends against controversy* in the very utterance that *ensures that a controversy will have taken place*: It institutes the controversy it warns against.

The flysheet argues that 'had the Council consulted the Philosophy Faculty, they would have realized how controversial the proposal is'; but would they? Don't the statement and the *non placet* flysheets generally actually comprise the performative utterance necessary to bring the controversy into being? The degree of controversy, that is, could not have been avoided by the council consulting the philosophy faculty: This is because if its consultation of the philosophy faculty had satisfied the council that the Derrida proposal was controversial (an outcome the philosophy faculty evidently believes would, and should, have taken place), there would, paradoxically, have been no controversy (the Derrida proposal would have been declined). Controversy would have been avoided by virtue of the philosophy faculty advising the council of the controversiality of the Derrida proposal. This is the logic of our statement, which tendentiously suggests that controversy can be nullified before it is constituted as a crisis.

Here is the third problem. I stated just now that 'The degree of controversy [. . .] could *not* have been avoided by the Council consulting the Philosophy Faculty', before arguing that if the council had consulted the philosophy faculty and been persuaded of the controversiality of the Derrida proposal before making it official, then there would have been no controversy. This seems like faulty reasoning: On the one hand, I apparently suggest that the council could *not* have avoided controversy by consulting the philosophy faculty, whilst on the other I apparently argue the opposite.

Here, I urge a nuanced distinction. Whilst I accept that controversy tout court might have been avoided by the council's prior consultation of the philosophy faculty, I stress that *the degree of controversy* could *not* have been avoided by such a consultation. This is an important distinction, because it is precisely the *degree* of controversy that our statement focuses on: 'Had the Council consulted the Philosophy Faculty, they would have realized *how* controversial the proposal is'. This is different from 'had the Council consulted the Philosophy Faculty, they would have realized *that* the proposal is controversial'.

How are these two expressions different? What is introduced by the question of the *degree* of controversy? The *how* of 'how controversial' seems to introduce a decisive, representative action, a *measurement* of the crisis of controversy. Had the expression been 'had the Council consulted the Philosophy Faculty, they would have realized that the proposal is controversial', no such action would have been introduced, because this expression permits the possibility that the council simply would have consulted the philosophy faculty, encountered resistance to the proposal, and concluded that it was controversial. However, the formulation 'how controversial' suggests that the philosophy faculty would have taken a measure of the degree of controversy, traced the contours of the controversy, shaped it in a dispassionate yet sovereign way – *narrated* it.

The *how* is therefore crucial because it supplements a further crisis: that of the location of the crisis attendant on the Derrida proposal. On the one hand, the *how* is introduced as a means of intensifying the crisis – intimating that it is not only controversial but a special case of controversy – but on the other hand, it has a simultaneous rhetorical function of localizing within the philosophy faculty the juridical act of shaping the crisis that way; the philosophy faculty gives the controversy dimensions and degrees. This double rhetoric indicates that the faculty would have its crisis and eat it – foreclose the crisis taking place as an event by constituting it as a crisis that has been measured, resolved, quarantined, brought to its dénouement. The *non placet* vote recommended by our statement's flysheet therefore is cast not as constitutive of the controversy, but as posterior to it. The vote is to internalize and neutralize the crisis, within the jurisdiction of the philosophy faculty, through an implicit profession of faith in the faculty's capacity to take its measure, to narrate it: to quarantine it.

Here is the fourth problem. If one acknowledges this narrative gesture, one should also recognize its disarticulation: 'Had the Council *consulted* the Philosophy Faculty, they would have *realized* how controversial the proposal is'. First, note how in this construction, the philosophy faculty is grammatically shielded from any enunciative agency – as opposed to, say, 'had the Council consulted the Philosophy Faculty, the Philosophy Faculty would have indicated how controversial the proposal is'. Both action ('consulted') and reaction ('realized') are attributed to the council. But this does not mean that the philosophy faculty is cast as passive, as acted upon – instead, it is impassive. Myths of unchanging, authoritative legibility or transparent readability entail, necessarily, an element of inscrutability: The transparency is what cannot be scrutinized. What this grammar – 'consulted . . . realized' – avoids is any enunciative act by the philosophy faculty. This effectively quarantines the faculty from the necessary partiality of the narrative gesture it nonetheless makes by topologizing and quarantining the 'controversy'. Consequently, the act of quarantine *is itself quarantined* in a process where 'consultation' leads to 'realization' without any intermediary dialogue.

The only way to parse this non-dialogic process is by a very partial construal of the term 'consultation', which occludes an entire genealogy in which it is understood to entail dialogue – to consult *with, of, upon, about*. Instead of this understanding, we have a consultation without preposition, predicated upon a dispassionate authority in that which is consulted. Our statement figures the philosophy faculty as something to be consulted, as one might consult a dictionary, map, or archive. In fact, it is the ideal of an archive: a body of reference impassive to the act of consultation. 'Consultation' is not an active intervention, but a passive process of being 'put right', a putting right so comprehensive in its ability to define, frame, and narrate the 'controversy' in question so as to defy representation – hence the absence of dialogue in the council's hypothetical process of 'realization' of the error of the Derrida proposal.

In our statement, the philosophy faculty figures itself as the perfect, dead archive. If, as Derrida argues, the possibility of *actual* archivization is also the possibility of the archive's destruction, then one might hypothesize an *ideal* archivization that would preclude the possibility of its destruction:

> if there is no archive without consignation in an external place which assures the possibility of memorization, of repetition, of reproduction, or of reimpression, then we must also remember that repetition itself, the logic of repetition, indeed the repetition compulsion remains, according to Freud, indissociable from the death drive. And thus from destruction. Consequence: right on that

which permits and conditions archivization, we will never find anything other than that which exposes to destruction, and in truth menaces with destruction, introducing, *a priori*, forgetfulness and the archiviolithic into the heart of the monument. Into the "by heart" itself. The archive always works, and *a priori*, against itself.[26]

This is Derrida's outline of the archive in its *actuality*. Yet the fantasy of an *ideal* archive is glimpsed in our statement: an archive that is not consigned externally, but internally, and that is constituted by the *impermissibility* of memorization, repetition, reproduction, and reimpression; an archive that cannot be visited, or forbids the iteration of its contents. If the actual archive is formally thanatological, the ideal archive would be necrological, its constituents petrified. The ways in which our statement portrays its audience as absolutely exterior, and its interlocutors as absolutely passive, suggests that the philosophy faculty from which it issues understands itself in this necroscopic fashion.

Problems one to four demonstrate the overdetermination of our *non placet* statement. The first referred to the philosophy faculty understood as the proper and only place for the diagnosis of controversy. The second unpacked the enunciative paradox of simultaneously diagnosing and recommending the foreclosure of controversy through a performative utterance of dissent. The third attempted to show that the *how* of the phrase 'how controversial' was the focal point of this paradoxical tendency: This *how*'s equivocal senses – at once *intensifying* the controversy (making it a special case of controversy) and presuming to *measure* it – render the controversy both critical, and curable through quarantine, by the philosophy faculty. And the fourth argued that the statement attempts a further quarantine, that of the philosophy faculty's diagnostic act, by figuring it as somehow not part of a dialogue, or, perhaps, not even an enunciative act at all – a text in a dead archive.

These overdeterminations serve a wish to award the philosophy faculty's diagnosis a status unburdened by any contingency (linguistic, perspectival, semantic). What is sought for the diagnostic capacity of the philosophy faculty is therefore instantaneous, *Gestalt* sovereignty – the law that is not a law among laws. As Derrida has argued, this noncontingent sovereignty finds its roots in the notion of a monarch's 'right of grace':

[The] right of grace is, as its name suggests, of the order of law, but a law which inscribes in the laws a power above the laws. The absolute monarch can, by divine right, pardon a criminal; that is to say, exercise in the name of the state a forgiveness that transcends and neutralises the law. Right [*droit*] beyond the law [*droit*]. As with the very idea of the sovereign, this right of grace has been reappropriated into the republican heritage.[27]

Derrida is consistent on this score, elsewhere discussing the importance of '"deconstructing" both the onto-theologico-political fantasies of an indivisible sovereignty and pro-nation state metaphysics',[28] and describing 'political sovereignty' as 'the Christian incarnation of the body of God (or Christ) in the King's body, the King's two bodies'.[29] Important here is the Idea, in the Kantian sense, of a law to which all others refer, but which itself is exempt from reference – from citation, iteration, or concatenation of any kind. The law that understands itself – and must be understood – as event itself, rather than as the enunciation, or representation *of* something. The overdetermination and paradox in our statement's understanding of the philosophy faculty signify something of this theological appropriation.

The way in which the belief in the sovereignty of the philosophy faculty's diagnosis can be grounded, despite this overdetermination and paradox, is through our statement's conditional future perfect tense: '*Had* the Council [of the Senate] consulted the Philosophy Faculty, they *would have* realized how controversial the proposal is'. This tense permits an inscrutable certitude – a certitude that cannot be subject to analysis – an impassive certitude (the realization *certainly* would have taken place). It also precludes the possibility of this certitude ever being arrived at, or reconciled with the present moment, even more than does the simple future perfect tense. Through the introduction of another, impossible world, the conditional future perfect could be seen visually as adding a dimension of 'depth', or a 'third dimension', to time flow, permitting parallels, comparisons, even hierarchies between time flows – and thereby making possible the fantasy of a law independent of the contingency of its articulation; a law that, in Derrida's term, is 'set aside', a programmable possible. That type of absolute law can only be sure of itself if it is certain it will never be tested, either as historical precedent or provable hypothesis. The conditional future perfect is a tense that cancels out either option, its conditionality enshrining its impassivity.

The conditional future perfect ensures that the philosophy faculty's diagnosis is always anterior: It has always already been made, but it is never visible in its moment of articulation. But in addition to this ancientness, the philosophy faculty is always already one step *ahead* of the rest of the university: Its diagnosis is only glimpsed at a moment of *peripeteia*, when the university does not follow the path the philosophy faculty has already deemed to be the correct one.

The hypothetical scenario conjured by our *non placet* statement apportions to philosophical jurisdiction a logic of a-temporal, a-topological 'ideality'. The narrative the philosophy faculty would have provided would have been a narrative without subject-position, sequence, grammar. The problem here stems from an attempt to enact the Socratic principle that 'knowledge of what is good leads automatically to doing what is good'.[30] That is, the philosophy faculty's diagnosis is impossible because it presupposes both the desirability and the possibility of unmediated translation from knowledge to action. And this presupposition itself reflects a negotiation with a philosophical quintessence, encountered as though it is law.

IMPOSSIBLE WORLDS

We can clarify the transition from conditional ('had the Council consulted the Philosophy Faculty') to certainty ('they would have realized how controversial the proposal is') with reference to possible worlds theory. Our statement gestures toward a 'possible world' that did not obtain during the Affair. This is straightforward enough at first: Possible worlds theory provides a method of analyzing 'if' scenarios like the one imagined by this *non placet* flysheet. Ruth Ronen defines possible worlds in these terms:

> Despite the diversity of philosophical opinions about possible worlds, the idea common to all of them is that non-actual possibilities make *perfectly coherent systems which can be described and qualified, imagined and intended and to which one can refer.*[31]

Ronen describes a 'perfectly coherent system' in terms of its capacity to be described, qualified, imagined, intended, and referred to. But in our statement, we encounter a fantasy of perfect coherence constituted by its being *in*describable, *un*qualified, *un*imaginable, and so forth. What is the status of a possible world conceived antithetically to this vocabulary of interpretation and representation? Later, Ronen refines her description of the possible world:

> There is more to the notion of possible worlds than just demonstrating various ways things might have happened but did not: possible worlds are destined to distinguish non-actual but possible states of affairs from impossible ones. A possible world cannot include contradictions and it cannot violate the law of the excluded middle.[32]

The law of the excluded middle is one of the 'laws of thought' Aristotle establishes in the *Metaphysics*. According to this law,

> Nor indeed can there be any intermediate between contrary statements, but of one thing we must either assert or deny one thing, whatever it may be. This will be plain if we first define truth and falsehood. To say that what is is not, or that what is not is, is false; but to say that what is is, and what is not is not, is true; and therefore also he who says that a thing is or is not will say either what is true or what is false. But neither what is nor what is not is said not to be *or* to be.[33]

This law is implicitly violated by the absoluteness of our statement, which envisions a diagnosis without even the slightest degree of partiality inherent in any assertion or denial. Because our statement disavows that the philosophy faculty's diagnosis is an interpretable assertion, it understands it as neither asserting nor denying one thing, but instead being of some greater order, passing judgement everywhere in a manner that cannot itself be interpreted.

As Wittgenstein insisted, Aristotle's establishment of the law of the excluded middle must comprehend the intermediate between contrary statements, in order to disavow it: 'In order to draw a limit to thought, we should have to find both sides of the limit thinkable'.[34] In the Aristotelian schema, this fusion of the comprehensive and the necessary is, unsurprisingly, emblematized by philosophy. The young Aristotle's influential *Protrepticus*, which only survives in fragments, contains an argument to the effect that, as Luca Castagnoli paraphrases it,

> "If your position is that one must philosophise, you are definitely on my side of the barricade, and safe from the snares of Isocrates' shallow rhetoric; if you contend, on the contrary, that one must not philosophise, you ought to vindicate this crucial choice of lifestyle, in front of me and yourself, by offering reasons for it; but don't you realise that choosing what to do (and then defending your choices) on the basis of reflection and argument, and not, say, by ballot, is already doing philosophy, and thus you have already jumped over the fence to my side?"[35]

Although it does not represent the intermediate between contrary statements, philosophy here is figured as the vantage point from which the condition of contradiction can be observed and analyzed: It interprets but is not interpretable. This is what Aristotle in the *Protrepticus* vaunts as philosophy's 'homelessness': its great advantage of being everywhere at home, resisting localization and particularization.[36]

This imagined unaccountability of the philosophical account is central to the incorporation in the modern university of the Kantian Regulative Idea of reason. In a late text entitled 'The "World" of the Enlightenment to Come (Exception, Calculation, Sovereignty)', Derrida considers such a conjuration as antithetical to the vital plurality of the contemporary university:

> If reason passes for being disinterested, in what is it still interested? Would this "interest" of reason still have to do with reason? With the rationality of a reason that is past, present, or still to come? If this architectonic vocation of reason is indeed systemic and unifying, what risks threatening it today are not only the figures of the antithesis in the antinomies of the transcendental dialectic. It is also the just as rational necessity, rational, that is, from the point of view of a history and of a development or becoming of the sciences, to take into account plural rationalities. Each of these has its own ontological "region," its own necessity, style, axiomatics, institutions, community, and historicity.

These plural rationalities thus resist, in the name of their very rationality, any architectonic organization. They do so through their distinct historicity, through the figures and conjurations that inform them, however they might be named or interpreted by means of such categories as *paradigm, themata, episteme*, the supposed *epistemological break*, and so on; and they do so through all the differences between mathematics, the natural or life sciences, the human sciences, the social sciences or the humanities, physics as well as biology, law and political economy, politology, psychology, psychoanalysis, and literary theory, along with all the techniques and institutional communities that are inseparable from their knowledge. Such an architectonic organization would do these violence by bending their untranslatable heterogeneity, one that is without analogy, and inscribing them in the unity of a "world" that Kant spoke of as a "regulative idea of reason"[.][37]

For Derrida, the 'disinterestedness' of Kantian philosophical enquiry and its architectonic form has never been disinterested, and actually *has* always been a matter for critical assertion or denial – illustrated by the unprecedented proliferation and hybridization of disciplines in the late twentieth and twenty-first centuries. Derrida questions the basic logic behind the arboreal metaphor whereby knowledge has 'branches', suggesting that the tacit Kantian root of this metaphor does violence (partly by dint of remaining *in* the metaphor, or at least in its register) to any potential for heterogeneity, or 'plural rationalities', within the modern university. It is specifically relevant here that Derrida draws on topographical vocabulary – 'ontological regions' of epistemology versus the Kantian 'world' of reason – to contend that this Kantian world is only perfectible through violence.

The universalizing ontological sphere dreamt by the philosophy faculty bears the trace of this violent 'bending' into uninterrupted sphericality of multifarious, 'regional' ontologies that are disavowed by, and in, that process. Our statement provides a clear example of this. For what, actually, does this hypothesis of the philosophy faculty represent, other than a troubling of the boundary between possibility and fictionality whose integrity – the fixity of that boundary – the hypothesis actually relies on? With Ronen,

> Possible worlds are based on a logic of ramification determining the range of possibilities that emerge from an actual state of affairs; fictional worlds are based on a logic of parallelism that guarantees their autonomy in relation to the actual world. [. . .] The fictional modal structure manifests the parallelism of fictional ontologies indicating that fictional facts do not relate *what could have or could not have occurred in actuality, but rather, what did occur and what could have occurred in fiction*.[38]

However, the figure of the philosophy faculty in our statement undoes this distinction. Our statement conjures up, *through* ramification, an autonomous possible world, one whose sovereign 'would have' is not only independent of any possible empirical verification, but, in fact, could not possibly be verified.

This would be the view of a philosopher on whose behalf the *non placet* flysheet ostensibly speaks, in its opposition to philosophy's continental drift. A. J. Ayer, seeking in the 1930s to secure philosophy's status as a discrete discipline (amidst, among other things, upheavals in the idea of 'English Literature' as a subject of study), critiques what he calls the 'metaphysical' tradition in philosophy for precisely this proclivity for the unverifiable – for propositions that are 'neither true nor false but literally senseless'[39]:

> we shall maintain that no statement which refers to a "reality" transcending the limits of all possible sense-experience can possibly have any literal significance; from which it must follow that the labours of those who have striven to describe such a reality have all been devoted to the production of nonsense.[40]

The nonsensical, non-philosophical, or fictive utterance par excellence, therefore, shares the form of our *non placet* statement. Furthermore, as a non-truth-functional conditional, our statement's structure, in Ayer's terms, would develop and multiply the terrain of controversy unforeseeably, rather than delimit it. That is, debating the value of one such conditional invariably will lead to the supplementation, either in support or detraction, of more of them:

> Very often the grounds on which one advances a non-truth-functional conditional are such that its acceptability remains open to debate. This is especially so when human behaviour is in question. [. . .] [Debates about the acceptability of a given non-truth-functional conditional] move from one non-truth-functional conditional to another, almost without touching the springboard of a fact.[41]

Or again:

> Very often we advance a conditional on the basis of nothing stronger than a statement of tendency. This applies especially to the field of human conduct, where our comparative lack of success in lighting upon universal laws leaves room for what may easily develop into rather idle speculation. [. . .] One party to such a dispute stresses one set of facts, another another; the generalizations on which they respectively rely are weak: supposition is added to supposition. In the end we are left to decide which piece of fiction seems to us to have the greater verisimilitude.[42]

A non-truth-functional conditional would be acceptable, for Ayer, 'if and only if it is supported more strongly than any of its rivals by a set of facts which include a true generalisation that we are willing to project'.[43] Allowing provisionally the extreme hypothesis that the entire Cambridge philosophy faculty voted *non placet* (it did not[44]), one still could not extrapolate from that information any generalization that could make acceptable the notion that the *degree* of controversy could have been provided by consultation with the philosophy faculty. The conditional in question is unacceptable in these terms; for what is more profoundly *fictional* than an ontology that does not pay lip service, an 'as if' that gives absolutely free rein to unaccountability, and the fantasy of an absolutely deregulated proposition? As Novalis shows, this type of articulation borders on impossible:

> Everything *Real* created out of *Nothing* (like numbers and abstract expressions for instance) – has a wonderful affinity with the things of another world – with the infinite series of singular combinations and relations – with a mathematical and abstract world in itself as it were – with a *poetical mathematical* and abstract world.[45]

Hence, by appealing to sovereign philosophical consensus through a non-truth-functional conditional, our statement cancels its own actuating force. In the *Poetics*, Aristotle argues for another overlap between philosophy and poetry on precisely this issue of unreality, indicating in another way philosophy's remove from the flysheet's hermetic designs on the discipline:

> The difference between the historian and the poet is not merely that one writes verse and the other prose – one could turn Herodotus' work into verse and it would be just as much history as before; the essential difference is that the one tells us what happened and the other the sort of thing that would happen. That is why poetry is at once more like philosophy and more worth while than history, since poetry tends to make general statements, while those of history are particular.[46] A "general statement" means [in this context] one that tells us what sort of man would, probably or necessarily, say or do what sort of thing, and this is what poetry aims at, though it attaches proper names; a particular statement on the other hand tells us what Alcibiades, for instance, did or what happened to him.[47]

For Aristotle, philosophy and poetry should share this fusion of certitude and possibility – probability and necessity – which elevates their status as disciplines at the cost of a residual shared 'DNA'. Christopher Norris argues that this fusion remains fundamental to philosophy's idiom, despite its co-option in the typical form of modern scientific hypotheses.[48] Our statement elevates the status of the philosophy faculty through this trope, irrevocably introducing a constitutive fictionality into its claim. As for the impossibility of the contention, Aristotle recommends three rebuttals to the charge of impossibility in poetry. The first stresses poetry's distinguishing formal idiosyncrasy,[49] whereas the second and third open its frontiers, pertaining respectively to its typical trade in 'general statements'[50] (which it shares with philosophy) and to a broader and more nebulous idea of consensus.[51] Nowhere does Aristotle specify the conditions for preferring one emphasis to the others; he seems to regard the three rebuttals as interchangeable. We see here an imbrication of disciplinary boundaries, which are provisional and strategic rather than fixed and organic.

INTERIORITY COMPLEX

At the beginning of this chapter, I considered Derrida's discussion of possibility in *Politics of Friendship*:

> For a possible that would only be possible (non-impossible), a possible surely and certainly possible, accessible in advance, would be a poor possible, a futureless possible, a possible already *set aside*, so to speak, life-assured. This would be a programme or a causality, a development, a process without an event. [. . .] What would a future be if the decision were able to be programmed, and the risk (*l'aléa*), the uncertainty, the unstable certainty, the inassurance of the "perhaps", were not suspended on it at the opening of what comes, flush with the event, within it and with an open heart?

It is clear from my analysis above that this programmed/programmable, 'set aside' possibility corresponds both to the grammatical form and the rhetoric of our *non placet* statement – even if my analysis challenges the historical consensus model that the contention implicitly attributes to philosophy. We can now give more thought to this metaphor of 'setting aside', which intimates a deeper heritage of the philosophy faculty's self-understanding. By critiquing a 'possible' that is at once 'futureless' (*sans avenir*) and 'set aside' (*mis de côté*), Derrida attributes a certain perspective on space and time to the reductive attitude to possibility as risk-free and 'life-assured' (*assuré sur la vie*). I will now illustrate the ways in which this spatio-temporal quality bestows upon the 'poor possible' (*mauvais possible*) a DNA it shares with a historically influential trope in metaphilosophical argument.

Saint Augustine's *Confessiones* is crucial to modern philosophies of time.[52] Specifically, its notion of the 'vanishing present' is both foundational for and recurrent in twentieth-century phenomenology, from Husserl through Heidegger and Derrida.[53] However, less attention has been paid to how this influential philosophy of time is shadowed, in Augustine's text, by a metaphilosophy of time and space.

In Book XI of the *Confessiones*, Augustine's most explicit elaboration of his conception of time, he asks God to provide a means whereby authentic philosophy can take place (XI: ii):

tuus est dies et tua est nox: ad nutum tuum momenta transvolant. largire inde *spatium meditationibus* nostris in abdita legis tuae, neque adversus pulsantes claudas eam.⁵⁴

Here is William Watts's 1631 translation of the passage:

> The day is thine, and the night is thine: at thy beck the moments fly past. Afford out of it some spare *time* for my meditation upon the hidden things of the Law; which I beseech thee shut not up against them that knock.⁵⁵

However, Edward Bouverie Pusey's translation of 1838, although avowedly based on Watts's,⁵⁶ renders the sense differently:

> The day is Thine, and the night is Thine; at Thy beck the moments flee by. Grant thereof a *space* for our meditations in the hidden things of Thy law, and close it not against us who knock.⁵⁷

Pusey follows the first English translation of the *Confessiones*, by Sir Tobie Matthew (1620), rendering *spatium meditationibus* as 'space for our meditations'.⁵⁸ Francis Joseph Sheed⁵⁹ (1942) and Henry Chadwick⁶⁰ (1991) also prefer *space* in their translations, as does Louis de Mondadon in his French translation from 1961⁶¹ – whereas Robert Arnauld d'Andilly's French translation (circa 1649) foregrounds the expression's temporal element.⁶² Alternatively again, Richard Sydney Pine-Coffin (1961) implicitly foregrounds the term's temporal aspect, but does so via a spatial metaphor:

> Yours is the day, yours the night. No moment of *time* passes except by your will. Grant me some *part* of it for my meditations on the secrets of the law. Do not close your door to those who knock.⁶³

Here, 'part' qualifies 'time', but in a manner that expresses time predominantly as something with physical, as opposed to temporal, extension. Time is represented in this translation as an area, or territory, the *spatium* of philosophy a sort of asylum.⁶⁴ Pine-Coffin's translation, therefore, figuratively situates 'part' on a spatio-temporal axis, or chiasmus.

Augustine is trying to work through the conceptuality of what he terms his *domicilio cogitationis*⁶⁵ (XI: iii), a modality proper to philosophy in which truth and meaning ineluctably cleave to one another due to a condition of non-somatic a-linguisticism:

> Audiam et intellegam, quomodo in principio fecisti caelum et terram. scripsit hoc Moyses, scripsit et abiit, transiit hinc a te ad te neque nunc ante me est. nam si esset, tenerem eum et rogarem eum et per te obsecrarem, ut mihi ista panderet, et praeberem aures corporis mei sonis erumpentibus ex ore eius, et si hebraea

voce loqueretur, frustra pulsaret sensum meum nec inde mentem meam quicquam tangeret; si autem latine, scirem quid diceret. sed unde scirem, an verum diceret? quod si et hoc scirem, num ab illo scirem? intus utique mihi, intus in *domicilio cogitationis* nec hebraea nec graeca nec latina nec barbara veritas sine oris et linguae organis, sine strepitu syllabarum diceret: "verum dicit," et ego statim certus confidenter illi homini tuo dicerem: "verum dicis." quum ergo illum interrogare non possim, te, quo plenus vera dixit, veritas, rogo, te, deus meus, rogo, parce peccatis meis, et qui illi servo tuo dedisti haec dicere, da et mihi haec intellegere.

Let me hear and understand how thou in the beginning hast made heaven and earth. This Moses wrote of; he wrote and passed away, he passed hence from thee unto thee, and he is not at this present before mine eyes. For if he were, then would I lay hold of him, and entreat him, and for thy sake would I beseech him to open these things unto me: yea, I would lay the ears of my body unto the sound bursting out of his mouth. And should he speak in the Hebrew tongue, in vain should he beat mine ears, and never should he come near my understanding: whereas if he spake Latin, I should know what he said. But how should I know whether he said truth or no? And if I could learn this too, should I know it from him? Yea, for certainly within me, in that *inward house of my thoughts*, Truth, neither Hebrew, nor Greek, nor Latin, nor of any other language, without helps of the mouth and tongue, without any sound of syllables, should tell me he says true; and myself thereupon assured of it, would confidently say unto that servant of thine: Thou speakest truth. Seeing, therefore, I have not now the means to confer with Moses, I beg of thee, Truth (inspired by whom he uttered these truths) of thee, my God, pardon of my sins: and thou that enabledst that servant of thine to deliver these truths, enable me also to understand them.[66]

The *spatium meditationibus* would be the place affording such a philosophical language uninhibited by the spatial and temporal particularities – the deixis – of mundane tongues. None of the translations consulted acknowledges the crucial fusion of space and time that Augustine's phrase introduces.[67] But the translation problems posed by Augustine's Latin imply that the place proper to philosophy is an enclosure which somehow entails the *gathering* of a spatio-temporal 'bothness' or coalescence which not only comprehends both modalities (space and time), but involves their interrelation in a manner that would not oblige either term's inflection by any contingency inflicted by the other.

Yet such inflections are precisely what is at stake in two temporal models developed and popularized by Augustine's text – those of *nunc movens* and *nunc stans*. Mark Currie explains these models' problematic duality:

> The notion that the future is ahead and the assumption that time goes forward are perhaps the most fundamental orientational metaphors we have, but the fact

is that they contradict each other. We might think of the first metaphor, with Lakoff and Johnson, as a human subject moving in a landscape, eyes facing the direction of travel, so that the future is ahead. In this case the subject is moving forward while the landscape moved through stands still. How do we reconcile this with the idea that time moves forward? It would seem that, in relation to a subject moving from left to right, from the past into the future, time must either be static or be moving in the opposite direction: the direction that would, in fact, be backwards if the person involved were to walk that way. These are perhaps best thought of as different orientational metaphors that we have to choose between, and the existence of this choice has been fully acknowledged in the history of philosophy as the distinction between a now that moves and a now that stands still. But the problem that we are getting at here is not the normal problem, often designated by the terms *nunc movens* and *nunc stans*, terms which can be traced back through Aquinas and Augustine at least as far as Plato, to name the opposition between the flow of time that humans experience and the divine perspective of an eternal now. The opposition of a moving and a standing now can also be used, in a quite different sense, to understand two basic physical orientations to which the human experience of time flow can be related: according to *nunc movens*, "now" moves through a static landscape like a person walking along a road; according to *nunc stans*, "now" stays still as time flows from the future into the past. Most of our metaphors for the passage of time contain a tension between these two conceptualisations of movement[.] [. . .] The notion of time as a spatial totality, of the kind that Augustine located in the mind of God and that Merleau-Ponty goes on to discuss as an objective field, by definition exceeds the grasp of any embodied orientation.[68]

If *nunc movens* figures the temporal experience as a changing spatial orientation traversing an unchanging temporal environment or ambience, whilst *nunc stans* entails a static spatial orientation encountered by a permanently mobile time flow, then one can say that both models, despite their dichotomy, image space and time in a *chiasmic* mutual orientation: Space traverses time, or vice versa. As Currie observes, there is a third conceptualization that 'exceeds the grasp of any embodied orientation', necessarily doing so to preserve its capacity to pertain to the divine. How though do we account for the *spatium meditationibus* and *domicilio cogitationis*, which, although not divine, seem to exceed any straightforward linguistic embodiment?

To start with, in a sense for Augustine the very use of experiential spatio-temporality as a governing trope, or idea (its function in both the *nunc movens* and *nunc stans* paradigms), would be ironic because both modalities (as experiences of the mundane) are effects of the postlapsarian condition. As Andrea Nightingale notes, '[According to Augustine] One must give praise for the natural world as God's creation but not settle down in it as a proper abode. The true dwelling for humans is elsewhere. [. . .] In Augustine's view, when Adam and Eve "fell" into earthly bodies, they also "fell" into time'.[69] Garry

Wills makes the related point that spatio-temporally situated objects of perception and experience are apprehended by Augustine as 'lower expression':

> In the very first verse of the Bible, [Augustine] sees that "At the Origin (*in Principio*) God made heaven and earth" cannot literally mean *at the beginning of time*, since God's creative act is outside time. So *Principium* means the origin of form, God's Wisdom, his Son, the second person of the Trinity, through whom he acts to give being to all the things he makes. And "heaven and earth" are not the visible things we see but their principles, the primal spirit and unformed matter that are the principles of creation. These are later given lower expression as sky and earth, but their first conception is outside time, as sound is a precondition of the song that shapes it.[70]

Empirical spatio-temporality is not an Idea in a Platonic or Kantian sense, but a trace of the present inaccessibility of the Idea. The operation of experienced space and time as a governing trope in metaphors of time would therefore testify to the limits of these representations for describing phenomena which transcend mortal experience. However, this is not to say that Augustine denigrates the phenomena of spatio-temporal experience per se; indeed, the partiality of such experience hints at some possible totality.[71] It is a question of identifying the conditions of the present nonrealization of this 'possible'. What are the tensions between the spatio-temporality proper to philosophy (the 'possibility' of philosophy), and the schemata in which this spatio-temporality can be apprehended?

For Quentin Meillassoux, these tensions can be marshalled as secular objections to predominant tropes in contemporary philosophy – tropes that, for Meillassoux, hinder philosophy's capacity to keep pace with modern science:

> [At] issue here is not the time of consciousness but the time of science – the time which, in order to be apprehended, must be understood as harbouring the capacity to engender not only physical things, but also correlations between given things and the giving of those things. Is this not precisely what science thinks? A time that is not only anterior to givenness, but essentially indifferent to the latter because givenness could just as well *never* have emerged if life had not arisen? Science reveals a time that not only does not need conscious time but that allows the latter to arise at a determinate point in its own flux. To think science is to think the status of a becoming which cannot be correlational because the correlate is in it, rather than it being in the correlate. So the challenge is therefore the following: to understand how *science can think a world wherein spatio-temporal givenness itself came into being within a time and a space which preceded every variety of givenness.*[72]

There is a homology here between the capacity of modern scientific thought (for Meillassoux) to comprehend conditions prior to the genesis (let alone the naturalization) of human metaphors of spatio-temporality, and the manner in which time in the mind of God (for Augustine) 'exceeds the grasp of any embodied orientation'. For both Augustine and Meillassoux, the task for philosophy is for its articulation to cohabit with its ideal subject-position, whose model is the divine (for Augustine) and/or the modern scientific (for Meillassoux). A related inquiry for both pertains to the epistemic circumstances or conditions limiting such cohabitation.

Appropriately, this idea is difficult to communicate. It is attempted by Heidegger, who suggests one point of contact between Augustine and Meillassoux. In his 1924 lecture 'The Concept of Time', Heidegger hints at the inarticulable and arguably unthinkable nature of the *spatium meditationibus*:

> The following considerations are not theological. In a theological sense – and you are at liberty to understand it in this way – a consideration of time can only mean making the question concerning eternity more difficult, preparing it in the correct manner and posing it properly. Nor, however, is the treatise philosophical, in so far as it makes no claim to provide a universally valid, systematic determination of time, a determination which would have to enquire back beyond time [hinter die Zeit] into its connection with the other categories.[73]

A (metaphysical) *philosophy* of time, therefore, must metaphilosophically situate itself in an unfeasible manner. It would have to enquire back beyond time, but surely this going 'back beyond' would have to do so in a manner not identifiable as temporal – otherwise time has not been relativized in the manner Heidegger suggests, but remains the governing modality. One would not enquire 'back in time' in order to elaborate upon time's 'connection with the other categories', but the method by which the appropriate (non-)perspective would be reached would be metaphilosophically radical and as yet unthought. Augustine's God and Meillassoux's ancestrality and arche-fossils[74] share this conflation of metaphilosophical spatio-temporal positioning (sometimes called 'thesis'[75]) and 'product'.

I introduced Meillassoux and Heidegger here to preempt the objection that the metaphilosophical aspects of Augustine's meditations on spatio-temporality can be figured as symptomatic of an epochally specific, theological 'incapacity topos'. On the contrary, such aspects can inform a consideration of the genealogy of the philosophical articulation in general – which genealogy can be fed back into the metaphilosophical statement we are examining in this chapter: 'Had the Council consulted the Philosophy Faculty, they would have realized how controversial the proposal is'.

This statement imagines a scenario in which articulation and meaning are ungainsayably correlative, or even mutually superimposed. More specifically, the imagined scenario is one in which the metaphilosophical aspects of the contention – the legislation of what philosophy *is* and *is not*, the articulation's capacity to demarcate with finitude its own interiority and exteriority

– cohabit absolutely with its signification. Hence, our statement is an extension of the Kant fragment with which we began: In this fantasy of philosophical 'presence', there are no enunciative contingencies ensuring the utterance is always struggling to guarantee the meaning it strives for. Instead, the subject of the philosophical enunciation, the time of its articulation, and its content are configured as *necessarily* imbricated ('necessary' understood in the Kantian sense as the basis of possibility). There are no chiasmic interrelations or inflections in the constitution of the *spatium meditationibus*; instead, all are presumed enclosed within its mysterious interiority, which must be understood as absolute, rather than as dependent for its signification on a putative exteriority. Boris Groys argues that 'The self-evidence of traditional philosophical discourse is supposed to be its inner quality – independent of any external factors'.[76] Augustine strives for this effect through an exemplarily insular metaphilosophy.

THE PHILOSOPHER AND THE INSIDE

This *necessity* of the philosophical articulation (beyond the importance of the content of any such articulation) is metaphilosophically emphasized by Kant in *Toward Perpetual Peace*, the text that introduces the higher/lower university faculty divisions he would prescribe more expansively in *The Conflict of the Faculties*, which we looked at in detail in the preceding chapter. Kant argues that it is necessary, in times of impending warfare, for states to consult 'the maxims of the philosophers concerning the conditions of possibility of public peace'.[77]

However, so that the state does not lose face, or the wider citizenry confuse the locus of authentic power, the consultation of the state's philosophers shall be done in secret:

> But it seems belittling to the legislative authority of a state, to which we must naturally attribute the greatest wisdom, to seek instruction from its own *subjects* (philosophers) on the principles of its conduct with regard to other states; yet at the same time it seems very prudent to do so. The state will thus *call upon* the latter *quietly* (by making a secret [ein Geheimnis] of it) to do so, which means as much as: the state will *let them speak* freely and publicly about the general maxims of waging war and making peace (for they will do this of their own volition, as long as one does not forbid it), and the agreement among states on this point does not require any special arrangement to this effect on the part of the states, rather it is based already on the obligation by universal (moral-legislative) human reason. – I do not mean to say that the state must favor the principles of the philosopher [den Grundsätzen des Philosophen] over the pronouncements of the lawyer (as a representative of state authority), but rather only that one *listen* to the philosopher [sondern nur das man ihn höre].[78]

Kant clarifies in the final sentence that the importance of this arrangement is that it provides a forum for the philosopher; what the philosopher actually comes up with is very much a secondary concern. What matters is the fact of the articulation being allowed for. This crucial dispensation attends the acknowledged origins of philosophy, as Hannah Arendt notes in *The Life of the Mind*.[79] Discussing Arendt's text, Sloterdijk relates that 'Socrates had the habit of "sinking" into thought, as if thinking involved a kind of trance or obsessive daydream', an activity that entailed 'breaking off contact with his environment and becoming "deaf to the most insistent address."'

> Although the ancient witnesses [Xenophon and Plato] did not give any clue about the content of Socrates's immersion in thought, they all respected the savant's condition of "absence" as an inseparable attribute of the business of thinking. The thoughts evidently interact to form such a dense relationship that they commandeer the thinker's consciousness and interrupt his link with the perception of circumstances. This seems to imply that in real thinking, thoughts belong more closely to their fellow thoughts than the thinker to the world around him. Anybody who experiences this in reality is uprooted from his or her everyday relationship to circumstances and totally absorbed in "internal" operations.[80]

In Sloterdijk's interpretation, respect for the pure interiority of Socrates's thought-practice is manifest by the observer or reader being rendered exterior to its content. Recall that this process is recapitulated in our *non placet* statement's exteriorizing pastiche of the Socratic dialogue: 'Consultation' engendering 'realization'. For Franz Rosenzweig, this exemplary image is the spatio-temporal condition of philosophy:

> The philosopher cannot wait. His kind of wonder does not differ from the wonder of others. However, he is unwilling to accept the process of life and the passing of the numbness wonder has brought. Such relief comes too slowly. He insists on a solution immediately – at the very *instant* of his being overcome – and at the very *place* wonder struck him. He stands quiet, motionless. He separates his experience of wonder from the continuous stream of life, isolating it.[81]

I see in these depictions of the philosopher-figure a constitutive dislocation that Kant reconciles with the modern university via a state-sanctioned autonomy. Importantly, this dislocation seems to entail, as it does in our statement, a bracketing of philosophy's dialogic element within something like a privileged cadre, if not a disavowal of it altogether.

The right to philosophy will be shored up by a secret guarantee of autonomy from the state; the autonomy of the philosophers is founded on a secret state provision. The secrecy suits both parties: The philosophers are not confused with the powerful (preserving the philosophers' vital disinterestedness), and the head of state is not confused with the powerless.[82] Although in *Toward Perpetual Peace*, this arrangement seems to apply exclusively to warfare and peacemaking, the *Conflict* recommends its general application. The earlier text, too, suggests striking this bargain where state affairs more broadly are concerned:

> One cannot expect that kings philosophize or that philosophers become kings. Nor is this desirable, for holding power unavoidably corrupts the free judgment of reason. Yet both kings and king-like peoples (those which rule over themselves in accordance with laws of equality), should not allow the class of philosophers [die Classe der Philosophen] to diminish or fall silent, but rather should have them speak publicly, for this enlightens the business of government, and, because by its very nature [Natur] it is incapable of forming mobs and clubs [Rottirung und Clubbenverbündung], this class is beyond suspicion of being mere *propagandists* [der Nachrede einer Propagande verbachtlos].[83]

This invites the objection that by making a secret deal with the state, the philosophers to an extent have already formed a 'club' of sorts, and therefore are not beyond the suspicion of being propagandists. This objection would approach the telling problem with the way in which Kant contrives a time and space proper to the philosophical articulation – that he wants philosophers to be able both to have and to eat their state-sanctioned cake. He wants their autonomy to be guaranteed by the state, but them not to be consequently indebted in any way to this guarantee or its guarantor. Derrida has shown that this stance, which is reiterated in the *Conflict*, influences subsequent iterations of philosophy's privilege in university facultative structures.[84] Here, though, I want to show how the Kantian instauration of philosophical privilege cannot avoid problematizing the spatio-temporal, metaphilosophical orientation of the philosophical articulation even as it seeks to stabilize it.

Does Kant hold that the philosopher's 'privilege' is not something provided by the state, but merely that it behoves the state to accommodate this privilege? This certainly seems to be the case: the privilege of the philosopher seems self-authorized, autonomous. However, if this is so, what are the conditions for this self-authorization? Who has the right to philosophy? Does a certain privilege predetermine the undertaking of philosophy, and if so, is philosophy just an effect of privilege? This hardly seems a formulation adequate to the dynamism integral to Kantian critique; but the alternative, that the undertaking of philosophy engenders a certain privilege, seems to recast philosophy as solely praxis, and hence to diminish Kant's confidence in the *Natur* of philosophers. To be sure, philosophy for Kant is democratic in principle, but at the same time he resists the idea that *Aufklärung* is entirely reducible to conscientious hard work. There remains a conviction that philosophy is a discipline qualitatively distinct from all others.

This aporia is illustrated in another late Kant text, 'On a Newly Arisen Superior Tone in Philosophy', which foregrounds the question of the proper presentation and representation of philosophy. In this respect, like *Toward Perpetual Peace*, the essay prefigures the focus of the *Conflict*.[85] Here, Kant critiques a body of contemporary philosophy that figures truth as something like a flash of intuition, which more or less distinguishes the philosophically 'elect' from everybody else (he calls the 'philosophizers' that belong to this trend 'philosophers of vision'). He finds the basis of this 'exalted philosophy' in Plato. Instead of this image of an irruptive, aristocratic event, Kant proposes the becoming- (and maintaining-) philosopher as a process of self-authorization (Kant calls this 'work' or 'labour': *Arbeit*). But how does he integrate into his metaphor the terminuses of this process? How does he recommend one regard the space and time of the philosopher-as-process?

Kant's essay has two main aims. On the one hand, it attempts to distinguish the philosopher of work (the authentic philosopher) from the philosopher of vision; on the other, it seeks to justify this distinction by describing what work is, and how it engenders authentic philosophy. Kant undertakes the first project in a manner familiar to historians of philosophy and its rhetoric: he aligns the inauthentic philosopher (here the philosopher of vision) with the contemporary, understood as crude and modish. Disputing the claim that an acquaintance with Platonic philosophy and related classical texts makes one a philosopher, Kant states:

> To reproach this claim did not seem to me to be superfluous in our times, when ornamentation with the title of philosophy has become a fashionable item [eine Sache der Mode], and the philosopher of *vision* [der Philosoph der Vision] (if one admits such a thing), because it is so easy to attain the peak of insight by a bold leap without effort, can surreptitiously gather a great following around himself (for boldness is contagious) – a phenomenon that the police in the realm of the sciences cannot tolerate [welches die Polizei im Reiche der Wissenschaften nicht dulden kann].[86]

Kant uses the language of metaphilosophical policing and border control we saw in the previous chapter in relation to the *Conflict*, and Derrida, in his discussion of this text, makes that link explicitly.[87] Kant writes as a member of, or at least in sympathy with, this *Polizei* (interesting, given his insistence in *Toward Perpetual Peace* that philosophers cannot form factions!), and his mandate is to ensure that the interior of philosophy remains authentic. But these metaphilosophical remarks arrive straight after his most explicit fulfilment of the essay's second aim, which establishes the discipline of philosophy as nothing other than the securing of the interior of philosophy, and the establishment of interiority as the destiny of *both the space and time of philosophy*:

> Now, I consider a man as he asks himself: What is in me that makes it so that I can sacrifice the most inner [innigsten] allurements of my drives and all the desires that proceed from my nature to a law that promises me no advantage as a replacement and threatens no loss if it is transgressed; indeed, a law that I honor all the more inwardly [inniglicher] the more strictly it bids and the less it offers in return? This question stirs up the entire soul through the astonishment over the greatness and sublimity of the inner [inneren] disposition of humanity and at the same time the impenetrability of the secret that it conceals (for the answer – it is *freedom* – would be tautological, precisely because freedom constitutes the secret itself). One cannot become tired of directing one's attention toward it and admiring in oneself a power that yields to no power of nature; and this admiration is precisely the feeling generated from Ideas that make human beings morally *better* if, beyond the doctrines of morals taught by schools and pulpits, the presentation of this secret still constituted a frequently repeated occupation of the teacher, if it penetrated deeply into the soul and was not neglected.
>
> Here is what Archimedes needed but did not find: a firm point on which reason can set down its lever, and indeed it is neither in the present nor in a future world [Welt] that he needed to set it down but, rather, in reason's inner [innere] Idea of freedom, which, on account of the unshakable moral law, stands there as a secure foundation [Grundlage] for setting the human will into motion by its principles, even against the opposition of nature in its entirety. Such is the secret that *can be felt* only after a long development of concepts of the understanding and carefully tested principles, thus only through work [Arbeit]. – It is not empirically given (set up for rational analysis) but is given a priori (as an actual insight within the limits of our reason), and it even widens rational knowledge to the supersensible, but only from a practical point of view: not by some sort of *feeling* that grounds knowledge (the mystical) but by clear *knowledge* that acts on feeling (moral feeling). – The tone of those who believe themselves in possession of this true secret cannot be superior.[88]

This passage first demarcates authentic from inauthentic interiority: The becoming-philosopher 'sacrifices' the non-philosophical inner compulsions of their 'drives' (which pertain to a base nature), for a more complex and authentic interiority, 'a law that I honor all the more inwardly the more strictly it bids and the less it offers in return'. The internalization of moral law and right reason is in principle infinitely perfectible, and this perfectibility is metaphorically figured as a movement *inward*. This archaeology will uncover 'a firm point on which reason can set down its lever'.

The spatial aspect of this passage, therefore, clearly collocates philosophical integrity and interiority. This is unsurprising – the collocation integrity-interiority is a common trope[89] – but becomes more remarkable if considered alongside the way in which Kant also figures temporality in this passage. The shift in emphasis from space to time occurs between the phrases 'a firm point on which reason can set down its lever, and indeed it is neither in the present nor in a future world that he needed to set it down but, rather, in reason's inner Idea of freedom'. Here is when and where the point in space becomes also a point in time. The movement inward is now figured according to a temporal schematic which proffers a possible world theory, with interiority presented as the alternative to experiential time. Space and time here are not figured chiastically (as inflecting one another), but they are coetaneous in this philosophical becoming.

The passage can be read as a speculative account of the genesis of the Augustinian *spatium meditationibus*, referring to the process of that genesis as 'work' or 'labour'. And if we were to accord to time no discrete value here, but instead regard it as a function of philosophy's comprising the inward bent of all imaginable modalities, then we would come close to Heidegger's contention in 'The Concept of Time' that a philosophical inquiry entails not taking a given modality or 'category' of *Dasein* (that is, a means of understanding the *Da*, or 'there' in the term) at face value, but in attempting to observe the shared conditions of being which produce the categorical or modal status.

Hence, philosophical 'privilege' attends this inward trajectory. It is as though Kant wants 'privilege' to be in some way absolutely simultaneous with the philosopher – neither prior nor subsequent to, but absolutely coetaneous with them. And yet this privilege must be actively self-authorized (differentiating it from the default privilege of a monarchical lineage, for example), but *without* this taking place according to the logic of a single, irruptive act locatable in space and time (if the latter logic obtained, we would revert to the hypothesis of privilege determining philosophy, or vice versa). Privilege is metaphilosophical, pertaining to the enunciative conditions ensuring that enunciation's *interiority* vis-à-vis philosophy – its right to philosophy.[90] What is imagined is an absolute cohabitation, or spatio-temporal continuity, of the metaphilosophical and the philosophical – a cohabitation possibilized by the interior bent of the becoming-philosophical.

The force of this cohabitation is that the philosophical cannot be demarcated, if the role of the metaphilosophical is to spatio-temporally demarcate and therefore describe the limit, or 'edges', of the philosophical. The philosophical, then, becomes pure, nondifferentiated interior. An impossible geometry, an embodied, recognizable space without dimensions or limits: the Augustinian *spatium meditationibus*.

However, precisely this figure *was* theorized in Kant's first published work. In *Thoughts on the True Estimation of Living Forces*, from 1747, Kant's seventh proposition is that 'Things can actually exist and yet not be present anywhere in the world'. He develops this with reference to a thing of pure interiority:

108   *Chapter 3*

> Since all connection and relation of substances existing outside one another are derived from the reciprocal actions which their forces exercise upon one another, we may take note of what truths can be deduced from this concept of force. Either substance is in a connection and relation with others outside itself or it is not. Since every self-sufficient being contains within itself the complete source of all its determinations, it is not necessary for its existence that it stand in relation to other things. Substances can therefore exist, and yet have no outer relation to others, nor stand in any actual connection with them. Now since there can be no position without external connections, locations and relations, it is quite possible that a thing actually exists and yet is nowhere present in the world. This paradoxical statement, although it is a consequence, and indeed a very obvious consequence, of the most familiar truths, has not hitherto, so far as I know, been noted by anyone. And other propositions, which are not less remarkable, and which capture the understanding so to speak against its own will, follow from the same source.[91]

The proposition that follows from this remarkable idea (Kant's eighth proposition) is a radical version of possible worlds theory based on impossible objects and their capacity for interrelation, which relies heavily upon a metaphilosophical legislation against the inauthenticity of prevalent contemporary philosophy:

> Since we cannot say that anything is a part of a whole if it stands in no connection with other parts (in that case no distinction could be drawn between an actual and an imaginary union), and since the world is a being whose constituents are actually interconnected, a substance which is connected with nothing in the world does not in any way belong to the world, though in thought it may be something. That is to say, it is not part of the world. If there are many such beings which stand in no connection with any thing in the world, but have a relation to one another, a quite special whole thence arises: they constitute an altogether separate world. Philosophers are in error, therefore, when they teach in their Schools that more than one single world, in the metaphysical sense of the term, cannot exist. It is actually possible that God has created many millions of worlds, taking the term world in its full metaphysical meaning. Consequently, it remains undecided whether or not they also actually exist. The error into which philosophers have thus fallen undoubtedly arises from their not having paid sufficient attention to the explanation of [what is meant by] the world. By definition, only that which stands in an actual connection with the other things which are in the world can be reckoned as belonging to the world. They forget this limitation when they apply their theorem to all existing things in general.[92]

The seventh proposition suggests that it is possible to conceive of a thing that exists in a nonreciprocal relationship with other worldly things; but that since the reciprocity of thing-thing relationships is the necessary condition for their worldliness, the nonreciprocal thing would, though extant, not be of this world.[93] And being not of this world entails being divested of any obligation to a recognized subject-position. The eighth proposition develops this insight by venturing the counterintuitive idea that it is possible to imagine some way in which non-worldly things may relate to one another that does not correspond to any order of worldly relation. This impossible type of relation would be the DNA of the possible world, and the one thing that can be said for sure about this DNA is that it comprises relations that are genuine but nonreciprocal.

Having advanced this hypothesis, Kant immediately turns to the perceived errors of professional philosophers in 'their Schools' on this score. It is a fascinating juxtaposition: an impossible interrelation of impossible (entirely interior) things comprising a possible world that is then figured as something merely professional philosophy cannot comprehend. The metaphilosophical, legislative gesture par excellence, that is, comes directly after the suggestion that things of pure interiority *can* exist and cohere. Yet it arrives – and this is what is problematic about this question in Kant – precisely where Kant takes leave of the world itself.

This early Kant text offers a framework that corresponds strongly with the possible world of the philosophical jurisdiction presupposed by the Cambridge philosophy faculty in our *non placet* statement. In the latter, the possible world is founded on the hypothesis of a subject-position, or 'privileged location'[94] of absolute interiority that nonetheless exists, and that grounds a metaphilosophical critique of bad or non-philosophy. The mutually constitutive aspects of this psychology, on the one hand *being inside* and on the other *narrating what is inside* ('philosophy' and 'metaphilosophy'), are reconciled by Sloterdijk into a blueprint for what he terms 'Western culture':

> It is the basic neurosis of Western culture to have to dream of a subject that watches, names and owns everything, without letting anything contain, appoint or own it, not even if the discreetest God offered himself as an observer, container and client. The dream persistently returns of an all-inclusive, monadic ego orb whose radius is its own thought – a thought that would easily pass through its spaces up to the outermost periphery, gifted with a wonderfully effortless discursivity that no real external thing could resist.
>
> The other side of this masterful panoptic egotism shows itself in the Jonah complex, whose subject would have created a happy exile for himself in the belly of a whale, like the thirteen-year-old whose phantasms the psychoanalyst Wilhelm Stekel described: in his daydreams, the young man longed to set foot in the monstrous inside of a giantess whose abdominal cavity presented itself as a vault ten meters high. In the center of her stomach there was supposed to be a swing on which the blissful Jonah would propel himself aloft, safe in the knowledge that even the wildest vigor would never carry him out of there. The first,

fixed ego, which contains everything in its view around itself, and the second ego, the swinging one that allows itself to be contained fully by its cavity, are related in character insofar as both attempt to withdraw from the folded, interlaced, participatory structure of the real human space. Both have annulled the original dramatic difference between inside and outside by placing themselves, in a fantastic manner, in the middle of a homogeneous sphere not challenged by any real outside or unappropriated other.[95]

This neurotic Janus offers a speculative psychological paradigm for the self-understanding of philosophy I have discussed in this chapter so far; the paradigm describes the principle of the deregulated narrative position discussed in the first section of this chapter in relation to the grammar of our Derrida *non placet* statement.

However, we might suggest in conclusion that this desire for spatio-temporal apposition is the desire for that which philosophy as a discipline will have rendered unattainable for its adherent. Moreover, the point when this apposition becomes unattainable perhaps marks the success of philosophical training. The case of Fichte's scholar, in 'On the Nature of the Scholar', is again pertinent here.

For Fichte, there are two types of true scholar: 'a complete and Finished Scholar, a man who *has studied* [ein vollendeter und fertiger Gelehrter, ein Mann, der ausstudirt hat]' (141/12), and the 'Progressive, [. . .] self-forming Scholar – *a Student*' [ein angehender und sich bildener Gelehrter, ein Studirender]' (142/12). The former has incubated the Divine Idea for sufficient time, and with sufficient responsibility, that it has assumed its optimum form in him. He is able to recall and deploy this form at any moment and in any circumstance. For the latter, this incubation is ongoing; the Idea, although assuming form, is incomplete. This is a variation on a commonplace distinction, but where the nature of the relation between the types of scholar is concerned, there is a tension.

The student, if truly inspired by the Idea – 'if he possess Genius and true talent' (168) – is, as we saw in the beginning of this chapter, beyond the remit of external legislation where his vocation is concerned; in this respect he is in the realm of philosophical legislation. Nobody may determine whether or not the student possesses this Genius which marks the gestation of the Idea within him. Nobody, that is, including himself – and indeed if a scholar can reflexively determine that he possesses Genius, that he is possessed by the Idea, then he is truly in the possession of neither. Self-satisfied reflection upon one's own believed-in possession of Genius tends to manifest itself in self-congratulation, complacency, and 'contemptuous disparagement of the personal qualities and gifts of others' (163–64). According to Fichte, 'the advancing Scholar can never determine for himself whether or not he possesses Genius [der angehende Gelehrte kann nie entscheiden, ob er in dem von uns angegebenen Sinne des Wortes Talent habe, oder nicht]' (168/70). This 'never' absolutely demarcates between studentship (progressive scholarship) and the status of 'Finished Scholar'. The demarcation is absolute because the apprehension of one's scholarship as 'finished' in fact confirms that it is not, and never will be, because such an apprehension would confirm a disposition unamenable to the formation of the Idea in its optimum form. The continuing, genuine disbelief in one's scholarly completion is the only possible mental attitude whereby that completion might take place. The postulated self-formation of the scholar is a final temptation which continually must be resisted in order for that self-formation to reach completion in a possible future.

However, alongside these distinctions between the student and the finished scholar is a differing relation to what Fichte calls 'circumstances', a difference that he does not address. In the finished scholar the optimal form of the Idea's love for itself manifests itself in knowledge of the Idea 'with a well-defined and perfect clearness'; in the student, the gestating form of the Idea manifests itself 'as a striving towards such a degree of clearness as it can attain under the circumstances [Umständen] in which he is placed' (158/49). The student experiences a 'presentiment [Ahnung]' of the Idea as it strives to manifest itself within him; this striving is felt as lack, and the student orients his 'essential life [eigenes Leben]' around the attainment of what is lacking, without being able to intellectualize what this is: 'He feels that every new acquisition which he makes still falls short of the full and perfect truth, without being able to state distinctly in what it is deficient, or how the fullness of knowledge which is to take its place can be attained or brought about' (159/50). This orientation, a 'supernatural' instinct or impulse (Uebernatürlichen Hinziehendes), relegates even personal, natural want to a secondary concern, and the result is a life marked by Genius: 'This impulse towards an obscure, imperfectly-discerned spiritual object, is commonly named Genius' (159/50); 'Genius is [. . .] the effort of the Idea to assume a definite form' (161).

However, at this stage the impulse remains directed toward a partial grasp of the Idea. Fichte suggests two explanations of the student's maturation to account for this partiality. It is either a case of 'inborn *specific* Genius [angeboren besondere Genie]', which would lay hold of the initial manifestation of the Idea it encountered upon the given individual's 'first appearance [. . .] in the world of sense', and would need gradually to extrapolate from that initial laying-hold in order to grasp further manifestations; or it is a case of 'originally universal Genius [Allgemeinen als Genialität überhaupt angeboren]', where peculiar Genius does not extrapolate from an initial scene, but develops according to the encounter between the individual power and 'that material which chance presents at the precise moment when the power is sufficiently developed'. Whether arguing from specificity or universality, what is constant is the incompletion of the Genius's grasp, in the student, of the Idea as de-particularized: Genius's impulse remains 'towards some particular side of the one indivisible Idea' (160/53–54).

The continuing impulse of Genius must be alloyed with 'persevering industry [Fleiß], uninterrupted labour' (161/59); this Industry is as important as Genius, because Industry provides the value of Time necessary for the Idea to disclose itself through material manifestations, of which Genius can then make sense. Industry 'spontaneously appears' where 'Genius is really present' (163). Genius and Industry are the twin processes through which the student can become a finished scholar, because these provide the conditions allowing the Idea to 'impress its image on the surrounding world', which is 'the object for which the living Idea dwelling in the True Scholar seeks for itself an embodiment' (161). This embodiment would entail for the finished scholar the truest worldly interiority; it would allow him or her an affinity with the world's animating principles:

> [The living Idea] is to become the highest life-principle, the innermost soul [innigste Seele] of the world around it; – it must therefore assume the same forms which are borne by the surrounding world, establish itself in these forms as its own proper dwelling-place [ihrer Behausung wohnen], and with a free authority regulate the movements of all their individual parts according to the natural purposes of each, even as a healthy man can set in motion his own limbs (161/56).

To this healthy symbiotic interiority experienced by the finished scholar, Fichte opposes the sickness of the one in whom 'the indwelling Genius proceeds but half-way in its embodiment, and stops there'. This termination – whether due to the inaccessibility of 'the paths of Learned Culture' or disdain for these – results in the opening of 'an impassable gulf' between himself and 'every possible age and the whole human race in every point of its progress' (161). This individual's aborted growth of Genius is experienced as alien: 'Whatever may now dwell within him, – or, more strictly speaking, whatever he might have acquired in the course of his progressive culture, – he is unable to explain clearly either to himself or others, or to make it the deliberate rule of his actions and thus realize it in the world'. What is lacking in the two types of incompletion – that of the student and that of the one whose growth of Genius is terminated – are '*Clearness* [Klarheit]' and '*Freedom* [Freiheit]'. Clearness is the self-reflexive cultivation of the mind whereby it can act as a transparent conduit for the divine source of thought, guiding this outward and directing it to 'all those points at which it has to manifest and embody itself in the visible world'; and freedom is the capacity to guide perception thus prepared by clearness (162/57).

Now Fichte clarifies the transition from the student or otherwise incomplete scholar, to the finished scholar: Fichte locates 'the point of perfection for the Scholar':

> [He] in whom the Idea perfectly reveals itself, looks out upon and thoroughly penetrates all reality [die ganze Wirklichkeit] by the light of the Idea. Through the Idea itself he understands all its related objects, – how they have become what they are, what in them is complete, what is still awanting, and how the want must be supplied; and he has, besides, the means of supplying that want completely in his power. The embodiment of the Idea is then for the first time completed in him, and he is a matured Scholar; – the point [Punkt] where the Scholar passes into the free Artist [den freien Künstler] is the point of perfection [Punkt der Vollendung] for the Scholar. Hence it is evident that even when Genius has disclosed itself, and visibly becomes a self-forming life of the Idea, untiring Industry is necessary to its perfect growth. (162/58).

The finished scholar would therefore provide a model for the place from which our *non placet* statement speaks: Able to derive the image of a perfect reality or possible world from the present state of reality, he has the capacity to supplement the discrepancy between reality and preferable possibility. However, the attempted actualization of this potential would entail the supposition that one had become a finished scholar, which for Fichte is inimical to finished scholarship. One way to resolve this tension is to suggest as Fichte does that the point of scholarly completion in fact is not only a point but also a moment of passage: This figure of a spaced-out point both marks the completed manifestation of Genius and reveals the infinite incompletion of the Industry that appeared with the beginnings of this manifestation:

> Hence it is evident that even when Genius has disclosed itself, and visibly becomes a self-forming life of the Idea, untiring Industry is necessary to its perfect growth. To show that at the point where the Scholar reaches perfection the creative existence of the Artist begins; that this, too, requires Industry, that it is infinite; – lies not within our present inquiry; we only allude to it in passing. (162)

For the perfection of scholarship as manifestation of Genius to be a point, but not thereby to reveal itself as actually a point of terminal imperfection ('the advancing Scholar can never determine for himself whether or not he possesses Genius'), it must also be part of a more extensive process: that of the infinite existence of the artist. Hence, the position of interiority – of symbiosis with the topography of reality – which our *non placet* statement granted for itself is revealed as anticipatory of a future which is beyond it. For although Industry initially is conditional on Genius, the former's infinitude renders the latter provisional. An ostensible philosophical description of the *non placet* perspective reveals that perspective only to obtain if it is preparatory to what exceeds it.

NOTES

1. Derrida, 'following theory: Jacques Derrida', *life.after.theory*, eds. Michael Payne and John Schad (London and New York: Continuum, 2003; repr. 2004), 27.
2. Malpas, *Heidegger and the Thinking of Place: Explorations in the Topology of Being* (Cambridge, MA and London: The MIT Press, 2012), 175.
3. Derrida, *'Honoris Causa*: "This is *also* extremely funny,"' trans. Marian Hobson and Christopher Johnson, Derrida, *Points...: Interviews, 1974–1994*, ed. Elisabeth Weber, trans. Peggy Kamuf et al. (Stanford: Stanford University Press, 1995; repr. 1999), 410.
4. *'Honoris Causa'*, 410–11.
5. *'Honoris Causa'*, 411/Johnson MS.
6. Martin Hägglund, *Dying for Time: Proust, Woolf, Nabokov* (Cambridge, MA and London: Harvard University Press, 2012), 1–7.
7. 'Flysheets Reprinted', *Cambridge University Reporter*, Vol. 122, No. 29 (Wednesday, May 20, 1992), 687.
8. I draw on S. R. Slings's introduction to his edition of Plato's *Clitophon* (Cambridge: Cambridge University Press, 1999), especially 59–63.
9. *Clitophon*, 90.
10. *Clitophon*, 91, 221.
11. Kant, 'On a Newly Raging Spirit of Domination in Philosophy', trans. Peter Fenves, *Raising the Tone of Philosophy: Late Essays by Immanuel Kant, Transformative Critique by Jacques Derrida*, ed. Fenves (Baltimore and London: The Johns Hopkins University Press, 1993), 106.
12. Kant, 'Vorarbeit zu Von einem neuerdings erhobenen vornehmen Ton in der Philosophie', *Kant's gesammelte Schriften, Bande XXIII*, ed. The German Academy of Sciences in Berlin (Berlin: Walter de Gruyter & Co., 1955), 195.
13. Something of this can be seen in Novalis's almost contemporary claim that a 'Philosophical arithmetic' would be a 'Pure – higher – specialized and applied arithmetic' (*Notes*, 70). Here, the relation between the two disciplines discussed by Kant is clarified: 'Philosophy' is the principle by which arithmetic or mathematics becomes pure, higher, specialized and applied. Philosophy is the means by which that field becomes principled: 'In the end, mathematics is only *common*, *simple* philosophy, and philosophy, is higher mathematics in general' (*Notes*, 86). Axiomatically, 'Every science is itself a specific philosophy. Philosophy is the reason of the scientific being, which likewise consists of a body and soul' (*Notes*, 111; also 133).
14. *Notes*, 77.

15. *The Tain of the Mirror*, 13.
16. Nancy, 'Borborygmi', trans. Jonathan Derbyshire, Nancy, *A Finite Thinking*, ed. Simon Sparks (Stanford: Stanford University Press, 2002), 122/'Borborygmes (soi de soi débordé)', Nancy, *La pensée dérobée* (Paris: Galilée, 2001), 57.
17. Sloterdijk, *The Art of Philosophy: Wisdom as a Practice*, trans. Karen Margolis (New York: Columbia University Press, 2012), 22.
18. *Notes*, 154/Novalis, *Das Allgemeine Brouillon: Materialien zur Enzyklopädistik 1798/1799* (Hamburg: Felix Meiner Verlag, 1993), 193.
19. Fichte, 'On the Nature of the Scholar and Its Manifestations: Lectures Delivered at Erlangen 1805', *Johann Gottlieb Fichte's Popular Works*, trans. William Smith (London: Trübner, 1873)/Fichte, *Ueber das Wesen des Gelehrten, und seine Erscheinungen im Gebiete der Freiheit. In öffentlichen Vorlesungen, gehalten zu Erlangen, im Sommer-Halbjahre 1805* (Berlin: In der Himburgischen Bucchandlung, 1806).
20. Sloterdijk suggests that Fichte's work indeed anticipates certain tenets of psychoanalysis; specifically, he regards Fichte's use of the term 'unconscious' as the inaugural instance of the 'systematic emphasis' on the word which 'would have such an impact on the modern culture of reflection' (*The Art of Philosophy*, 72).
21. *The Art of Philosophy*, 71–76.
22. D. H. Mellor, *Matters of Metaphysics* (Cambridge: Cambridge University Press, 1991), 2.
23. Derrida, 'How to Avoid Speaking: Denials', trans. Ken Frieden and Elizabeth Rottenberg, Derrida, *Psyche: Inventions of the Other, Volume II*, eds. Peggy Kamuf and Elizabeth Rottenberg (Stanford: Stanford University Press, 2008), 164.
24. Derrida, *The Politics of Friendship*, trans. George Collins (London and New York: Verso, 1997; repr. 2005), 29/*Politiques de l'amitié suivi de l'oreille de Heidegger* (Paris: Galilée, 1994), 46.
25. Mark Currie, *The Unexpected: Narrative Temporality and the Philosophy of Surprise* (Edinburgh: Edinburgh University Press, 2013), 35.
26. Derrida, *Archive Fever: A Freudian Impression*, trans. Eric Prenowitz (Chicago and London: University of Chicago Press, 1998), 11–12.
27. Derrida, 'On Forgiveness', Derrida, *Cosmopolitanism and Forgiveness*, trans. Mark Dooley and Michael Hughes (London and New York: Routledge, 2001; repr. 2005), 45–46.
28. Derrida, 'Fichus', Derrida, *Paper Machine*, trans. Rachel Bowlby (Stanford: Stanford University Press, 2005), 172.
29. Derrida, 'What Is a "Relevant" Translation?', trans. Lawrence Venuti, *Critical Inquiry*, Vol. 27, No. 2 (Winter 2001), 197.
30. See *Clitophon*, 15.
31. Ronen, *Possible worlds in literary theory* (Cambridge: Cambridge University Press, 1994), 25 (my italics).
32. *Possible worlds*, 54.
33. Aristotle, *Metaphysics*, IV. vii. 1, *The Metaphysics, Books I-IX*, trans. Hugh Tredennick (London: William Heinemann, 1933), 199–201.
34. Ludwig Wittgenstein, *Tractatus Logico-Philosophicus*, trans. D. F. Pears, B. F. McGuinness (London and New York: Routledge, 2001), 3.

35. Castagnoli, *Ancient Self-Refutation: The Logic and History of the Self-Refutation Argument from Democritus to Augustine* (Cambridge: Cambridge University Press, 2010), 193.

36. See Hannah Arendt, *The Life of the Mind, One: Thinking*, ed. Mary McCarthy (London: Secker & Warburg, 1978), 199–200.

37. Derrida, 'The "World" of the Enlightenment to Come (Exception, Calculation, Sovereignty)', trans. Pascale-Anne Brault and Michael Naas, *Research in Phenomenology*, 33 (2003), 12–13.

38. *Possible worlds*, 8–9.

39. A. J. Ayer, *Language, Truth and Logic*, Volume 1 of the Palgrave Macmillan Archive Edition of *A. J. AYER: WRITINGS ON PHILOSOPHY* (Basingstoke and New York: Palgrave Macmillan, 2004), 9.

40. *Language, Truth and Logic*, 14.

41. Ayer, *Probability and Evidence*, Volume 3 of the Palgrave Macmillan Archive Edition of *A. J. AYER: WRITINGS ON PHILOSOPHY* (Basingstoke and New York: Palgrave Macmillan, 2004), 125–26.

42. Ayer, *The Central Questions of Philosophy*, Volume 7 of the Palgrave Macmillan Archive Edition of *A. J. AYER: WRITINGS ON PHILOSOPHY* (Basingstoke and New York: Palgrave Macmillan, 2004), 152.

43. *Probability and Evidence*, 129.

44. This can be verified by consulting the *placet* and *non placet* voting cards in the Cambridge University Library archives (EAD/GBR/0265/VOTES 8) and cross-referencing these with *Resident Members of the University 1992/1993* (*The Cambridge Review Special Issue*, Vol. 113).

45. *Notes*, 160.

46. Anthony Kenny's 2013 translation has 'poetry utters universal truths, history particular statements' (Aristotle, *Poetics*, trans. Kenny [Oxford: Oxford University Press, 2013], 28). This movement between 'statements' and articulable 'truths' again broaches the problematic distinction I am investigating in the case of the *non placet* thesis.

47. Aristotle, *Poetics*, trans. Margaret E. Hubbard, *Classical Literary Criticism* (Oxford: Oxford University Press, 1972; repr. 2008), 62. The square brackets in this passage are editorial emendations.

48. Christopher Norris, 'Hawking contra Philosophy', *Philosophy Now* 82 (January/February 2011), 24.

49. 'If the poem contains [, for instance,] an impossibility, that is a fault; but it is all right if the poem thereby achieves what it aims at[,] […] that is, if in this way the surprise provoked either by that particular passage or by another is more striking' (*Poetics*, 85; editorial emendations).

50. 'In answer to the charge of not being true, one can say, "But perhaps it is as it should be"' (*Poetics*, 85).

51. 'If it is neither true nor as it should be, one can reply, "But it is what people say"' (*Poetics*, 85).

52. See Mark Currie, *About Time: Narrative, Fiction and the Philosophy of Time* (Edinburgh: Edinburgh University Press, 2007), 7, 62; see also *The Unexpected*, 33, 62.

53. *About Time*, 13. For a short discussion of the *Confessiones*' relevance to and recurrence in phenomenological accounts of time, see Garry Wills, *Augustine's Confessions: A Biography* (Princeton and Oxford: Princeton University Press, 2011), 144–46. See also Andrea Nightingale, *Once Out of Nature: Augustine on Time and the Body* (Chicago and London: University of Chicago Press, 2011), 7–9.

54. *St. Augustine's Confessions, with an English Translation by William Watts, Volume II* London: William Heinemann, 1912; repr. 1946, 212 (my italics).

55. *St. Augustine's Confessions*, 213 (my italics).

56. *The Confessions of St. Augustine*, trans. Edward Bouverie Pusey (London and Toronto: J. M. Dent & Sons, 1907; repr. 1932), xxviii.

57. *The Confessions of St. Augustine*, 253 (my italics).

58. 'The day is thine and the night is thine, at thy beck the moments fly away. Grant therefrom a *space* for our meditations in the hidden things of thy law, and do not shut them up against such as knock'. *The Confessions of Saint Augustine. In the translation of Sir Tobie Matthew, Kt.*, ed. Roger Hudleston (London: Burns Oates and Washbourne, 1923), 295 (my italics).

59. 'Thine is the day, and Thine is the night: at Thy will the moments flow and pass. Grant me, then, *space* for my meditations upon the hidden things of Thy law, nor close Thy law against me as I knock'. *The Confessions of Saint Augustine*, trans. Francis Joseph Sheed (London: Sheed & Ward, 1943), 249 (my italics).

60. 'The day is yours and the night is yours (Ps. 73:16). At your nod the moments fly by. From them grant us *space* for our meditations on the secret recesses of your law, and do not close the gate to us as we knock'. Augustine, *Confessions*, trans. Henry Chadwick (Oxford: Oxford University Press, 1992; repr. 1998, 2008), 222 (my italics).

61. 'Maître du jour et maître de la nuit, tu fais un signe: aussitôt les instants prennent leur vol. Élargis donc le *champ* de mes réflexions dans les arcanes de ta Loi! Ne la ferme pas à qui frappe!' Saint Augustin, *Confessions*, trans. Louis de Mondadon, ed. André Mandouze (Paris: Éditions Pierre Horay, 1982), 303 (my italics). Mondadon's translation figures the *spatium meditationibus* as a 'champ', or field; Augustine's prayer is for it to be spatially extended (élargit).

62. 'Le jour et la nuit sont à vous, et les momens volent et s'enfuient comme il vous plaît. Accordez-moi quelques-uns de ces momens pour pouvoir méditer les secrets de votre loi, et ne fermez pas cette sainte porte à ceux qui frappent pour y entrer'. Saint Augustin, *Confessions*, trans. Robert Arnauld d'Andilly, *Choix d'ouvrages mystiques*, ed. Jean Alexandre C. Buchon (Paris, 1835), 179.

63. Augustine, *Confessions*, trans. Richard Sydney Pine-Coffin (London: Penguin, 1961; repr. 1963), 254 (my italics).

64. This demarcation is not without caveats. The etymology of 'part' indicates that, whilst classical Latin reserved for the term a spatial designation, post-classical Latin already recognizes it as temporally inflected: 'Part' could delimit a unit of time as well as space.

65. *St. Augustine's Confessions*, 216. Cf. Watts, 217 ('the inner retreat of my thoughts'); Pusey, 255 ('within me, within, in the chamber of my thoughts'); Matthew, 296 ('that very house of my thought'); Sheed, 250 ('the inner retreat of my

mind'); Chadwick, 223 ('the lodging of my thinking'); de Mondadon, 304 ('en dedans, au siège de ma pensée'); d'Andilly, 180 ('dedans de moi, et dans le plus secret de ma pensée'); Pine-Coffin, 256 ('deep inside me, in my most intimate thought'). Note how, between translations, the sense wavers concerning whether *domicilio cogitationis* refers to a type *of* thought or a place *for* thought.

66. *St. Augustine's Confessions*, 214–16/215–17 (my italics).

67. The same noun, *spatium*, recurs later in Book XI: xv, in the phrase 'praesens autem nullum habet spatium' (*St. Augustine's Confessions*, 244). Watts ('As for the present, it takes up not any space' [243–45]), Pusey ('The present hath no space' [264]), Matthew ('but as for time present, it hath no space' [308–9], and Chadwick ('But the present occupies no space' [232]) all translate it as 'space' here. Pine-Coffin renders it as 'When it is present it has no duration' (266), conceiving of it in terms of temporal extension. Sheed (260) has 'the present has no length', foregrounding temporality. D'Andilly (186) and De Mondadon (314) render the phrase similarly as, respectively, 'Le présent n'a donc aucune étendue', and 'mais dans le présent nulle étendue'; these refer to the present's non-extension, and thus retain an ambivalence between space and time. In Sheed's and Chadwick's translations, this complicates matters further; what underpins the unannounced shift from topology to chronology, and vice versa, in their renderings of *spatium*?

68. *The Unexpected*, 26–28.

69. *Once Out of Nature*, 7. On the relation between time and evil in Augustine, see Jaroslav Pelikan, *The Mystery of Continuity: Time and History, Memory and Eternity in the Thought of Saint Augustine* (Charlottesville: University Press of Virginia, 1986), 30–33.

70. *Augustine's* Confessions, 121–22.

71. See Roland J. Teske, *Paradoxes of Time in Saint Augustine (The Aquinas Lecture, 1996)* (Milwaukee: Marquette University Press, 1996), 32–38.

72. Quentin Meillassoux, *After Finitude: An Essay on the Necessity of Contingency*, trans. Ray Brassier (London and New York: Continuum, 2008; repr. 2011), 21–22.

73. Heidegger, 'The Concept of Time', trans. William McNeill, Heidegger, *The Concept of Time/Der Begriff der Zeit* (Oxford: Blackwell, 1992), §2E.

74. 'I will call "ancestral" any reality anterior to the emergence of the human species – or even anterior to every recognized form of life on earth. [...] I will call "arche-fossil" or "fossil matter" not just materials indicating the traces of past life, according to the familiar sense of the term "fossil", but materials indicating the existence of an ancestral reality or event; one that is anterior to terrestrial life' (*After Finitude*, 10).

75. Per Jeff Malpas, '*thesis* [...] can mean position, but also orientation, setting, or placing' (*Heidegger and the Thinking of Place*, 100). Additionally, the *OED* attests that the original ancient meaning of the term denoted 'The setting down of the foot or lowering of the hand in beating time, and hence (as marked by this) the stress or *ictus*'. The metaphorical consolidation of the word seems to have forgotten the crucial role that *temporality* played in the term originally. This dimension is restored by Heidegger, for whom *thesis* is reconfigured as 'bringing *hither* into unconcealment,

bringing *forth* into what is present, that is, allowing to lie forth' (Heidegger, 'The Origin of the Work of Art', quoted in *Heidegger and the Thinking of Place*, 101); the foregrounding of tense here reintroduces the element of time into *thesis*.

76. Groys, *Introduction to Antiphilosophy*, trans. David Fernbach (London and New York: Verso, 2012), ix.

77. Kant, *Toward Perpetual Peace: A Philosophical Sketch*, Kant, *Toward Perpetual Peace and Other Writings on Politics, Peace, and History*, trans. David L. Colclasure, ed. Pauline Kleingeld (New Haven and London: Yale University Press, 2006), 93.

78. *Toward Perpetual Peace*, 93/Kant, *Zum ewigen Frieden, Kant's gesammelte Schriften Bande VIII*, ed. The Royal Prussian Academy of Sciences (Berlin: Georg Reimer, 1912), 369.

79. *The Life of the Mind, One*, 197.

80. *The Art of Philosophy*, 27–28.

81. Franz Rosenzweig, *Understanding the Sick and the Healthy: A View of World, Man, and God*, ed. Nahum N. Glatzer (Cambridge, MA and London: Harvard University Press, 1999), 40 (my italics).

82. Leo Strauss argues that something of philosophy's essence lies in its aversion to authority: 'By calling nature the highest authority, one would blur the distinction by which philosophy stands or falls, the distinction between reason and authority. By submitting to authority, philosophy would lose its character; it would degenerate into ideology, *i.e.*, apologetics for a given or emerging social order, or it would undergo a transformation into theology or legal learning' (Strauss, *Natural Right and History*, quoted in Harry Neumann, 'Civic Piety and Socratic Atheism: An Interpretation of Strauss' *Socrates and Aristophanes*', *The Independent Journal of Philosophy*, Vol. 2 [1978], 35). This distinction is supported by the specifically Kantian facultative paradigm: if it is in cahoots with 'authority', philosophy risks 'degeneration' into a 'higher faculty' – two of which, for Kant, are law and theology.

83. *Toward Perpetual Peace*, 93–94/*Zum ewigen Frieden*, 369–70.

84. See Derrida, 'Mochlos ou le conflit des facultés', Derrida, *Du droit à la philosophie* (Paris: Galilée, 1990). Derrida calls the *Conflict* the 'discours pré-inaugural' of the modern university (407), and the trope of pre-history recurs more than once in 'Mochlos', in the terms 'avant-première' (411) and 'pré-contractuelle' (423). See also Derrida, 'L'âge de Hegel' in the same volume (181–227). For the role of 'privilege' in the Kantian and Derridean universities, see Michael O'Sullivan, 'L'Université sans profession (the University without profession): The Privilege of the Conflict of the Faculties', *Parallax*, Vol. 12, No. 3 (2006), 112–24.

85. For two complementary accounts of Kant's essay, see Carolyn D'Cruz, *Identity Politics in Deconstruction: Calculating with the Incalculable* (Aldershot and Burlington, VT: Ashgate, 2008), 57–59, and *Introduction to Antiphilosophy*, 73–89.

86. Kant, 'On a Newly Arisen Superior Tone in Philosophy', trans. Peter Fenves, *Raising the Tone of Philosophy*, 69/Kant, 'Von einem neuerdings erhobenen vornehmen Ton in der Philosophie', *Kant's gesammelte Schriften VIII*, 403–4.

87. 'This dream for a knowledge police could be related to the plan for a university tribunal presented in *The Conflict of the Faculties*', Derrida, 'On a Newly

Arisen Apocalyptic Tone in Philosophy', trans. John P. Leavey, *Raising the Tone of Philosophy*, 130.

88. 'Superior Tone', 68–69/'vornehmen Ton', 402–3.

89. For Sloterdijk, this analogy is evidence of 'the crushing heritages of the metaphysics of substance and the isolated thing', among whose effects are that 'Substance is that which maintains the cohesion of the world at its innermost point. Indeed, for general opinion, the only things that warrant our speaking of them are the ones bearing the predicate "substantial"'. See Sloterdijk with Hans-Jürgen Heinrichs, *Neither Sun nor Death*, trans. Steve Corcoran (Los Angeles: Semiotext[e], 2011), 138–39.

90. Appropriately, therefore, Kant's 'four stages of reason' (humankind's nourishment, sex, anticipation of future, and self-understanding as the 'end of nature') culminate in Kantian man's becoming 'aware of a privilege [*eines Vorrechtes*] that he, by virtue of his nature, had over all animals'. Reason's realization possibilizes privilege. Hence, Kant's allegorical history comprehends the necessary conditions for philosophy, without elaborating upon its sufficient conditions. See Kant, 'Conjectural Beginning of Human History', *Toward Perpetual Peace and Other Writings on Politics, Peace, and History*, 28/'Mutmasslicher Anfang der Menschengeschichte', *Kant's gesammelte Schriften VIII*, 109–23.

91. Kant, *Thoughts on the True Estimation of Living Forces* (*Selected Passages*), *Kant's Inaugural Dissertation and Early Writings on Space*, trans. John Handyside (Chicago and London: Open Court, 1928), 8.

92. *Forces*, 9.

93. Kant seems to be developing the influential medieval dictum that 'nature abhors a vacuum'. This dictum states that the four elements' affinity lies with their cooperation in order to avoid a vacuum. Edward Grant summarizes the logic supporting this as 'the assumption that matter necessarily and inevitably rushed in to fill places or spaces that were in danger of becoming void and would do so even if required to move in directions contrary to its natural inclinations'. The possible world about which Kant speculates does not appear bound to this principle, possibilizing 'unnatural' void and thus a radical type of interiority. See Grant, *Much Ado About Nothing: Theories of space and vacuum from the Middle Ages to the Scientific Revolution* (Cambridge: Cambridge University Press, 1981), 69.

94. See Jeff Malpas, *Place and Experience: A Philosophical Topography* (Cambridge: Cambridge University Press, 1999), 122.

95. Sloterdijk, *Bubbles: microspherology*, trans. Wieland Hoban (Los Angeles: Semiotext(e), 2011), 86–87.

Chapter 4

Repudiations
Derrida and Thatcher

'(Is this not the very desire of philosophy, the destruction of the delay
[...]?)'[1] —Derrida

In the previous chapter, I argued that philosophy and its metaphilosophical legislation are mutually constitutive, but in fraught, problematic and impossible ways. This chapter follows on from there, looking at this impossible philosophical interiority in terms of homesickness – the desire for an idealized spatio-temporal stability. My overarching claim is that, in the case of the Cambridge Affair, Thatcherite upheavals of the university in the 1980s are crucial to the emergence of this philosophical homesickness in the 'Derrida *non placet*' case.

PHILOSOPHY IN REHAB

Homesickness should be understood as having spatio-temporal dislocation as both its focus and condition. Jeff Malpas explains this:

> From its origins in the eighteenth century to its usage today, the meaning of "nostalgia" seems to have shifted. Part of that shift involves the disappearance of the term, along with other terms like "melancholia" itself, from the language of medicine. Nostalgia, like melancholia, is no longer recognized as an illness to be medically diagnosed and treated. But a more significant, although associated shift, is in the way the term is seen as related to the spatial and the temporal. Understood precisely as a pain associated with desire for *home* – and as home is neither a space nor a time, but a place that holds space and time within it – so nostalgia can never be understood as spatial or temporal alone[.]
> [. . .] Yet having originally referred to a condition resulting primarily from

spatial displacement (the soldier serving in a foreign land), "nostalgia" has come instead to signify a condition usually taken to involve, first and foremost, *temporal* dislocation (our estrangement from our past, and especially our childhood), so that even the migrant who reflects "nostalgically" on her homeland is typically reflecting back on memories of a place that, while perhaps spatially removed, is also more significantly and specifically temporally distinct. One might say, then, that understood as a form of homesickness, nostalgia is that particular form of longing for home that arises in circumstances in which the return home is somehow made impossible.[2]

What makes nostalgia a species of homesickness, more specifically than its general relation to impossibility, is its *posteriority* to impossibility. There seems to be a temporality peculiar to homesickness that is both related to and distinct from the temporality of its object. Not only is homesickness a longing for what is temporally removed, it is also a *temporally removed longing* for this, because homesickness seems to arise from, and thus after, the constitution of home as impossible. The time lapse is both theme and property of homesickness. The one who suffers homesickness is always belated by the smallest imaginable increment of time, and so actually longs for timeliness itself – for the coalescence of *meaning* (home as sufficiently meaningful to make one sick for it) and *intention* (the conscious desire for home). Is homesickness thus a conceptual longing? That is, in its general form, is homesickness the desire for a particular intimacy between intention and signification?

The impossible philosophical interior dreamt by Augustine, Kant, and Fichte, and glimpsed in the other cases of philosophical self-grounding studied in the previous chapter, corresponds to a certain, ultimately surprising, experience of homesickness. The conjunction of philosophy and homesickness is a famous one: It is among several definitions or accounts of philosophy sketched by Novalis in his *Notes for a* Romantic Encyclopaedia.[3] Novalis states, 'Philosophy is really homesickness – *the desire to be everywhere at home* [Die Philosophie ist eigentlich Heimweh – *Trieb überall zu Hause zu seyn*]' (155/194). This aphorism deserves close attention, because it is not really an aphorism at all, but a series of redefinitions, or substitutions, which serves to carry philosophy away from itself: 'Philosophy' to 'homesickness'. 'homesickness' to 'the desire to be everywhere at home'.

How does this structure of redefinition and relocation correspond to the experience of homesickness it elaborates? And what do we make of how the most canonical treatment of this insight, at the outset of Heidegger's lecture course on the *Fundamental Concepts of Metaphysics*, reenacts this tendency to relocation, as though that were the principal import of the insight?

> Philosophy – an ultimate pronouncement [eine letzte Aussprache] and interlocution on the part of man that constantly permeates him in his entirety.

Yet what is man, that he philosophizes in the ground of his essence, and what is this philosophizing? What are we in this? Where do we want to go? Did we once just stumble into the universe by chance? Novalis on one occasion says in a fragment: "Philosophy is really homesickness, an urge to be at home everywhere." A strange definition, romantic of course. Homesickness – does such a thing still exist today at all? Has it not become an incomprehensible word, even in everyday life? Has not contemporary city man, the ape of civilization, long since eradicated homesickness? And homesickness as the very determination of philosophy! But above all, what sort of witness are we presenting here with regard to philosophy? Novalis – merely a poet, after all, and hardly a scientific philosopher. Does not Aristotle say in his *Metaphysics*: [. . .] Poets tell many a lie?

Yet without provoking an argument over the authority and significance of this witness, let us merely recall that art – which includes poetry too – is the sister of philosophy and that all science is perhaps only a servant with respect to philosophy.[4]

Heidegger's reading begins from the assertion that philosophy is 'an ultimate pronouncement', an assertion not shared by Novalis. Instead of this ultimate character, philosophy, for Novalis, is a necessary process of intervention in other human sciences whose purpose is a refinement, or perfecting: 'There is no philosophy *in concreto*. Philosophy, like the philosopher's stone – the squaring of the circle etc. – is simply a necessary task [Aufgabe de Szientifiker] of the scientist – the *ideal of science* in general' (116/145). This philosophical refinement brings the sciences to, or prepares them for, the point of attainment of another, somehow qualitatively distinct, state. But the actual point of this attainment marks its transformation into poesy: 'Every science will be poesy – after it has become philosophy [Jede Wissenschaft wird Poësie nachdem sie Philosophie geworden ist]' (125/156). Philosophy names the process whereby a science is perfected, yet the perfected form is poesy. This is a central tenet of Novalis's encyclopaedic project, perhaps even its point of cohesion.[5]

Yet Novalis keeps poesy in the future tense ('Every science will be poesy'), and so the figure of the 'philosophical poet' or 'poetic philosopher' is introduced, seemingly to designate the one who writes and recognizes poesy:

The logician proceeds from the predicate – the mathematician from the subject, the philosopher from the copula. The poet from both the predicate and subject. *The philosophical poet from all three simultaneously* [Der *philosophische Poët* von allen dreyen zugleich]. (140/175)

If the philosopher proceeds from the manner in which subject and predicate are linked (the copula), and the poet (not to be confused with, nor automatically stated to be, the one responsible for 'poesy') proceeds from a creative linking of the predicate and subject that does not require a copula to be pre-given, then the *philosophical poet* is the one able to fuse analysis of the relations between things (copulae) with a productive generation of those relations. The result of this, 'poesy', is perhaps yet to come in Novalis's schema – or at least a schematic of its derivation remains unthought. Its perfection gives it the pre- or supra-theoretical status of geometry: 'The poetic philosopher [poëtische Philosoph] is *en état de Créateur absolu*. A circle, a triangle are already created *in this manner*. Nothing can be added to them, save what the Creator has already given to them etc' (140/175).

Given this relation between philosophy and poesy, it is surprising that Heidegger begins his discussion of Novalis's fragment with the assertion that philosophy is 'ultimate' – because a running theme in Novalis's text is philosophy's necessary incompletion: it desires the bringing to completion of its object of analysis (in this case a given science, or field), but what this completion marks is the progression of that object beyond philosophy's exclusive jurisdiction, and the progression of those through whom this completion takes place into philosophical poets. Their 'poesy' is no longer rooted in a specific genealogy, but it is epistemologically and formally free and therefore comprehensible everywhere: 'The perfected form of the sciences must be poetic. Every proposition must have an independent character – a self-evident aspect, the husk of a witty inspiration'.[6] Ultimate in Novalis's thought, then, is not philosophy, but the *surpassings* of philosophy and the state of being-philosopher:

> The diversity of the methods increases – the thinker eventually knows how to make everything, out of *each thing* – the philosopher becomes a poet [der Philosoph wird zum Dichter]. The *poet* is but the highest degree of the thinker, or senser etc. (Degrees of poet.)
>
> The separation [Trennung] into poet and thinker is only apparent – and to the *disadvantage* of both – It is a sign of sickness – and of a sickly constitution [Es ist ein Zeichen einer Kranckheit – und Kranck-haften Constitution]. (132/166)

It is in this context that we can read the fragment, 'Philosophy is really homesickness – *the desire to be everywhere at home*'. Now, it starts to look like it means that philosophy is really the desire for the self-grounding of poesy. Philosophy, as a preparatory process, becomes the handmaid of poesy.

When we consider Novalis's fragment in this way, we understand something of Heidegger's recuperative treatment of it. But Novalis, as shown, hardly denigrates philosophy: He regards it as indispensable to poesy and as the chief agent in the genesis of poesy. You could even argue that, by 'poesy', Novalis simply wishes to give *his* conception of philosophy a name that differentiates it from others, or to distinguish philosophy as practice or education from philosophy as product of that training. Heidegger's recalibration of

Novalis in the *Fundamental Concepts of Metaphysics* is therefore most appreciable when we see its chief divergence being on the matter of philosophical sovereignty. For Heidegger, 'all science is perhaps only a servant with respect to philosophy', whereas in Novalis one finds the opposite polarity: Philosophy only exists insofar as it is the improvement of other disciplines, and therefore it depends on them. Heidegger rejects this contingency for an idea of philosophy as something that is neither a priori nor a posteriori (both designations sharing a character of dependency or at least contiguity), but fundamental and, crucially, somehow *despite*:

> Philosophizing is not some belated reflecting on nature and culture as something at hand, nor is it a thinking up of possibilities and laws that can subsequently be applied to whatever is at hand.
> All these are views which make an occupation and a business out of philosophy, albeit in a very exalted form. In contrast to this, philosophy is something that lies prior to every occupation [vor allem Sichbeschäftigen liegt] and constitutes the fundamental occurrence of Dasein [das Grundgeschehen des Daseins ausmacht], something autonomous [eigenständig] that stands on its own and is quite different in nature to the kinds of comportment within which we commonly move. (22/33–34)

Heidegger clarifies this nonchronological priority of philosophy by contradistinguishing philosophy from any link to 'occupation' or 'business'. This echoes his earlier remarks on homesickness:

> Homesickness – does such a thing still exist today at all? Has it not become an incomprehensible word, even in everyday life [alltäglichen Leben]? Has not contemporary city man, the ape of civilization, long since eradicated homesickness [Denn hat nich der heutige städtische Mensch und Affe der Zivilisation das Heimweh längst abgeschafft]? And homesickness as the very determination [Bestimmung] of philosophy! (5/7)

For Heidegger, reducing philosophy to a spatio-temporal variable – or spatio-temporally specifying its role as Novalis does, which for Heidegger amounts to the same thing – would localize it, bringing it into line with vulgar modernity. And this modernity would be responsible for the eradication of homesickness.

Does Heidegger lament this eradication? Arguably, by aligning homesickness and his own understanding of philosophy according to what they repudiate – the modern and urban – Heidegger can distil philosophy as a sovereign, non-deictic form from Novalis's definition of it. That is, Heidegger's appropriation of 'Philosophy is really homesickness' entails a rhetorical purification which acts both upon philosophy and homesickness: He works on the copula 'is really', vindicating Novalis's view of where philosophical analysis can be located. Heidegger agrees with Novalis's formula, but alters what philosophy and homesickness *are really* by suggesting that both terms have been nullified by a metropolitan modernity, which extends to Novalis's integration of philosophy into a spatio-temporally determinable process of completion, education, perfection, preparation – training.

Lamenting that homesickness is dead, Heidegger articulates the acutest homesickness of all: homesickness *for* homesickness. More specifically, this can be expressed as the nostalgia for philosophy-as-homesickness; but if there is already an element of lack in Novalis's definition of 'homesickness' and its structure of desire – a desire or drive (*Trieb*) to be everywhere at home – then Heidegger ignores this lack:

> *Philosophy in each case happens in a fundamental attunement* [*Grundstimmung*]. Conceptual philosophical comprehension is grounded [gründet] in our being gripped [Ergriffenheit], and this is grounded in a fundamental attunement. Does not Novalis ultimately [am Ende] mean something like this when he calls philosophy a homesickness? Then this poet's [Dichters] word would not be at all deceptive [lügenhaft], if only we extract [herausholen] what is essential from it. (7/10)

The explanation of homesickness as *Grundstimmung* erases Novalis's desire or drive, so we might express Heidegger's paraphrase as 'Philosophy is really homesickness – a desire to be at home everywhere'. In this sense, Heidegger's nostalgia is for philosophy's autonomy from any structure of desire.

However, Heidegger's glossing of Novalis surely evinces the very desire from which it casts philosophy as independent. What he calls extraction of an essence is actually a supplementation of the very experience of desire that it seeks to repress. Simply put, this is because Heidegger is trying to make Novalis mean what he wants (or desires) him to mean, whilst appearing to be in the process of separating what is meaningful in Novalis's formulation *from* its structure of desire. Heidegger desires a formulation of philosophy that does not depend on a privative structure of desire.

Homesickness, though, is not usually thought in terms of this dynamic structure of desire. It is more often understood, logically enough, as a type of sickness that only goes in one direction. However, in Heidegger, there appears a homesickness that more closely resembles the play of presence-absence constitutive of psychoanalytic desire. The type of sickness that accommodates this play is *dopesickness*, which names the manner in which the narcotic addict is at once sick *from* the drug to which he is addicted and sick *for* the drug that has made him sick. Seen this way, Heidegger's philosophical homesickness is really philosophy in rehab – its status as nondependent always overdetermined.

Heidegger's appropriation of Novalis's aphorism exemplifies a historico-philosophical self-deception: the myth of philosophy's function and concomitant autonomy as the manifestation of natural law. Philosophy is believed to be distinct insofar as it corresponds to what is unwritten, non-deictic, without home. But Heidegger's codification of this maxim betrays a fundamental ailment at the core of this self-belief, evinced by the overdetermination of what philosophy *is* and *is not* – an economical, strategic, written, deictic self-definition that does not simply frame philosophical content but participates in its constitution. Philosophy is thus a diary of narcotic convalescence masquerading as the journal of one who was never addicted. Does philosophy really yearn for the purity of origins, or does it actually long for the rediscovered rapture of the very first hit?

PHILISTINES

This double structure of philosophical 'homesickness' is most obviously illustrated by philosophy's denigration or mistrust of literature and the written word as entailing the possibility of untruth, as against the classical determination of philosophy as but one form of *poesis*. Because in the latter designation philosophy is a *manifestation*, its material, representational, conceptually localizable character – and thus its 'written-ness' – must be understood as fundamental to its constitution, and not as derivative, secondary, or (in more modern terms) an effect of commercial exigency. That philosophy is written is not a necessary evil, but its necessary condition.

If we accept this interpretation, the stated opposition to Derrida on behalf of Cambridge's philosophy faculty can partly be considered as a response to the anamnesis his work performs in relation to this written status – not only (arguably not even chiefly) in relation to its thematic element, but in relation to its very form. What are often dismissed as 'puns' or 'neologisms' in Derrida's texts become a reminder of that written status – narcotic measures waved before the addict in remission. How else can we explain the philosophy faculty's disproportionate focus on how Derrida writes, on Derrida's 'charms', and on Derrida's status as a contemporary craze? However, this reading also highlights a broader problem for the *non placet* case, namely that the repudiation of Derrida in order to indicate the philosophy faculty's sovereignty entails the demarcation as 'elsewhere' of something that, in fact, is constitutive. This is at work in the *non placet* elisions of deconstruction and Thatcherite neoliberalism.

A *Times Higher Education Supplement* editorial about the Cambridge Affair saw a diametric opposition between Derrida's honorary and the one refused to Margaret Thatcher by Oxford in 1985:

> [If] Cambridge rejects [Derrida] the outcome will be seen, by some and certainly by the press, as a reprise of – better, a riposte to – Oxford's refusal to award Margaret Thatcher an honorary degree five years ago. The scores will have been levelled between left and right in the wars of the dons and the battles of the fly-sheets!

The editorial downplays this interpretation, but retains the oppositional logic, arguing that, while Thatcher's *non placet* was a political gesture in protest against the restriction of academic freedoms and resources, politics were not in question in Derrida's case:

> The Derrida affair is very different. A vote to refuse him an honorary degree would be an act of intellectual censorship, however feeble its actual effect. Derrida exercises no political power over Cambridge or any other British university. His influence is confined to the persuasiveness or plausibility of his ideas. The proposal having been made to award him an honorary degree, his rejection at this stage could only be interpreted as an attempt to suppress, or muffle, that influence.

The editorial concludes by suggesting criteria by which the distinction between the cases of Derrida and Thatcher ought to be made:

> Politicians, industrialists and other lay people, and also scholars and scientists more strongly identified with extra-academic activities than their own work, must expect to be the focus of controversy if universities propose to honour them in this way. Such proposals send, and presumably are intended to send, powerful messages about institutional priorities, even values. They are statements of where a university stands – or at any rate, would like to stand. But Derrida, despite the push and pull of arguments about "deconstruction", falls in none of these categories. Therefore he is entitled to dignified respect rather than to be the object of petty-minded prejudice.[7]

As I have argued throughout this book so far, however, the flysheets pertaining to Derrida's honorary, particularly on the *non placet* side, did not share this delimitation of his work's current or potential efficacy. Instead, the *non placet* flysheets read Derrida's nomination as a statement about Cambridge's 'institutional priorities, even values', and this is the ultimate basis for their injunctions to vote 'no'.

The editorial's distinction between the cases of Derrida and Thatcher is questioned implicitly by the two letters that responded to it, published in the *THES* the following week. The first, by Graham McCann,[8] expresses admiration for Derrida's work ('I think Jacques Derrida is an extremely talented person who has written some excellent essays'), but states its author's intention to vote *non placet* (which he subsequently did[9]). McCann writes that when

Derrida's nomination was first announced, he did not consider opposing it. What prompted his change of mind is revealed to be the perceived consequences of Derrida's 'fail[ure] to discourage some very destructive ideas associated with his work', a failure that has engendered a disproportionate sense of its broader significance and political applicability.

McCann argues that the *placet* campaign is hyperbolic in two ways: First, it exaggerates the stakes of a local and relatively minor issue – 'When [Colin] MacCabe was being treated so shabbily his job was at stake. All Derrida is facing is the possible loss of walking along King's Parade in a funny hat and meeting Prince Philip' – and second, this exaggeration indexes a set of ethical priorities whose insular bent Derrida's work encourages. McCann refers to a familiar orthodoxy in the reception of Derrida – 'that interpretation is a rich and complicated process in which it is extremely difficult to accept crude notions of "good" and "bad", "true" or "false"' – and suggests that whilst this 'may have been quite a revelation to someone who spent their formative years at Eton or Shrewsbury, [. . .] down my way it was never an issue'. Down McCann's way, 'What *was* an issue was the need to make sense of a fairly wretched situation, and do all one could to improve it. This is a need which is muffled, to say the least, in Derrida (and has been all but smothered to death by his vastly more conceited group of followers)'. Although McCann imagines he would agree with 'the Derrida campaigners [. . .] on most matters', he sees the amplified relativism attendant on Derrida's reception in Britain as correlative to a diminishing material attention. Derrida's 'followers' comprise 'an extraordinarily privileged community, which seems so much more concerned with ideas than with people', and it is 'sad' that they 'should now (of all times) seem so ready to fight so zealously on behalf of someone who appears so disinterested in other people's suffering'.

McCann objects to the currentness of Derrida's work and its reception on the grounds of its advocacy of a political quietism ignorant of sociopolitical circumstances. We can determine that McCann is referring to unemployment rates under the Conservative Party from his assertion that, 'If I do vote, I will have to walk past the two teenage boys who are now living in the street outside my faculty; I really cannot believe that they count for so little when Derrida's degree counts for so much'. In this construction, participation in the vote overlooks more immediate material issues in favour of a much less urgent debate, and this gesture is one that Derrida's work permits. Although it should be noted that according to McCann's own logic, the most appropriate thing to do would be to refrain from voting, rather than vote *non placet*, what is interesting here is the link made between Conservatism and Derrida based on a perceived shared negligence.

McCann's argument is an especially polemical instance of a homology made throughout the Affair. Brian Hebblethwaite, in his retrospective on the

Affair, juxtaposes Derrida and Conservatism owing to a perceived shared philistinism:

> Our universities are held in contempt anyway by a government of philistines, as Michael Dummett, in a preface to another book, has powerfully lamented. There seems to be little we can do to reverse this. But I should have thought we could have avoided the internal contempt we bring upon ourselves when instead of repudiating the enemies of reason, truth and objectivity, we honour them.[10]

In making this connection, Hebblethwaite exemplifies many of the themes of my previous chapter. First, he opines that universities are *held*, or fixed, in contempt by Conservatism – which he terms 'a government of philistines'. Second, he reverts to that familiar structure of conditional versus actual ('I *should have* thought we *could have* avoided' versus 'the internal contempt we *bring* upon ourselves when [. . .] we *honour* them'). Third, the shift from the conditional structure to what Hebblethwaite thinks actually happened is a crossing of a threshold he names 'internal contempt' – or contempt for the interior of philosophy whose inviolable nature is at stake. Hebblethwaite's second and third points refer to a logic that we have explored at length. I will deal here with his first – the juxtaposition of Derrida and Conservatism.

Hebblethwaite supports his first point with the preface to Michael Dummett's book, *Frege: Philosophy of Mathematics*. This preface, completed in July 1990 in Oxford, laments that 'British universities are in the course of being transformed by ideologues who misunderstand everything about academic work'. This is a familiar complaint at the time, but perhaps the reason Hebblethwaite chooses it is because it goes on to narrow the focus of the threat posed by Conservatism – specifically Thatcherite policy on higher education – from the university at large, to the philosophy faculty:

> The plan of the ideologues is to increase academic productivity by creating conditions of intense competition. [. . .] [Academics'] output is monitored by the use of performance indicators, measuring the number of words published per year. Wittgenstein, who died in 1951 having published only one short article after the *Tractatus* of 1922, would plainly not have survived such a system. [. . .] It is obviously as objectionable in a capitalist as in a communist country that politicians should decide how the universities are to be run; but it is catastrophic when those politicians display total ignorance of the need to judge academic productivity on principles quite different from those applicable to industry. Our masters show some small awareness that, as in industry, quality is relevant as well as quantity: their performance indicators are sometimes modified by the use of more sophisticated criteria, such as counting the number of references made by other writers to a given article. Frege would never have survived such a test: his writings were very seldom referred to in his lifetime. [. . .] [O]verproduction defeats the very purpose of academic publication. It long ago became

impossible to keep pace with the spate of books and of professional journals, whose number increases every year; once this happens, their production becomes an irrelevance to a working academic, save for the occasional book or article he happens to stumble on. *This applies particularly to philosophy. Historians may be able to ignore much of their colleagues' work as irrelevant to their periods; but philosophers are seldom so specialised that there is anything they can afford to disregard in virtue of its subject-matter. Given their need for time to teach, to study the classics of philosophy and to think, they cannot afford to plough through the plethora of not bad, not good books and articles in the hope of hitting on the one that will surely cast light upon the problems with which they are grappling; hence, if they are sensible, they ignore them altogether.*[11]

There are many important points here. First, the relation of present to conditional tense: the actuality of the government is opposed to a negative conditionality of the philosophical canon: 'Wittgenstein [. . .] *would plainly not have survived* such a system. [. . .] Frege [. . .] *would never have survived* such a test'. The authentically philosophical becomes what *would not survive* if transplanted into the actual; it becomes in a sense negatively *subjunctive*. This shares the grammar of our *non placet* contention from the previous chapter, and how it positions philosophy.

Second, Dummett develops this subjunctive nature of the philosophical by distinguishing between the philosopher and the historian – closely following Aristotle's distinction, and updating it for the modern university. The historian deals in particulars and so is reconcilable with the Thatcherite university, whereas the philosopher's work is ideally so general as to be completely irreconcilable not only with the Thatcherite programme, but with other academic disciplines. The only thing breaking the symmetry is that here the homology between philosophy and poetry has been forgotten: This forgetting is the effect of an Aristotelian distinction (philosophy-poetry/history) encountering a Kantian one (philosophy/everything else).

Third, it is not immediately clear whether Dummett's final sentence is a lament or a threat. Either way, he seems to state that the only feasible course for philosophy to take at this point is to abscond from the present entirely. The opposition between teaching, studying 'the classics of philosophy' and thinking, on the one hand, and 'plough[ing] through the plethora' of what is being produced in the present in the name of the discipline, on the other, is important. Dummett figures the academic discipline of philosophy as Thatcherism's scapegoat, by virtue of its singular scope – or rather he claims that the survival of authentic philosophy is unthinkable under the auspices of a government which considers the university within its purview.

This last claim is one with which Derrida would, and did, agree.[12] However, it is problematic that Dummett immediately uses the notion of 'overproduction' to imply two classes of philosophical producer: the authentic philosopher, and a philosophical hoi polloi, who contribute to the discipline only this disabling aspect of overproduction. The first class, crucially, is *subjunctive* from the perspective of the Thatcherite programme: It teaches, studies the canon, and thinks, but does not apparently actually produce any work (the activity required to make it 'actual', from the perspective of performance indicators and so forth). The second class *does* produce, abundantly and witlessly, but the implication is that it does not do any teaching, canon-studying, or thinking.

Dummett's text elides a widespread and understandable objection to Thatcherism with a disingenuous assertion that a position of elitism has been forced on philosophers by that government, as though intellectual atavism is the only possible course of action. Dummett does not actually use the word *philistine* (he prefers *ideologue*, which recalls, ironically, terminology in the contemporary Thatcherite hunt for 'Marxist' elements in further and higher education[13]), but that is the term by which Hebblethwaite translates his arguments. For Dummett and Hebblethwaite, the 'philistinism' of the government is shown by its implementation of measures that seek to dissolve the putative distinction between authentic philosophy and excess – that seek to bloat the body philosophic beyond recognition. And there is an aesthetic subtext here: A philistine, as Malcolm Bull observes via Michael Thompson, is one who welcomes 'the absolute negation of the aesthetic'.[14] Moreover, the philistine embraces the devaluation of the aesthetic in its Kantian inflection as an experience of cognition that is 'set aside'. This revisits a motif discussed in chapter 2, of Kant representing the last major historical stand against the fall of philosophy. Murray Krieger condenses this complaint into just a few sentences, with reference to deconstruction:

> It may well be that the post-structuralist mood [with which Krieger identifies the 'Yale School'] is the most appropriate one to account for the revolutionary art produced in our culture these last decades: an anti-aesthetic for an anti-art. The philosophical assault on man's symbols may both mirror and justify what man has been of late doing with them – or refusing to do with them. It would hardly be a flattering comment to suggest that, if post-structuralism turns out to be a theoretical partner of recent activities in the arts, they deserve one another. And I trust it is more than just reactionary comment to suggest that the recent wars on metaphysics and art alike have hardly produced in the arts worthy successors to the tradition they would destroy.[15]

A review of Krieger's *The Institution of Theory* avers that 'one of deconstruction's most startling discoveries [is] that *all* texts, fictional, nonfictional, poetic, etc., are "dependent on a series of tropes" leading back ultimately to the sun. *All* texts, from the Bible to Locke's *Essay* to Stephen King's latest, all are, finally, *narratives* – they tell a story; how they are *judged*, i.e., as low or high art, sacred or profane, scientific or science fiction, is beside the point. They all employ rhetorical and tropological figures to make their case'.[16] This description corresponds to Bull's delineation of the philistine's position:

> The philistine should argue not that existing objects are of temporary as opposed to durable aesthetic value, or that, although they may once have been or may yet become valuable, all existing objects are valueless, but that all objects are permanently aesthetically valueless. In consequence, any object whose value is derived solely from its classification as an art-object is fit only for recycling.[17]

The description of deconstruction above elides devaluation and recycling in suggesting that *all* texts' fundamental characteristic is merely a recycled ancient heliotropism.[18] The equalizing commodification that results from this understanding of texts is homologous with the 'overproduction' that Dummett and others read as the key Thatcherite impact upon professional academic research. 'Philistinism', here, signifies at once 'modernity', the decline of 'authentic' philosophy, and having no time for the 'unquantifiable' dimensions of texts.[19] Through the melding of these three meanings, the same charge of philistinism can be, and is, levelled at Derrida and Thatcher.

It is worth comparing Hebblethwaite's and McCann's homologies between Derrida and Conservatism because, despite reaching the same conclusion, they diverge importantly. Hebblethwaite bases the homology on a shared philistinism, whereas McCann bases it on a lack of philistinism. McCann's anecdote about homelessness, where sympathy with the *placets* overlooks actual suffering in favour of being preoccupied with a rarefied conceptual matter, amounts to accusing such sympathy of anti-philistinism. This is not just because 'philistine' was a German term for a townsperson or nonstudent, but because more generally it is a term by which a perceived lack of education is made into a point of qualitative distinction – the gesture that McCann makes, despite his avowed sympathy with 'the two teenage boys who are now living in the street outside my faculty'. For McCann, deconstruction corroborates Conservatism in its anti-philistine priorities.

The heterology between these homologies is significant, because it offers another focused instance of what I have argued throughout this section of the book: the critique of Derrida founders precisely where it seeks to demarcate what ought to be proper to philosophy. For McCann, what most urgently needs to be thought are materially disadvantageous circumstances that deconstruction and Conservatism neglect in favour of the more abstracted concerns of the academy; for Hebblethwaite, deconstruction and Conservatism's shared neglect is, instead, a lack of respect for the rarefied atmosphere of the university. But where these homologies *are* homologous is in their presupposition of an ideal interiority undergirding this thinking: For McCann, universities should be places where social justice can be strategized; for Hebblethwaite, they should be places for work guaranteed autonomy from government intervention. In both cases, deconstruction threatens this interiority. For McCann, deconstruction's greater concern with 'ideas' than with 'people' severs the relation to the outside by which the inside is constituted – the university ought to be where one thinks about the people who exist outside of it – whereas for Hebblethwaite, deconstruction threatens to legitimize a plebeian compromise of the ineffable dimensions of university work.

The ambivalent relation between these homologies derives, ironically, from their attempts to preserve the university from the ambivalence of deconstruction and Conservatism through an appeal to the interiority proper to the university. The form of this argument contains an element that is hostile to it, which is manifest through the attempt to immunize the university from what is hostile to it. I conclude this chapter by arguing that this complex incoherence derives from the fact that the homology between Derrida and (Thatcherite[20]) Conservatism is compromised because it shares its outlook with the very species of Conservatism it seeks to disown.

DERRIDA AND THATCHER

Thatcher's premiership's 'unprecedented' degree of interest in education and its institutions has been the subject of much scholarship.[21] My interest here is not in elaborating this, but in indicating that the *non placet* homologies between deconstruction and Thatcherism in fact inherit from Thatcherism their condition of possibility – a condition they misrecognize as belonging to 'philosophy'.

The broader question of what the 'Thatcherite' version of Conservatism signifies is predominantly seen as a question of psyche. Peter Riddell lauds Thatcherism as 'an application of Mrs Thatcher's instincts, values, and, above all, energy to the solution of successive problems', arguing that any identification of a 'coherent hegemonic process' is merely an après-coup imputation based around 'the dire linguistic legacy of Marx and Gramsci'.[22] Similarly, Martin Holmes avers that the primary characteristic of Thatcherism 'was the Prime Minister's near total dominance over economic policy formation. The initial strategy, the refusal to change course, the Cabinet purges of the wets, the reliance on the key personnel were all at the behest of Mrs Thatcher's own initiative and reflected her personal political strategy'.[23]

In *Why War? – Psychoanalysis, Politics and the Return to Melanie Klein*,[24] Jacqueline Rose concurs with the logic of this interpretation[25] (referring to Thatcher's 'utter certainty of judgement'), if not its trajectory, diagnosing a possible psychic basis for the Thatcherite inscription. Centring her interpretation on Thatcher's support for the return of capital punishment, Rose argues that the consequences of this stance offer one working definition of 'Thatcherism':

> One of the things that Thatcher presented us with is an inflated version of the rationality which can be the only basis for distinguishing between legal and illegal violence. For if the law partly allows for the murderer who is deemed to be out of her or his mind, punishing above all a violence which stems from a self-knowing calculation, it is also because violence as rational is the form of violence which it reserves to itself. (59)

Analogically, this offers an explanation of the images of Derrida as bad philosophy, non-philosophy, or non-philosophical philosophy that emerge in the *non placet* literature. If, from the *non placet* perspective, Derrida were simply considered not to be a philosopher, then the *non placet* flysheets as they are would not have been written. That Derrida's honorary is immediately brought into the purview of the philosophy faculty suggests that the objection to Derrida is not that he is straightforwardly irrational, but that his offence is to encroach, rationally, upon the very terrain – Rose calls it 'rational violence' – that the philosophy faculty would reserve for itself. For Rose, this reservation of rational violence '[refuses] any possible gap between reality and intent' in Thatcherite discourse, and the paradoxical consequence of this (Rose quotes Richard Hofstadter) is a reality that 'is nothing if not coherent, far more coherent than the real world, no room for mistakes, failures, ambiguities, if not rational intensely rationalistic' (61).[26] This paints a picture that is uncannily similar to what, in the previous chapter, I called the non-derivative possible world conjured by the *non placet* literature.

Here, Thatcherism shares with the *non placet* statement we analysed there an instantiation of 'reason in excess'; the dimension of fantasy common to both is that the acceptable form of this excessive reason 'is not opposed to the threatening [form], but depends on it' (62). Furthermore – again the resemblance is unmistakeable – the logic structuring this fantasy 'is not some rational/irrational dualism – but a logic of fantasy in which violence can operate as a pole of attraction at the same time as (to the extent that) it is being denied' (64). If this paradox – the (acceptably) violent foundations of the purgation of (threatening) violence – expresses 'a paradox inherent to the organization of the social itself' (64), it is difficult to see how our *non placet* statement does not ground itself in this social paradox, even as it articulates its aspiration to transcend it.

Rose's analysis is instructive because it explains denials, such as Riddell's and Holmes's, that Thatcherism was in any way ideological. It elucidates Thatcherism's basis, as a 'parody of government as reason' (61), in the textbook hegemonic gesture, according to Ernesto Laclau and Chantal Mouffe, of redistributing 'floating elements' into oppositional 'camps' in a continual articulatory process.[27] Riddell's insistence that Thatcherism was not hegemonic misrecognizes hegemony as an a priori distribution of elements ('There was no master plan'[28]), whereas hegemony actually should be understood as reactive and adaptive 'construction[s] of new systems of differences'. Crucially, this adaptive quality permits the formal convergence between the philosophy faculty and Thatcherism:

> A hegemonic formation also embraces what opposes it, insofar as the opposing force accepts the system of basic articulations of that formation as something it negates, but the *place of the negation* is defined by the internal parameters of the formation itself.[29]

This accounts for the specific form of the oppositions to Thatcherism from McCann and Hebblethwaite. The objection to Thatcherism is formulated in terms that tacitly accept its hegemonic process of ongoing narration: For what is the *non placet* statement examined in the previous chapter, other than an especially bald articulation of hegemony? 'Had the Council consulted the Philosophy Faculty, they would have realized how controversial the proposal is': In my analysis of the grammar of this statement, I underscored its subjunctive fantasy, its desire to be at home everywhere, to be able to comprehend any opposition to it on its own terms. But this self-understanding itself is predicated on the very Thatcherite grammar to which that self-understanding posits itself as a qualitative alternative; and it posits itself as this alternative by eliding the hegemony to which it formally consents with the object it rejects. This final gesture naturalizes the process, disavowing its political contingency in a movement confirmative of the hegemonic[30]; with Anna Marie Smith, 'To the extent that a project achieves a hegemonic status, it appears that virtually any problem can be resolved within its framework. [. . .] It imposes itself as the universal framework for the interpretation of experience by ruthlessly eliminating alternative interpretations, but it conceals this violent ground in that it pretends to perform merely the a-political and innocent recognition of "facts."'[31] Smith describes the grammar of our *non placet* statement here much more accurately than the statement's own appeal to some incorruptible philosophical interior.

Desmond Ryan[32] argues that what Smith calls the act of paradigmatic imposition is especially pertinent to the Thatcherite involvement in higher education. Like Rose, Ryan argues that Thatcher's premiership cultivated a language that brooked no opposition, '[giving] the impression of participating in a communicative exchange, when in reality the messages were all one-way' (18). Ryan states that this broke with traditional Conservatism where it sought to redefine the internal parameters of governance, which redefinition was rhetorically supported by the alibi of a myth of autochthony:

> Electorally impregnable after 1983, the Tories withdrew from the traditional conservative engagement to keep the inherited institutional framework in working order, in favour of imposing a dogmatic vision. This was the vision of a reborn industrial Britain. But the rhetoric of competition was not supported by policies – for instance a position on exchange rates – genuinely supportive of manufacturing industry; it served rather to cloak and justify attacks on established institutions seen by the Conservative leadership as "over-mighty subjects": the unions, the professions, local government. (18)

Universities are a scapegoat by which Thatcherite self-entrenchment is functionalized. The public appeal of an industrial renaissance lent legitimacy to the typical features of Thatcherite discourse concerning higher education, including: the claim to act on behalf of public dissatisfaction with universities' negligible role in economic growth, thereby justifying government intervention in universities' internal operation[33]; the assertion that any such intervention was forced on the government by university negligence concerning the market (echoed by the first *non placet* flysheet's 'we regret any embarrassment caused by the request for a vote'); and what Ryan terms 'the double-bind of such interventions, requiring institutions to alter their ways of working to meet such new needs at the same time as "protecting" those ways that have supported traditional excellences, of which the government declares itself proprietorially proud' (18). The 'originality' of this government's incursions into higher education was to turn that market into 'an arm of the centralization of power' (16); the underlying strategy was 'to break the constitutional independence of the university', 'driven by a belief that the government should be sovereign, not needing to "consult or negotiate with anyone else"' (27).[34] This recalls the flysheet's modification of the figure of 'consultation' I discussed in the previous chapter – consultation shedding any dialogism in favour of a sovereign narration of the 'inside'.

These analyses of Thatcherite rhetoric, and its important intensification where institutions of higher education are concerned, ground a decisive homology between that rhetoric and the perspective the philosophy faculty grants to itself during the Cambridge Affair. The citation from Derrida with which the previous chapter began, about philosophy's potential to be inflected by a certain conservatism, astutely perceives the conditions of possibility for the philosophy faculty's understanding of itself as, precisely, immune to such inflections. The unique threat of Thatcherism to the philosophy faculty resided in its striving to govern in a manner that is actually homologous to that which the philosophy faculty would reserve for itself. With Ryan once more,

> Mrs Thatcher's government sought to destroy the 'privileges' of established institutions so as to enlarge the relative weight of the governing party. Ignoring the existence of the Great British University Miracle meant that the government could shackle those recalcitrantly expensive institutions with ways of working which would both drive up the indicators of university "productivity" and also symbolically reinforce the work ethic of the Factory System. This in turn would reinforce their claim that to be the guardians of what they declared was the true economic interest of the nation – the culture of enterprise – and thus secure their re-election as the only party fit to govern. Driven by the power they had, drawn on by the power they wanted, the Thatcher governments were building a state that only they could govern. (30)

This account of the ulterior motive for university 'reform' in the 1980s implies that Thatcherism strove for an almost identical sovereignty to that of philosophy as it is presented in the *non placet* literature. The capacity for governance sought by Thatcherism in this account is not only a capacity pertaining to authority, but a capacity pertaining to capability – and the fusion of these terms is the exemplary feature of the 'lower' sovereignty of the philosophy faculty. The effect of this complex sovereignty, according to Ryan, is the attempted creation of a state regarding which the government retains exclusive legislation, whilst remaining irrevocably inside of it.

Ironically, it may be that the *non placet* flysheets were actually mobilized by the kind of institutional and disciplinary concerns that Derrida had voiced repeatedly for many years prior to the Affair. If Thatcherism's self-interested, interventionist approach to the university in the 1980s haunts certain aspects of the Affair, this is because the central *non placet* presupposition – that philosophy can only be legislated according to a metaphysics of pure interiority – actually echoes a theme present in much of Derrida's work on the university in the late 1970s and throughout the 1980s. The difference, however, is that in Derrida it functions not as a presupposition but as a proposition to be deconstructed, 'For there may be no inside [dedans] possible for the university, and no internal coherence [cohérence interne] for its concept'.[35] Derrida's scepticism on this score distinguishes the form of his thought from *non placet* philosophy and Thatcherism, whose mutual repudiation displaces a fundamental kinship.

NOTES

1. Derrida, *Athens, Still Remains: The Photographs of Jean-François Bonhomme*, trans. Pascale-Anne Brault and Michael Naas (New York: Fordham University Press, 2010), 51.
2. *Heidegger and the Thinking of Place*, 162.

3. *Notes for a* Romantic Encyclopaedia: *Das Allgemeine Brouillon/Das Allgemeine Brouillon: Materialien zur Enzyklopädistik 1798/1799.*

4. Heidegger, *Fundamental Concepts of Metaphysics*, trans. William McNeill and Nicholas Walker (Bloomington and Indianapolis: Indiana University Press, 1995), 5/*Die Grundbegriffe der Metaphysik. Welt – Endlichkeit – Einsamkeit, Gesamtausgabe, Band 29/30* (Frankfurt am Main: Vittorio Klostermann, 1983), 7.

5. See *Notes*, 254, n300.

6. *Notes*, 254, n300 (citation from Novalis's *Vorarbeiten*).

7. 'The Derrida affair', *THES*, No. 1018 (Friday, May 8, 1992), 12.

8. *THES*, No. 1019 (Friday, May 15, 1992), 13. I do not discuss the second letter, by Susan Wilsmore, which is principally an objection to deconstruction's putative elision of 'differences', and hence of the capacity for rational discernment crucial to university education.

9. EAD/GBR/0265/VOTES 8.

10. 'Derrida Non Placet', 111.

11. Michael Dummett, *Frege: Philosophy of Mathematics* (London: Duckworth, 1991) viii–x (my italics).

12. In February 1988, Derrida was invited by Jennifer Birkett to speak on the topic of Thatcherism and the university at the Standing Conference of Arts and Social Sciences (SCASS) at the University of Strathclyde. Although he declined to intervene directly, he issued a statement of solidarity, in which he clearly states that he believes Thatcherism to be involved in a utilitarian compromising of the autonomy of research and teaching:

> The solidarity that I wish to express has another motivation: the politics to which you are opposed only elevates to its most perilous degree today a general tendency which one sees at work in the politics of all western government, whatever the differences which continue to distinguish them from one another: the violent and unreflective implementation of a principle of general techno-economic profitability which is poorly understood and interpreted in a narrow fashion, irrespective of all thought, of all work, of all questioning which would not be programmable and calculable outside the university, ignorance or scorn of that academic tradition which only survives in liberty, and an openness concerning promises of the future which would not be determinable by an established authority (technical, economical, political). From this perspective, your reflections, your disquiet, your mobilization closely resemble those in which certain of my friends and colleagues have felt ourselves engaged for a long time. In taking account of the fact that these resemblances are no accident, from now on we ought to combine or coordinate our efforts. Irvine, Box 62, Folder 2; my translation. I am grateful to Jennifer Birkett for providing information about the SCASS event.

13. See especially Julius Gould, *The Attack on Higher Education: Marxist and Radical Penetration. Report of a Study Group of the Institute for the Study of Conflict* (London: The Institute for the Study of Conflict, 1977). For a discussion of this in the wider context of Thatcherism, see Matthew Salusbury, *Thatcherism Goes to College: The Conservative Assault on Higher Education* (London: Canary Press, 1989).

14. Bull, *Anti-Nietzsche* (London and New York: Verso, 2011), 4. Bull's argument is informed by Michael Thompson, *Rubbish Theory* (Oxford: Oxford University Press, 1979), 103–30.

15. Krieger, *Poetic Presence and Illusion: Essays in Critical History and Theory* (Baltimore and London: The Johns Hopkins University Press, 1979), 112–13. See also Krieger, *Arts on the Level: The Fall of the Elite Object* (Knoxville: University of Tennessee Press, 1981), 62–64, and Krieger, *Words about Words about Words: Theory, Criticism and the Literary Text* (Baltimore: The Johns Hopkins University Press, 1988), 75.

16. Mark Youngerman, 'Murray Krieger. *The Institution of Theory*', *International Studies in Philosophy*, Vol. 28, No. 4 (1996), 118.

17. *Anti-Nietzsche*, 3.

18. This reading of Derrida's 'White Mythology' does something that as early as 1980 Barbara Johnson was able to identify as typical of certain construals of deconstruction: the mistaking of the interrogation of a binary for an attempt to reverse it – 'if you are not for something, you are against it'. This false dilemma, arguably indissociable from dogma and even outright militarism, caricatures deconstruction according to its own simplistic logic. In reality, as Johnson notes, 'Instead of a simple "either/or" structure, deconstruction attempts to elaborate a discourse that says *neither* "either/or", *nor* "both/and" nor even "neither/nor", while at the same time not totally abandoning these logics either. The very word *deconstruction* is meant to undermine the either/or logic of the opposition "construction/destruction."' But it is not meant to reverse it. See Johnson, *A World of Difference* (Baltimore and London: The Johns Hopkins University Press, 1987), 12.

19. Christopher Ricks's distinction between literary 'theory' and literary 'principles' exemplifies this tendency. See Ricks, 'In theory', *London Review of Books*, Vol. 3, No. 7 (April 16, 1981), 3–6 and Ricks, 'John Crowe Ransom, *Selected Essays*', Ricks, *Reviewery* (London: Penguin, 2003), 141–42.

20. Although this specification is not made in the *non placet* literature, it is accurate to state that both the unemployment alluded to by McCann and the university incursions referenced by Hebblethwaite are seen as related to a longer-term Conservatism than John Major's premiership, which at the time of the Cambridge Affair was only a year and a half old and had begun toward the end of what otherwise would have been Thatcher's third full term in office. Major's first white paper on education was not published until July 1992. See Peter Dorey, 'The legacy of Thatcherism for education policies: markets, managerialism and malice (towards teachers)', *The Legacy of Thatcherism: Assessing and Exploring Thatcherite Social and Economic Policies*, eds. Stephen Farrall and Colin Hay (Oxford: Oxford University Press, 2014), 116–19.

21. See Stefan Collini, *What Are Universities For?* (London: Penguin, 2012), 33–34; Thomas Docherty, *For the University: Democracy and the Future of the Institution* (London and New York: Bloomsbury Academic, 2011), 103–6; Jane Mulderrig, *The Language of Education Policy: from Thatcher to Blair* (Saarbrücken: VDM Verlag Dr. Müller, 2009), 97–112; Desmond Ryan, 'The Thatcher Government's Attack on Higher Education in Historical Perspective', *New Left Review*, No. 227 (January–February, 1998), 3–32.

22. Peter Riddell, *The Thatcher Era and Its Legacy* (Oxford and Cambridge, MA: Blackwell, 1989; repr. 1991), 11, 4.

23. Martin Holmes, *The First Thatcher Government 1979–1983: Contemporary Conservatism and Economic Change* (Brighton: Harvester Press, 1985), 199.

24. Jacqueline Rose, *Why War? – Psychoanalysis, Politics, and the Return to Melanie Klein* (Oxford and Cambridge, MA: Blackwell, 1993).

25. Against the image of Thatcher as straightforwardly a 'conviction politician', see Bruce Arnold, *Margaret Thatcher: A Study in Power* (London: Hamish Hamilton, 1984), 116–17. For Thatcher's cultivation of the semblance of being a 'conviction politician', see 268–74.

26. Richard Hofstadter, *The Paranoid Style in American Politics and Other Essays* (London: Cape, 1966), 271; quoted in *Why War?*, 61.

27. Laclau and Mouffe, *Hegemony and Socialist Strategy: Towards a Radical Democratic Politics, Second Edition* (London and New York: Verso, 2001), 135–36.

28. *The Thatcher Era*, 5.

29. *Hegemony*, 138–39.

30. In a critical discourse analysis of the language of Thatcherite education policy, Jane Mulderrig demonstrates that it differed from Major's and Blair's in terms of self-representation: In the Thatcherite text, there typically is 'a stylistic division of labour' whereby 'the more personalised and referentially ambivalent *we* helps present the vocationalist agenda in terms of shared needs, while the more traditional institutional authority of *government* is evoked to narrate a crisis in education'. Major's education policy tended to refer to 'the government', whereas the Blairite text prefers 'we' (see *The Language of Education Policy*, 90–101, 112). Mulderrig's analysis suggests that Thatcherite discourse concerning education policy performed an elision of the sovereign ('government') and the appeal to consensus ('we') formally analogous with that of the *non placet* contention under study. For Blair as a 'disciple of Derrida', see Vanessa Feltz, 'Philosophy made for spin-doctors', *Daily Express*, October 12, 2004.

31. Smith, *New Right discourse on race and sexuality: Britain, 1968–1990* (Cambridge: Cambridge University Press, 1994), 36. For comparison, these are the precise terms in which Christopher Ricks formulates 'literary theory': 'The case against literary theory begins with its overbearing insistence that there is no genuine case for anything else. The advocates of theory often declare that we are all theorists whether we realise it and acknowledge it or not' ('In theory', 3), and 'So thorough does theory set out to be, so complete within its own terms, that it can only ever achieve this by the most pointed of exclusions' ('John Crowe Ransom', 142).

32. Desmond Ryan, 'The Thatcher Government's Attack on Higher Education in Historical Perspective', *New Left Review*, No. 227 (January–February, 1998), 3–32.

33. For example, the founding of the Universities Funding Council in the Education Reform Act of 1988 stipulates of the governing body comprising the council that between six and nine of its members be present or past 'providers' of higher education, but that the remaining members be selected on the basis of their 'experience of, and […] capacity in, industrial, commercial, or financial matters or the practice of any profession'. *Education Reform Act 1988* (London: Her Majesty's Stationery Office, 1989), 135.

34. Ryan cites Aubrey Jones, *Britain's Economy: The Roots of Stagnation* (Cambridge: Cambridge University Press, 1985), 140.

35. 'Mochlos, or The Conflict of the Faculties', 92/'Mochlos ou le conflit des facultés', 410.

Part 3

Chapter 5
'Préférance'

Je préfère chez Freud des analyses partielles, régionales, mineures, les coups de sonde les plus aventurés. Ces percées réorganisent parfois, au moins virtuellement, tout le champ du savoir.[1]

Préférez toujours la vie et affirmez sans cesse la survie.[2] —Derrida

The previous section of this book looked in detail at the case against Derrida outlined in the Cambridge Affair, in terms of the understanding of philosophy that undergirded it. This section addresses the Affair's other fundamental topic: Derrida and the question of belonging to an institutional community. This matter was not considered during the Affair by *placet* or *non placet* writers; the Affair proceeded from a supposed desirability of such belonging, and in this section I show how Derrida resists this presupposition. The present chapter is called 'Préférance', echoing 'différance', because I try to show that the presupposition resisted by Derrida is resisted inasmuch as it is preferential but has sublimated its foundational gesture of preference.

In this chapter, I focus primarily on an important essay by J. Hillis Miller, '"Don't Count Me In": Derrida's Refraining', which argues that Derrida's thinking of alterity entails a sort of monadology. That one cannot say confidently that there is any means of accessing, or even approaching the other, is for Miller the ne plus ultra of Derrida's ethics, and informs what Miller calls a gesture of 'refraining' from any and all iterations of community. I concur with Miller up to this point, because he, like Martin Hägglund, bucks a tendency one finds in many discussions of Derridean ethics, whereby obstacles to the approach of the other (in the double sense) are somehow transmuted into injunctions or even prescriptions to behave in a recognizably charitable manner (Ernesto Laclau makes this point in an essay on *Specters of Marx*, before immediately doing the very thing he purports to be critiquing; I return to Laclau's text below). However, there is a tension in Miller's piece, because he argues that Derrida's gesture of 'refraining' is his 'fundamental and defining act, his ground without ground'. I argue that this phrasing, which is crucial to the perspicacity of Miller's argument, also marks its own limit, by which the gesture of refraining identified in Derrida by Miller shall not be circumscribed. This both corroborates his argument and contradicts it. Thus, it has much in common with the construals of Derrida by Martin Hägglund and Ernesto Laclau, whose arguments also founder on their own rectitude.

Hägglund, Laclau, and Miller all identify in Derrida's thought something that questions any naturalized model of the community or institution; but all three contradict themselves where they attempt to communicate or institute this questioning. In the following chapter, I argue, with Derrida, that this observation does not identify a weakness in the three readings, because there is an inevitability of such a contradiction in any text that thinks seriously about institution and institutions.

PREFERENCE 1: MARTIN HÄGGLUND

Difficult to reconstruct its exact trajectory.[3] —Geoffrey Bennington

Martin Hägglund's *Radical Atheism: Derrida and the Time of Life*[4] is reckoned by Jonathan Culler an 'especially admirable' account of Derrida's work, and a 'decisive rejoinder to those seeking to capture deconstruction for religion'.[5] Hägglund locates the ethical nucleus of Derrida's thinking in a process he calls autoimmunity. Hägglund postulates that nothing is exempt from temporal finitude, and that Derrida's work coheres through this point. Central to his thesis is the term 'autoimmunity', through which Hägglund reads Derrida's counterposition both to theology (including negative theology), and to a history of philosophical argument that Hägglund regards as theological, often despite itself. Schematically, '[Derrida's] notion of autoimmunity spells out that everything is threatened from within itself, since the possibility of living is inseparable from the peril of dying'. Without this peril, something is not living, and hence autoimmunity is 'inscribed at the heart of life', not just as a confirmation that things are living, but also as an explanation of why they live: 'The tracing of time is the minimal protection of life, but it also attacks life from the first inception, since it breaches the integrity of any moment and makes everything susceptible to annihilation' (9). Reading autoimmunity as Derrida's first principle, allowing him to '[rethink] the condition of identity, ethics, religion, and political emancipation', is not an especially controversial position, but this sentence's conclusion is what indicates the singularity of Hägglund's contribution: This rethinking takes place 'in accordance with the logic of radical atheism' (9–10). I am interested here in how Hägglund casts Derrida's work as 'radical atheism', imputing to it a 'logic', and the tensions that result.

For Hägglund, autoimmunity is the outcome of the logic of the trace in Derrida's work: 'Derrida defines the trace in terms of a general co-implication of time and space: it designates the becoming-space of time and the becoming-time of space, which Derrida abbreviates as spacing (*espacement*)'.[6] This mutual becoming of time and space indicates that each concept (time and space) is impossible without the other one, against the 'classical distinction between space and time', which holds that 'The spatial can remain the same, since the simultaneity of space allows one point to coexist with another', whereas 'the temporal can never remain the same, since the succession of time entails that every moment ceases to be as soon as it comes to be and thus negates itself'.[7] For Hägglund, this distinction errs twice: it does not account for the temporal dimension of the understanding or perception of spatial coexistence, and it does not account for the spatial dimension of the understanding or perception of time as negation. Accounting for these unaccounted-for questions ultimately leads to a 'co-implication of time and space', which outlines the structure of the trace:

> Time is nothing but negation, so in order to be anything it has to be spatialized. There is no 'flow' of time that is independent of spatialization, since time has to be spatialized in order to flow in the first place. Thus, everything we say about time (that it is 'passing', 'flowing', 'in motion' and so on) is a spatial metaphor. This is not a failure of language to capture pure time but follows from an originary *becoming-space of time*. The very concept of duration presupposes that something remains across an interval of time and only that which is spatial can remain. Inversely, without temporalization it would be impossible for a point to *remain* the same as itself or to exist *at the same time* as another point. The simultaneity of space is itself a temporal notion. Accordingly, for one point to be simultaneous with another point there must be an originary *becoming-time of space* that relates them to one another.[8]

Hägglund's argument is lucid, but there is a problem where he states that spatial metaphors not only are in some way natural and fundamentally homogenous, but are also spatial metaphors of spatial metaphoricity. That is, a spatial metaphor for time is not 'a failure of language to capture pure time but follows from an originary *becoming-space of time*'; this 'follows from' is itself a spatial metaphor for time, to which, in Hägglund's account, all metaphors for time testify. I flag this tension here to introduce a more general problem with Hägglund's delimitations of Derrida.

Developing this interrelation of space and time in *Radical Atheism* allows Hägglund to challenge, principally, the idea that the spatial can remain the same. Rejecting the notion of any fixity whatsoever in the spatio-temporal matrix gives place for autoimmunity as the fundamental condition of being, 'where nothing is immune from its own destructibility' (196); there is 'an autoimmune threat intrinsic to everything' (119). The 'deconstructive logic of identity', for Hägglund, is therefore that 'the essence of X is *not* to be identical to itself' because X is marked at all times, from all angles, by the structure of the trace (30). Hägglund's Derrida is atheist because theism, as belief in 'God', entails a desire for a state or a being that would lie outside the effects of tracing and hence would not be conditioned by autoimmunity. In a reading of 'Faith and Knowledge', Hägglund outlines Derrida's thinking about religion as he sees it:

> Derrida defines religion as premised on the idea of "the unscathed" (*l'indemne*), which he glosses as the pure and the untouched, the sacred and the holy, the safe and sound. The common denominator for religions is thus that they promote a notion of the unscathed, regardless of whether the unscathed is posited as transcendent or immanent and regardless of whether it is called God or something else. As Derrida puts it, "every religion" holds out a "horizon of redemption, of the restoration of the unscathed, of indemnification." Accordingly, the religious promise of the good would be the promise of something that is unscathed by evil. The good may be threatened from the outside – by corruption, idolatry, misunderstanding, and so on – but in itself it is exempt from evil.[9]

That religion can suppose, as 'God', an internal fixed state of good (or evil) makes it incompatible with Derrida's thinking as Hägglund reads it, in which the structure of the trace falsifies any idea of 'the unscathed' by establishing autoimmunity (the risk of change and death at any moment and at any point) as the condition for life. Radical atheism, Hägglund argues, maintains that 'every moment of life is a matter of survival, since it depends on what Derrida calls the structure of the trace' (1).

Hägglund's Derrida has an emphatically political dimension: 'Nothing can matter to you in a state of immortality. There can be no urgency to do anything, to cultivate anything, or to strive for anything, since nothing of value can be lost or fail to take place. You cannot even be motivated to pursue a single activity, since it would not count as a loss for you if you did not engage in the activity or if it ceased to be'.[10] For Hägglund, Derrida's philosophy must be understood as a mortal undertaking: 'Anyone who is committed to something that can be lost is mortal',[11] and such notions as autoimmunity and the trace indicate that Derrida is the thinker of precisely this commitment.

However, if for Hägglund Derrida's oeuvre coheres through the figure of autoimmunity, then we can ask whether this thesis – that Derrida's oeuvre is unwaveringly consistent on the matter of autoimmunity – is problematized, according to the logic of autoimmunity, by the very autoimmunity from which it draws its force. Hägglund's reading of Derrida founders on the fact that what makes possible this reading is a necessary arrestation of autoimmunity or indeed any formulation of contingency, where Derrida's oeuvre is concerned. In *Radical Atheism*'s first sentence, Hägglund describes his project as 'a sustained attempt to reassess the entire *trajectory* of Derrida's work' (1; my italics).

There is a discrepancy here between Hägglund's attribution of a 'trajectory' to Derrida's oeuvre, and the content he ascribes to that trajectory – namely, a commitment to mortal life as a refusal of absolutist claims, which would entail the views that (a) a trajectory, because it is a spatio-temporal phenomenon, necessarily is not contemporaneous with itself; and (b) that this non-contemporaneity amounts to destruction (this is the basis of Hägglund's critique of Quentin Meillassoux, who does not maintain that the necessary contingency entailed by the passage of time necessarily has to obey the logic of temporal destruction). Since, by Hägglund's lights, a trajectory should be characterized in these terms, does this pose a problem to his reading of Derrida? If Hägglund's observation of a trajectory in Derrida's work is formally consistent with the characteristics of a trajectory given by the content derived from this observation, then the observation of a trajectory is strictly impossible. Either this, or Hägglund's interpretation proceeds from a strategic arrest of the argument informing that interpretation, something noted by Michael Naas, who labels *Radical Atheism*'s opening sentence 'a pretty big claim, laid out in a rather bold declarative sentence without equivocation, qualification, or periphrasis'.[12]

This note of caution is sounded by Derrida himself. In an interview of 1983 with Catherine David, he responds to a remark about his oeuvre ('To read you, one has to have read Derrida'):

> But that's true for everyone! Is it so wrong to take account of a past trajectory [un trajet passé], of a writing that has part sealed itself, little by little? But it is also interesting to undo, to unseal. I also try to begin over again in proximity to the simplest thing, which is sometimes difficult and dangerous.[13]

This partly refers to the familiar idea that the more one reads of a writer's corpus, the better capable one will become of understanding it. But two things complicate this: the image of a 'past trajectory' as a partially and gradually self-sealing writing ('une écriture qui s'est en partie scellée elle-même, peu à peu'); and Derrida's suggestion that not only is he ambivalent about this sealing process, but that his oeuvre itself might develop according to an impetus that seeks to make it contingent – to undo and unseal ('de défaire, de desceller'[14]). Derrida himself actually offers an account of the trajectory of his work that is more of a piece with the trajectory of Hägglund's argument than Hägglund's self-identical model of the trajectory with which Hägglund frames this argument.[15] This implies that something of Derrida has been sealed off in Hägglund's construal.[16]

Hägglund's persuasive account of Derrida's ethics – a commitment to something that can be lost – always takes place in the present tense indicative: His derivation through Derrida of the primacy of autoimmunity can only take place due to his construal of Derrida's work as consistent on this point and therefore exempt from the autoimmunity it posits. For example, Hägglund's insistence that Derrida's *The Work of Mourning*[17] coheres around a 'secular faith' – a refusal of recourse in this mourning to any conception of time that would transcend the mortal – misses one crucial sentence in Derrida's oeuvre.[18] This sentence is found in 'Final Words', a short text that Derrida wrote to be read at his funeral. The text in full reads:

> Jacques n'a voulu ni rituel ni oraison. Il sait par expérience quelle épreuve c'est pour l'ami qui s'en charge. Il me demande de vous remercier d'être venus, de vous bénir, il vous supplie de ne pas être tristes, de ne penser qu'aux nombreux moments heureux que vous lui avez donné la chance de partager avec lui.
>
> Souriez-moi, dit-il, comme je vous aurai souri jusqu'à la fin. Préférez toujours la vie et affirmez sans cesse la survie . . .
>
> Je vous aime et vous souris d'où que je sois.[19]

The English translation of this text,[20] which otherwise largely accords with Hägglund's presentation of Derrida, does not render the tense of its final word. Derrida's dernier mot, 'sois', is in the subjunctive, and thus cannot be interpreted according to any single space or time: A nearer English translation would read 'wherever I may be'.[21] The status of this 'sois', at the terminus of a text written almost entirely in the present tense, asks some questions of its relation to the temporality that it qualifies (if 'qualify' is the right word for the effect achieved), and of the function of the plural, 'Derniers mots'.

John D. Caputo, responding to Hägglund's reading of Derrida, states, 'God is not the hyperousiological I know not what of negative theology, but a call from I know not where. God is not an unlimited being but a name uttered in all limit situations'.[22] Caputo's position, where 'God' names 'not the might of omnipotence but the *subjunctive* "might" of might-be',[23] would allow for Derrida's subjunctive, whereas Hägglund's would require that it be translated into a rigorously present tense.[24] This subjunctive marks a novel *kairos*: It is the moment that the subjunctive in a sense becomes the law. Derrida from then on no longer *is* anywhere (he is dead); there is no longer a simple tensile recourse, nor a deixis, and the value of the 'trajectory' is put in question. The subjunctive of 'Final Words' outmanoeuvres the logical architecture of

Hägglund's reading, which must resort to a constative ideal (the postulation of a self-same 'trajectory' in Derrida's work) even as its larger argument is presented as a critique of the possibility of such an ideal.

Derrida's subjunctive asks difficult questions of Hägglund's reading, and illuminates Hägglund's affinity with the readings of Derrida's ethics he disputes. In *Radical Atheism*, Hägglund argues that pseudo-ethical mistakes are made when one conflates openness to the other as a material circumstance with the prescription that one must act in a manner that somehow conveys openness to the other (31). Hägglund would challenge a formulation such as this:

> For Derrida, the undecided possibility of what is "to come" allows for acts of unexpected invention that might break with the old and any fixed horizon of expectation. Radically undecided, Derrida's "out of joint" time welcomes that which remains still to come but which can make no promise of its coming. [. . .] The provisionality of this undecided future is important insofar as it loads the commitment to that future with risk; there can be no guarantee of correct outcomes, no promise of either utopia or apocalypse, designations of neither winners nor losers without closing the unformed possibility of what is to come.[25]

This account privileges acts of invention over conservation or degradation independent of any action: It prescribes an attitude of 'welcoming' the à-venir; and despite arguing against prescriptivism concerning the future, it nonetheless preloads that argument with the noblesse of 'commitment' and 'risk'. However, far from avoiding the form of such prescriptivism, Hägglund presents the converse to its content.

As Caputo notes, unconditional hospitality in Derrida is 'the pure concept of hospitality, "the very idea" of hospitality, regardless of the circumstances in which it is "put into practice."' But Hägglund's reading cannot admit this 'regardless'; it must reintroduce specific circumstances by arguing that since the 'wholly other' has no pregiven content or character, it cannot be said either to be 'good' or 'bad', and instead describes 'our "violent exposure"' to the unforeseeable', against which one must 'take all due precautions'.[26] For Hägglund, 'Derrida's notion of unconditional hospitality designates the exposure to the unpredictable, which can always be violent and to which one cannot know in advance how one should relate' (104). This formulation, which turns the risk of violence into a maxim that colours in advance the horizon of alterity ('can *always* be violent'), typifies Hägglund's reading of Derridean hospitality, which transmogrifies passivity before the approach of the other into a curtain-twitching waiting game, which does not stop even when the other has been welcomed, or, more aptly, 'welcomed': 'Even the other who is welcomed as peaceful may turn out to be an instigator of war, since the other may always change' (104). Hägglund's construction, again, is sceptical: If the chronology of war and peace in this example were reversed, it would have consequences for his argument but not for Derrida's.

This can be clarified where Hägglund states that 'Derrida says that unconditional hospitality is at once indissociable from *and* heterogeneous to conditional hospitality'. Hägglund's construal of this indissociability is significant: 'Unconditional hospitality is *indissociable* from conditional hospitality, since it is the exposure to the visitation of others that makes it necessary to establish conditions of hospitality, to regulate who is allowed to enter' (104). Given that the idea of necessity in Hägglund's reading is axiomatic, it is pertinent that here he is arguing for the establishment of necessary conditions of hospitality as a corrective to the nonprescriptive character of unconditional hospitality. According to this argument, unconditional and conditional hospitality cannot be dissociated because unconditional hospitality does not give a priori grounds for its implementation – such grounds being given marks the incipience of conditional hospitality. This is true, but it does not follow necessarily that the 'regulations' Hägglund recommends are themselves indissociable from unconditional hospitality.

Because, for Hägglund, everything comes down to a question of time, it pays to look closely at the temporality of his argument for indissociability: 'It *is* the exposure to the visitations of others that *makes* it necessary to establish conditions of hospitality, to regulate who *is* allowed to enter'. These present tenses are not strictly compossible: What is actually achieved is a foreclosure of what is to come. One cannot have 'exposure to the visitations of others', in the present tense, *and* the regulation of 'who *is* allowed to enter', also in the present tense. One cannot be passive before the other within a jurisdictional framework, exposed temporarily and in a controlled environment to the visitation of the other, before deciding by committee and according to preexisting regulations whether to admit the other more permanently (of course, one *can*, and in many cases one *does*, but this already would be conditional hospitality). If the exposure and the regulation are indissociable for Hägglund, then this amounts to the mode of exposure being circumscribed in advance by the regulation, and since this exposure is always entailed in Derrida's invocation of the à-venir (the thought of the future he *prefers*), then Hägglund's argument cannot do without an analogous circumscription of this à-venir.[27] As Caputo argues, the a priori delimitation of unconditional hospitality would be Hägglund's 'unconditional hospitality': The superimposition conveys the necessity, for Hägglund's argument but not Derrida's, of figuring the future as qualitatively homologous to the present moment.[28]

In its institution of Derrida's irreducibility to extant paradigms, Hägglund's argument delimits itself, and does so instructively. Hägglund is not alone in having his argument marked or even constituted by this strange rebound.

PREFERENCE 2: J. HILLIS MILLER

In arguing that the 'fundamental and defining act' in Derrida is one of 'refraining', J. Hillis Miller draws together the questions of institutionalization and preference with which this chapter is concerned. In his essay, '"Don't count me in": Derrida's Refraining',[29] Miller develops Simon Morgan Wortham's argument that Derrida enjoyed a 'with-against' relation to the academic institution, elaborating it via remarks made by Derrida in *A Taste for the Secret*, his interviews with Maurizio Ferraris and Gianni Vattimo between 1993 and 1995.[30] In an introductory phrase relevant to my reading of Miller's essay, Wortham defines this relation as 'a turning toward and away from, a measure both of distance and proximity (inordinately difficult to calculate, and therefore in *constant need of reckoning*)',[31] a logic in '*continual* play' for a '*ceaseless* negotiation' with the question of the institution of the university.[32] Through attention to this logic, Miller arrives at his notion of 'refraining'.

On the one hand, writes Miller, Derrida's 'fidelity' to academic institutions is apparent from his teaching commitments, institutional engagements, and writings. Focusing on the first of these, Miller cites Derrida's teaching work at the École normale supérieure and the École des hautes études en sciences sociales, at the latter of which, as director of studies, Derrida oriented his research and teaching around the topic of 'Philosophical Institutions'. The 'rigor' of this work (Miller's example is the 'immense proportion' of Derrida's seminars based around extremely close readings of Heidegger) is partly an institutional inheritance: As well as a commitment to the procedures of Husserlian thought carried over from his time as a student,[33] Derrida also shows the influence of what Miller calls 'the French tradition of microscopic reading as a way of identifying the systematic hanging together of philosophical writings', learnt from Martial Guéroult, who taught at the ENS (176–77).

After this outline of Derrida's 'commitment to the institutions already firmly in place' (177), Miller introduces an ostensible 'on the other hand', which it transpires is a decoy. This concerns Derrida's interest in 'counter-institutions', which appears opposed to the first type of institutional commitment. The counter-institutional facet of Derrida's work most obviously concerns the four such institutions of whose founding Derrida was instrumental: GREPH (1974), the Estates General of Philosophy (1979), the Jan Hus Association (1981), and CIPH (1983). Miller identifies four defining characteristics of these counter-institutions. First, they were not 'counter-' in a strong sense[34]: Rather than being 'wholly different, subversive, revolutionary, unfaithful' to existing institutions, they were interested uppermost in restoring to the study of philosophy a fidelity to the tradition of that study which those institutions were seen to be betraying. Second, Derrida's involvement with these counter-institutions did not last long, and his position in them typically became increasingly marginal during his membership. Third, none of these counter-institutions has had much 'actual' effect or impact upon the institutional contexts in which they intervened. Fourth, Derrida's association with these counter-institutions basically enacted a hyper-fidelity to the procedures he had learnt from the existing institutions, which had the effect of deconstructing the pedagogical assumptions founding those procedures: 'In Derrida's case, the age-old assumption that a great philosopher's works form a system, plus the exhortation to micrological reading, led him to try to fit everything in. Behold! He found that you cannot do that' (178).

Developing this fourth counter-institutional characteristic, Miller argues that this scrupulous fidelity engenders deconstruction itself:

> As any schoolchild knows, nothing can be more insolent or subversive than a slightly ironic exact repetition of what someone in authority has said. Derrida, as an *agrégé-répétiteur* at the École Normale was supposed to perform such iteration in his teaching. He was supposed to avoid thinking for himself. He was supposed just to repeat what Plato, Hegel, Kant, or Husserl had said. (179)

The basic tenet of iterability for Derrida is that no repetition is *not* ironic: There is always, at least, an alteration of 'socio-institutional context' and 'historical time' between an iteration and its repetition/s (179). For Miller, this logic of supplementarity informs the continuity and rupture that mark the relation between institution and counter-institution: 'The counter-institution supplements the institution by more adequately fulfilling its goals, that is, the goal of a collective working together on the basis of some kind of consensus. At the same time, the counter-institution brings into the open what keeps the institution from ever fulfilling its goals' (179). Concluding this ersatz 'on the other hand', Miller conjectures that the reason Derrida's counter-institutional involvements were brief may have had something to do with the same logic of supplementarity from which they derived their appeal: 'Nevertheless, a counter-institution is still an institution, with its own destined incompletion. That may explain why Derrida tended to remain for so short a time in each of his counter-institutions' (179). Miller suggests something quite recondite here. The counter-institution – in terms both of its form and of the work possibilized therein – can mark and perhaps unleash, through its iteration, repetition and supplementation of the 'goal' or object of the existing institution, the différance possibilizing that object; but it can only do so by retaining a fidelity to that object and the consensus by which that fidelity is determined. A counter-institution remains an institution, and Miller's 'on the other hand' was a decoy. The deconstruction at work in the counter-institution's relation to the institution remains 'on the one hand'.

Miller proceeds: 'Everything I have said so far still follows from my earlier "on the one hand," that is, a tracing out of Derrida's allegiance to professional institutions. I have not yet got to the other hand. I hope my readers have noticed that and have been waiting with bated breath for the other shoe to drop or for me to turn from one hand to the other' (180). This is a strikingly mixed figure from the author of *Tropes, Parables, Performatives*: Why is he holding his shoes? Has he confused his hands with his feet? And what of his last image, that of 'turn[ing] from one hand to the other'? Does Miller mean the other *hand*, or is he referring to the other in a 'bigger' sense? This catachresis, before Miller finally shows his hand, is a performative jolt or halt preparing what follows – Derrida in animal form:

> *On the other hand*, then, Derrida remains, in spite of his allegiance to institutions and counter-institutions, deeply suspicious of any form of collectivity or togetherness, any institution, however "counter." His most deep-seated and spontaneous reaction to invitations to join something is what William Faulkner, using a Southernism or at least a "Faulknerism," calls "refraining." This is, for example, the violent gesture made by a horse when it rears back, rolls its eyes, arches its neck, and resists being put in a truck or corral. The resistance to saying "X" without also immediately saying "not X" or "at the same time Y" is the stylistic marker of this refraining. Why is this? Why all this rearing back? What is the logical or illogical or logical-illogical basis of this refraining? (180)

If the first 'hand' of Miller's argument pertained to deconstruction's institutional significance in terms of what it lets happen, then the 'refraining' Miller proposes at the outset of the second 'hand' pertains to a moment of decision which is no simple mediation between available alternatives: a 'resistance to saying X without also immediately saying not X, or, at the same time Y'. This form of decision is the negative of choice – the latter being 'the reflex selection of pre-loaded options', as Nick Mansfield has it.[35] The significance of Miller's making this point through a bestialization of Derrida, or more specifically through the trope of an animal's resistance to – and within – its ongoing domestication, becomes apparent in his subsequent argument.

Miller states that Derrida's resistance to any idea of a community – its presuppositions (the common, the 'comme-un'), and its concomitant beliefs about intersubjectivity – is absolute: 'Everything in Derrida's thought follows from the fundamental assumption that every self or Dasein is absolutely isolated from all the others' (181). For Miller, Derrida is 'unusual', even 'almost unique', in denying that Mitsein is the aboriginal condition of Dasein[36]; for him, every community is 'phantasmal' (182). This would be a monadology without Leibniz's redemptive principle of divine compossibilization (184–86); instead, the image of the community is conjured by 'dispositifs' nowhere given in nature, which would express a false commonality,[37] not only between its members, but within each of its members. Miller argues that this is literally *disingenuous*, indicating thereby the significance of Derrida's refraining:

It is because I am so absolutely different from my neighbor, enisled in my own ego, that I can understand you and that you can understand me. [. . .] It would seem that each person understands what his or her neighbor means because the two have something, quite a lot in fact, in common – a common language, for example. It would seem that this, in turn, turns on the way you and I both go on being the same person from moment to moment, day to day, year to year. Derrida, however, insists that I am always, each moment, ingenuous, like a newborn, always new. He insists, paradoxically, moreover, that it is just because we are infinitely different that we understand one another. (185)

Is Miller's phrasing – 'I am always, each moment, ingenuous' – only a more optimistic version of Hägglund's construal of Derridean 'autoimmunity', or does he envisage a different process? As I suggested, in Hägglund's account of Derrida's ethics the fear of the ingenuousness of the other is prominent, whereas Derrida could not be much clearer when he says, for example, 'I take the responsibility for myself for an other; whether in myself or outside, it makes no difference'.[38] Miller's reading of Derrida, accordingly, ascribes to the community an irrevocable thanatosis, even a death drive, whereas refraining from this model would entail ingenuousness. Yet this question is complicated by Miller's subsequent reference to Herman Melville's Bartleby as Derrida's refraining antecedent:

Like Melville's Bartleby, Derrida just says no, or rather, he says no without saying no, or yes either. "He doesn't say no and he doesn't say yes," says Derrida of Bartleby. Derrida says, like Bartleby, politely but firmly, "I would prefer not to." (187)[39]

Although Miller goes no further with the Bartleby analogy, it takes us down an interesting route: how to square what Miller is saying (Derrida is saying) about the ingenuous character of refraining, with the repetitive, death-driven figure of Bartleby? Bartleby refrains through refrain; his refrain(ing) is a refrain(ing), and its exclusively repeated articulation leads to his death. Despite Bartleby ostensibly refraining from any commonality or community, at the same time the form of the refrain seems isomorphic with the form of the community, with 'this death drive that is silently at work in every community'.[40] This ambivalence is pertinent, not least because, although it is unremarked by Miller, it corresponds to the ambivalence that marks the tropology of this second 'hand' of his argument (that Derrida refrains from any idea of the community): the mixing of hands and feet as a way of defamiliarizing the 'on the one hand . . . on the other hand' argumentative form, and the rhetorically familiar figure of the domesticated horse describing Derrida's resistance to the familiarity presupposed by the idea of the community. If, as Miller argues, Derrida's 'refraining' is his 'fundamental and defining act, his ground without ground' (190), how might we understand this in relation to the ambivalence of Bartleby?

This more ambivalent construal of Bartleby is developed, interestingly enough, by Gilles Deleuze in an essay called 'Bartleby; or, The Formula'.[41] For Deleuze, Bartleby, rather than just expressing a resistance to the community, shows the community to itself. His 'prefer not to' expresses 'a logic of negative preference, a negativism beyond all negation', which is 'not a will to nothingness, but the growth of a nothingness of the will [non pas une volonté de néant, mais la croissance d'un néant de volonté]' (71/92). If the will to nothingness corresponds to the community's death drive, 'the growth of a nothingness of the will' would '[hollow] out an ever expanding zone of indiscernibility or indetermination between some nonpreferred activities [des activités non-préférées] and a preferred activity [un activité préférable]' (71/92). Since the 'prefer not to' initially applies to Bartleby's refusal to collate, it also makes copying impossible, but Bartleby continues his copying work until after the sixth instance of the utterance. His 'prefer not to' is not initially a refusal to copy, but becomes one in a delayed apprehension that this was at issue all along – not an a priori refusal to copy, but an emergent realization that this is what was being refused:

> And yet he will never say that he prefers not to (copy): he has simply passed beyond this stage. And doubtless he does not realize this immediately, since he continues copying until after the sixth instance. But when he does notice it, it seems obvious, like the delayed reaction that was already implied in the first statement of the formula: "Do you not see the reason for yourself?" he says to the attorney. The effect of the formula-block is not only to impugn what Bartleby prefers not to do, but also to render what he was doing impossible, what he was supposed to prefer to continue doing. (70/91–92)

Deleuze generalizes this figure of copying to signify the linguistic conformism of a community, so that the reiteration of 'I would prefer not to' is always in the process of becoming an articulation of refraining, rather than being posited as such from the start. This movement comprehends Bartleby's achievement: an utterance that, resisting the interlocutive presuppositions that condition all committed speech, 'excludes all alternatives'; it demurs without saying no, but also does not say yes to this demurral: It 'devours what it claims to conserve no less than it distances itself from everything else' (73/95). The effect will have been 'to carve out a kind of foreign language within language [creuser dans la language une sorte de langue étrangère], to make the whole confront silence, make it topple into silence' (72/94).

Deleuze identifies three things here: Bartleby's refraining as not an a priori refusal to copy or conform; an absolutely exclusive language thereby made possible; and that speech's function as a mirror held up to a language community from within it. The ensuing disorientation is not announced at the outset, nor at any other stage, but is felt by the community due to Bartleby reflecting what it understands itself to be. As an absolutely exclusive utterance, 'I would prefer not to' is the utterance of the ideal community, articulating exclusion without being an excluding articulation. It is already structured by exclusion without having an incipient instance of exclusion, and hence takes on the appearance of the 'natural'. Bartleby performs to the letter the genesis of the community which is embarrassed and unsettled by him.[42] It is unsurprising, therefore, that Derrida foregrounds Bartleby's relevance for, and disorientation of, psychoanalysis: 'Without saying anything, [Bartleby] makes others speak, above all the narrator, who happens to be a responsible man of the law and a tireless analyst'.[43]

This reading of Bartleby, via Deleuze, departs from, and at the same time remains faithful to, Miller's. Bartleby is seen to refrain even from Miller's postulation of his incipient, ingenuous refraining: Bartleby also says, '"at present I would prefer not to make any change at all."'[44] Deleuze's emphasis on the 'prefer not to' as not a priori resonates with a complication of the conventional idea of the 'foreigner' that Derrida, in 'Step of Hospitality/No Hospitality', articulates through Sophocles,[45] whereby 'foreignness' is not a pre-given characteristic but a process determinable retrospectively:

> Usually, the foreigner, the foreign citizen, the foreigner to the family or the nation, is defined on the basis of birth: whether citizenship is given or refused on the basis of territorial law or the law of blood relationship, the foreigner is a foreigner by birth, is a born foreigner. Here, rather, it is the experience of death and mourning, it is first of all the law of burial that becomes – let us say the word – determining. The question of the foreigner concerns what happens at death and when the traveller is laid to rest in a foreign land.[46]

This 'foreignness' is foreign to the foreign as it is familiarly defined. The possibility of this figure exposes a contingency in that construction of foreignness that is the founding gesture of any community – and it is a possibility insisted on by Bartleby[47] as much as by Derrida. This suggests that the logic of Miller's argument – whereby 'refraining' is Derrida's 'fundamental and defining act' and marks a relation to Bartleby – mobilizes a reading that problematizes Miller's argument *because* it vindicates it. Put simply, doing exactly what Miller says they do, Bartleby/Derrida exceed the logic of Miller's statement; the refraining is not fixed even by Miller's insistence that it amounts to a refusal of fixity, but that very insistence makes possible an observation of its deferral. That the matter of *preference* echoes in all of this multiplies the complication: What are the stakes, and what is the point, of a preference deferred?

PREFERENCE 3: ERNESTO LACLAU

Miller's essay invites a deconstructive reading of itself that can address an aporia that Ernesto Laclau identifies concerning deconstruction and the question of institution. Laclau's review of *Specters of Marx*, '"The Time is Out of Joint,"'[48] converges in part with Miller's construal of Derridean ethics. For Laclau, Derrida's discernment between the messianic and messianism in that text can and has been too hastily used as a basis to derive a set of ethical principles, based on the former term's apparent secularism. Derrida's preference for the messianic – 'we prefer to say *messianic* rather than *messianism*, so as to designate a structure of experience rather than a religion [*messianique*, préférons-nous dire, plutôt que *messianisme*, afin de designer une structure de l'expérience plutôt qu'une religion]'[49] – expresses a resistance to ontic closure, rather than replacing one form of that closure with another. Nicholas Royle describes this preference as a 'stress' ('Derrida stresses the notion of "the *messianic* rather than *messianism*"'[50]), but I would argue, according to the complexity of 'preference' outlined above, that Derrida's actual phrasing subtly destabilizes the model of optative insistence connoted by 'stress'. It certainly does so in the case of Laclau's reading of *Specters of Marx*.

For Laclau, Derrida's conception of 'the promise as a (post-) transcendental or (post-) ontological (non-) ground' relates to 'the ethical and political contents of an emancipatory project' in an uncertain manner, but Derrida's 'ambiguity' concerning this relation can give rise to an illogical synthesis of the (non-) ground of the promise and an emancipatory agenda. Such a synthesis would entail (and has entailed, according to 'many defenders of deconstruction') an uncritical gesture of prescription, or simple preference, which according to Laclau does not necessarily follow from the messianic:

> The illegitimate transition is to think that from the impossibility of a presence closed in itself, from an "ontological" condition in which the openness to the event, to the heterogeneous, to the radically other is constitutive, some kind of ethical injunction to be responsible and to keep oneself open to the heterogeneity of the other necessarily follows. (77)

If the messianic suggests a general structure of experience constituted by an absence of an 'immanent tendency to closure and full presence', it does not follow to privilege one derivable ethical injunction over all others (the most rigid messianisms, including certain Marxisms, have equally followed from this general structure), since all of these would have the same structural effect, if not the same material outcome – they artificially would bring about closure 'from the outside' (78).[51] For Laclau, this ambiguity is the 'main stumbling block' to a deconstructive intervention in the Marxist tradition: 'Once this ambiguity is superseded, however, deconstruction can become one of the most powerful tools at hand for thinking strategically' (82). Here, Laclau commits the very fallacy he critiques: Just as there is nothing immanent to the messianic promise that would legitimize a prescription to remain open to the heterogeneity of the other, there equally are grounds neither for putting this problem in Hegelo-Marxist terms of 'supersession', nor for the valuation of 'supersession' subtending that.

If Laclau is to argue that supersession would mark an organic intervention in the messianic that would resolve the ambiguity that keeps it inchoate, in a manner that does not amount to an artificial closure that contradicts its very postulation (and would be a corrective to the artificial closures he sees visited on the messianic), then in principle he must posit supersession as a stage in the temporal destination of the messianic. Doing so corresponds, at a conceptual level, to a phenomenon Laclau sees in localized emancipatory struggles, whereby 'within a certain social space, some signifiers assume a role of general representation', becoming increasingly indeterminate as the emancipation ontologizes itself:

> The symbols of an emancipatory struggle, in a certain context, assume the representation of something wider than any particular demand and are to that extent quite indeterminate. Sometimes, when a certain oppressive regime has been overthrown, people live for some time under the illusion that what has been overthrown is oppression in general, and the limits within which the signifiers of liberation operate are thus indeterminate.[52]

This passage folds back to describe a logic at work in Laclau's reading of *Specters of Marx*, where the Marxian corrective to deconstructive syntheses of the messianic amounts to a forgetting of the structural contingency it shares with these. Laclau's Marxian foreclosure of the future opened by the messianic corresponds to an interpretive orthodoxy he and Chantal Mouffe elsewhere observe in Marxian dialectics: '[Marxian] "dialectics" exerts an effect of closure in those cases where more weight is attached to the necessary character of an a priori transition, than to the discontinuous moment of an open articulation'.[53]

Hägglund's institution of a new Derrida lapses into the logic it purports to supersede at its moments of institution; Miller's delineation of Derrida's preference-not-to (his 'refraining') constitutively must allow itself to be breached by that refraining; and Laclau's critique of this refraining can only proceed by the very misstep whose occurrence he attributes to the inscrutability of Derrida's preference-not-to. These contradictions are symptomatic – not of some ecstatic excess on the part of Derrida or his readers, but of a process of institution that systematically is accounted for by Derrida in his lecture 'How to Avoid Speaking: Denials', on which I focus in the final chapter of this book.

NOTES

1. Derrida and Élisabeth Roudinesco, *De quoi demain . . . : Dialogue* (Paris: Flammarion, 2001), 280.
2. Derrida, 'Derniers mots', *Rue Descartes*, Vol. 2, No. 48 (2005), 6.
3. Geoffrey Bennington, 'Hap', *The Oxford Literary Review*, Vol. 36, No. 2 (December 2014), 174.
4. Martin Hägglund, *Radical Atheism: Derrida and the Time of Life* (Stanford: Stanford University Press, 2008).
5. Jonathan Culler, 'Preface to the 25th Anniversary Edition', Culler, *On Deconstruction: Theory and Criticism after Structuralism, 25th Anniversary Edition* (London and New York: Routledge, 2008), (no page number).
6. Hägglund, 'The Arche-Materiality of Time: Deconstruction, evolution and speculative materialism', *Theory After 'Theory'*, eds. Jane Elliott and Derek Attridge (Oxford and New York: Routledge, 2011), 265.
7. 'Arche-Materiality', 269.
8. 'Arche-Materiality', 270. See also Hägglund, 'Radical Atheist Materialism: A Critique of Meillassoux', *The Speculative Turn: Continental Materialism and Realism*, eds. Levi Bryant, Nick Srnicek, Graham Harman (Melbourne: re.press, 2011), 118.
9. Hägglund, 'Derrida's Radical Atheism', *A Companion to Derrida*, eds. Zeynep Direk and Leonard Lawlor (Chichester: Wiley Blackwell, 2014), 167.
10. Hägglund, 'On Chronolibido: A Response to Rabaté and Johnston', *Derrida Today*, Vol. 6, No. 2 (November 2013), 185–86.
11. 'On Chronolibido', 185.
12. Michael Naas, 'An Atheism That (*Dieu merci!*) Still Leaves Something to Be Desired', *CR: The New Centennial Review*, Vol. 9, No. 1 (Spring 2009), 47.
13. Derrida, 'Unsealing ("the old new language")', trans. Peggy Kamuf, Derrida, *Points . . . : Interviews, 1974–1994*, ed. Elisabeth Weber, trans. Peggy Kamuf et al. (Stanford: Stanford University Press, 1995; repr. 1999), 117/Derrida, 'Desceller ("la vieille neuve langue")', Derrida, *Points de suspension: Entretiens*, ed. Elisabeth Weber (Paris: Galilée, 1992), 125.
14. 'Desceller', 126.
15. This discussion of sealing and unsealing in Derrida is informed by Naas's discussion of the trope vis-à-vis Derrida's untitled one-line poem, or 'Petite fuite alexandrine', published in 1986. See Naas, *Derrida From Now On* (New York: Fordham University Press, 2008), 213–26.
16. This is a criticism made of *Radical Atheism* by Derek Attridge. Attridge avers that Hägglund overlooks the risk valorized in Derrida's ethical commitments (particularly to hospitality) – the risk at work in Derrida's sense of the 'unconditional'. According to Attridge, there is a certain timidity in Hägglund's approaches to this facet of Derrida's work. See Attridge, 'Review of Martin Hägglund, *Radical Atheism: Derrida and the Time of Life*', *Derrida Today*, Vol. 2, No. 2 (November 2009), 271–81.
17. Derrida, *The Work of Mourning*, eds. Pascale-Anne Brault and Michael Naas (Chicago and London: University of Chicago Press, 2001).

18. These remarks were made by Hägglund in his keynote paper, 'Secular Faith', at the 2014 'Derrida Today' conference at Fordham University, which began with the discussion of C. S. Lewis that can be read in 'On Chronolibido', 182–85.

19. 'Derniers mots', 6.

20. The translation reads:

> Jacques wanted no rites and no orations. He knows from experience what an ordeal it is for the friend who takes on this task. He asks me to thank you for coming and to bless you. He beseeches you not to be sad, to think only of the many happy moments you gave him the chance to share with him.
>
> Smile for me, he says, as I will have smiled for you until the end. Always prefer life and constantly affirm survival.
>
> I love you and am smiling at you from wherever I am. Jacques Derrida, 'Final Words', trans. Gila Walker, *Critical Inquiry*, Vol. 33, No. 2 (Winter 2007), 462.

21. Leslie Hill and Michael Naas also translate the phrase in this way. See Hill, *The Cambridge Introduction to Jacques Derrida* (Cambridge: Cambridge University Press, 2007), 11; *Derrida From Now On*, 234. Naas also refers to its 'perfectly appropriate subjunctive mood'.

22. Caputo, 'The Return of Anti-Religion: From Radical Atheism to Radical Theology', *Journal for Cultural and Religious Theory*, Vol. 11, No. 2 (Spring 2011), 39.

23. 'Anti-Religion', 45 (my italics).

24. In addition to Caputo, Attridge and Naas argue that although Hägglund's arguments make sense according to their own stated logic, they prove reductive if confronted with more expansive readings of Derrida's work. See 'Review', 271–81 and 'An Atheism', 45–68.

25. Shahidha K. Bari, *Keats and Philosophy: The Life of Sensations* (New York and London: Routledge, 2012), 140–41.

26. 'Anti-Religion', 75.

27. See Attridge, 'Review', 277, for a discussion of the same passage: 'The moral [for Hägglund] appears to be: be circumspect when you welcome a stranger, because the unruly force of unconditionality can always disrupt your careful plans'. See also Caputo, 'Derrida and the Trace of Religion', *A Companion to Derrida*, eds. Zeynep Direk and Leonard Lawlor (Chichester: Wiley Blackwell, 2014), 477–78: 'Hägglund's argument against ethics is that deconstruction is not an ethics of [the] coming of the other since the other who is coming might well be evil and so cannot be regarded as the "good as such."'

28. 'Anti-Religion', 75.

29. Miller, '"Don't Count Me In": Derrida's Refraining', Miller, *For Derrida* (New York: Fordham University Press, 2009).

30. Derrida and Maurizio Ferraris, *A Taste for the Secret*, trans. Giacomo Donis, eds. Giacomo Donis and David Webb (Cambridge: Polity, 2001), 1–92.

31. Wortham, *Counter-Institutions: Jacques Derrida and the Question of the University* (New York: Fordham University Press, 2006), 1 (my italics).

32. *Counter-Institutions*, 10 (my italics).

33. See Edward Baring, *The Young Derrida and French Philosophy, 1945–1968* (Cambridge: Cambridge University Press, 2011), especially 82–181.

34. For an enumeration of the manifold senses of 'counter' operative in the term 'counter-institution', see *Counter-Institutions*, 36–43.

35. Nick Mansfield, 'Refusing Defeatism: Derrida, Decision and Absolute Risk', *Social Semiotics*, Vol. 16, No. 3 (September 2006), 477. See also William W. Sokoloff, 'Between Justice and Legality: Derrida on Decision', *Political Research Quarterly*, Vol. 58, No. 2 (June 2005), 342.

36. Miller, 'Derrida Enisled', *For Derrida*, 102, 132. See also Miller and Éamonn Dunne, 'Interview: For the Reader-to-Come', Dunne, *J. Hillis Miller and the Possibilities of Reading: Literature After Deconstruction* (New York and London: Continuum, 2010), 131.

37. 'Enisled', 121.

38. Derrida, '*As if* I were Dead: An Interview with Jacques Derrida', *Applying: To Derrida*, eds. John Brannigan, Ruth Robbins, Julian Wolfreys (Basingstoke: Macmillan, 1996), 222.

39. Miller cites *A Taste for the Secret*, 27.

40. Derrida, 'Faith and Knowledge: The Two Sources of "Religion" at the Limits of Reason Alone', trans. Samuel Weber, Derrida, *Acts of Religion*, ed. Gil Anidjar (New York and Oxford: Routledge, 2002), 87.

41. Gilles Deleuze, 'Bartleby; or, The Formula', trans. Michael A. Greco, Deleuze, *Essays Critical and Clinical*, trans. David W. Smith and Michael A. Greco (London and New York: Verso, 1998)/'Bartleby, ou la formule', Deleuze, *Critique et clinique* (Les Éditions de Minuit, 1993).

42. This performative or parodic aspect is where my reading of Bartleby diverges from Giorgio Agamben's, which demonstrates, however ingeniously, Bartleby's belonging at face value to a basically Aristotelian philosophical genealogy, explaining how Bartleby's phrase comes to 'acquire its full sense (or alternatively, its nonsense)' (261). See Agamben, 'Bartleby, or On Contingency', Agamben, *Potentialities: Collected Essays in Philosophy*, ed. and trans. Daniel Heller-Roazen (Stanford: Stanford University Press, 1999), 243–71.

43. Derrida, 'Resistances', Derrida, *Resistances of Psychoanalysis*, trans. Peggy Kamuf, Pascale-Anne Brault, Michael Naas (Stanford: Stanford University Press, 1998), 24. For a psychoanalytic reading of 'Bartleby' untroubled by this question of refraining, which straightforwardly sees the preference-not-to as 'a sophisticated version of Freud's paradigm for aesthetic/emotional judgement [. . .] a spitting out of something', see Adam Phillips, 'On Eating, and Preferring Not To', Phillips, *Promises, Promises: Essays on Literature and Psychoanalysis* (London: Faber & Faber, 2000), 282–95.

44. Herman Melville, 'Bartleby, The Scrivener', *Melville's Short Novels*, ed. Dan McCall (New York and London: W. W. Norton & Company, 2002), 30.

45. Derrida, 'Step of Hospitality/No Hospitality', Derrida and Anne Dufourmantelle, *Of Hospitality: Anne Dufourmantelle invites Jacques Derrida to respond*, trans. Rachel Bowlby (Stanford: Stanford University Press, 2000), 85–87: 'Antigone the foreign woman who accompanies her father outside the law at the point where he is crossing a border and speaking to foreigners to ask them for hospitality; Antigone whose blind father, at the end of *Oedipus at Colonus*, again illustrates this strange experience of hospitality transgressed, through which you die abroad, and not always at all as you would have wanted'.

46. 'Step of Hospitality/No Hospitality', 87.

47. It should be recalled that Bartleby himself 'is laid to rest in a foreign land', one that is foreign to the opposition home/foreign: He dies in the Manhattan Halls of Justice, (and) 'the heart of the eternal pyramids'. See 'Bartleby', 31–33.

48. Laclau, '"The Time Is Out of Joint,"' Laclau, *Emancipation(s)* (London and New York: Verso, 1996).

49. Derrida, *Specters of Marx: The State of the Debt, the Work of Mourning and the New International*, trans. Peggy Kamuf (New York and London: Routledge, 1994; repr. 2006), 210–11/*Spectres de Marx: L'État de la dette, le travail du deuil et la nouvelle Internationale* (Paris: Galilée, 1993), 266.

50. Royle, 'The Private Parts of Jesus Christ', *Writing the Bodies of Christ*, ed. John Schad (Aldershot: Ashgate, 2001), 162.

51. See also Slavoj Žižek, 'The Real of Sexual Difference':

> The "radicality" of Derridean politics involves the irreducible gap between the messianic promise of the "democracy to come" and all of its positive incarnations: on account of its very radicality, the messianic promise forever remains a promise – it cannot ever be translated into a set of determinate, economico-political measures. Žižek, 'The Real of Sexual Difference', *Reading Seminar XX: Lacan's Major Work on Love, Knowledge, and Feminine Sexuality*, eds. Suzanne Barnard and Bruce Fink (Albany: SUNY Press, 2002), 66.

Despite seeing the messianic as a figure without prescription, Žižek retains a prescriptivism—concerning what the messianic promise 'cannot ever' do – whose negative mode does not annul its recourse to the very calculable futurity which the messianic puts in question. Similarly, Luke Ferretter argues that Christian eschatology has a privileged relation to the messianic, based on the assertion that, 'In "Faith and Knowledge", Derrida speaks of the "phenomenal form" of the messianic, as peace and justice, and asserts that it "always" takes this form' (Ferretter, *Towards a Christian Literary Theory* [Basingstoke: Palgrave Macmillan, 2003], 34). However, this misrepresents what Derrida writes in that text:

> The messianic exposes itself to absolute surprise and, even if it always takes the phenomenal form of peace or of justice, it ought, exposing itself so abstractly, be prepared (waiting without awaiting *itself*) for the best as for the worst, the one never coming without opening the possibility of the other. Derrida, 'Faith and Knowledge', 56.

Ferretter conflates the form of the messianic with the form the messianic historically takes when it is conceptualized or articulated; the adjective 'phenomenal' is a clue here, since 'Faith and Knowledge' is a text concerned with phenomenological construals of religion. This is not to say that there is anything necessarily erroneous about phenomenal apprehensions of the messianic, but simply that Ferretter's ascription of a pacific and just form to the messianic remains one such apprehension and does not schematize the messianic as such, even though it purports to.

52. Laclau, 'Is Radical Atheism a Good Name for Deconstruction?', *diacritics*, Vol. 38, Nos. 1–2 (Spring/Summer 2008), 188.

53. Laclau and Mouffe, *Hegemony and Socialist Strategy: Towards a Radical Democratic Politics, Second Edition* (London and New York: Verso, 2001), 95.

Chapter 6

Dénégations

'How to Avoid Speaking: Denials' and 'Interpretations at War: Kant, the Jew, the German' are two related lectures, originally given by Derrida at international conferences in Jerusalem. Giving the former in 1986, Derrida proposed that the theme of the next such conference be 'The Institutions of Interpretation', a phrase that occurs in 'How to Avoid Speaking' but is used more prominently in 'Interpretations at War', the lecture given at that next conference.[1] I am interested here in the function of this phrase in Derrida's argument, and in the relation between the two senses of the phrase: an institution in which interpretation takes place, and the act of instituting an interpretation. Are these senses dissociable, or is the idea of an institution that merely makes possible interpretation, without always-already delimiting it, a fantasy? My reading of 'How to Avoid Speaking' tries to account for the emergence of an interest in institutional interpretation in that lecture, and to outline how this illuminates the Cambridge Affair.

NEGATIVE THEOLOGY, DECONSTRUCTION, AND EXEMPLARITY

In 'How to Avoid Speaking',[2] Derrida clarifies the relation between negative theology and his own work. He resists identifying with the former because of what he regards as its constitutive 'ontological wager of hyperessentiality [surenchère ontologique de l'hyper-essentialité]' (147/541). Although Derrida applies this expression specifically to the negative theologies of Pseudo-Dionysius the Areopagite and Meister Eckhart, it affects everything he says here about the institution of interpretation. This 'wager' is seen at once to be closely related to deconstruction, to be infinitely distant from it, and to be something like the temptation of deconstruction. Hyperessentiality is how 'God' is figured in negative theology, and provisionally describes the 'family resemblance' of negative theologies. It describes a thought of God to which no predicative language would be adequate, to the point that 'only a negative ("apophatic") attribution can claim to approach God, and prepare us for a silent intuition of God'. Hyperessentiality, however, also marks the point at which the 'traits' of negative theology exceed the boundaries of its generic constitution, such that one sees a relation between negative theology and 'every discourse that seems to have recourse in a regular and insistent manner to this rhetoric of negative determination, endlessly multiplying the defenses and the apophatic warnings'. Hence, there is a superficial resemblance between negative theology and deconstruction:

> this, which is called X (for example, the text, writing, the trace, differance, the hymen, the supplement, the *pharmakon*, the *parergon*, etc.), "is" neither this nor that, neither sensible nor intelligible, neither positive nor negative, neither inside nor outside, neither superior nor inferior, neither active nor passive, neither present nor absent, not even neutral, not even dialectizable in a third term, without any possible sublation (*Aufhebung*). (144)

Derrida questions this resemblance by foregrounding two aspects of negative theology, or apophatic discourse, that deconstruction does not share. First, negative theology privileges two areas of language: 'the indestructible unity of the word [and] the authority of the noun or the name'. It must hypostasize language, even if the principle of that hypostasis is language's inadequacy, insisting on a necessary functional sameness of all language. Furthermore, if the condition of language is its incapacity to approach 'God', then the absent name of God retains the structure of the name in gesturing to something singular, even if that singularity is beyond predication. For Derrida, the propositional bias conveyed by this view of language is what 'a "deconstruction" must start by reconsidering' (147).

Second, negative theology 'seems to reserve, beyond all positive predication, beyond all negation, even beyond being, some superessentiality, a being beyond being' (147). This allows it to understand itself as 'exceed[ing] the alternative of a theism or an atheism that would only come to oppose each other around what one calls, sometimes ingenuously [ingénument], the existence of God' (147/541). (Note the resemblance Derrida underscores between the ontological excess of the 'God' posited by negative theology, and negative theology's avowed supersession of positivist theological debate.) This second aspect of negative theology invites the discussion of Eckhart's 'ontological wager of hyperessentiality', which states that 'God works above being in vastness, where he can roam. He works in nonbeing.

[. . .] He is as high above being as the highest angel is above a gnat' (148).[3] Superficially, this hyperessentiality shares with deconstruction a reference to something heterogeneous to codification of any kind whose insistence is felt by the negation such codification entails, but the resemblance founders on this logic of the *hyper*, whereby heterogeneity is too quickly formulated in terms of the beyond:

> it was because of this movement of hyperessentiality that I believed I had to refrain [je croyais devoir me défendre] from writing in the register of "negative theology." What "difference," "trace," and so on, "mean to say" – which consequently *does not mean to say anything* – would be "before" the concept, the name, the word, "something" which would be nothing, that would no longer pertain to being, to presence or to the presence of the present, nor even to absence, and even less to some hyperessentiality. (148/542, translation modified)

To the beyond of negative theology, Derrida opposes the anteriority toward which deconstruction orients itself, suggesting that negative theology is in a way more distant from deconstruction than discourses that take for granted notions of 'being' or 'presence'. The 'beyond' is not a different way of thinking what is heterogeneous to givenness, but instead is a hyperbolic givenness.

However, Derrida acknowledges the insistence and even inevitability of analogies between deconstruction and negative theology, which are not facile but stem from the difficulty or even impossibility of deconstruction framing its project in a manner that is not formally ontotheological and that does not need strategically to share with ontotheology an interest in what is non-present:

> Yet the ontotheological reappropriation always remains possible – and doubtless *inevitable* insofar as one is speaking, precisely, in the element of ontotheological logic and grammar. One can always say: hyperessentiality is exactly that, a supreme being that remains incommensurable with the being of all that is, that *is* nothing, neither present nor absent, and so on. If in fact the movement of this reappropriation appears irrepressible, its ultimate failure is no less necessary. But I concede that this question remains at the heart of a thinking of differance or of a writing of writing. (148)

There will always be grounds for insisting on deconstruction's hyperessentiality, but this possible errancy is borne by deconstruction and is necessary to its operation. This is one reason for the title of Derrida's lecture: Is it possible to avoid, and finally to have avoided, speaking of negative theology, given that its apophasis is never entirely dissociable from any utterance, and certainly not from deconstruction? And if negative theology entails a denial of any metalanguage (insisting on the impossibility of any articulation that by implication would be more adequate to the ineffable if it were able to conceptualize linguistic inadequacy to the ineffable), then is any attempt to speak *of* it not already ignorant of this insight, which is also an important tenet of deconstruction, and at the same time, should we not be careful with this similarity? 'Is one not compelled to speak of negative theology according to the modes of negative theology, in a way that is at once impotent, exhausting, and inexhaustible? Is there ever anything other than a "negative theology" of "negative theology"? [Y a-t-il jamais autre chose qu'une <<théologie négative>> de la <<théologie négative>>?]' (152/546).

If Derrida, provisionally, remains if not within then at least not outside of negative theology, this is because we might see in negative theology a way of speaking when and where, by rights, there should not be one: 'The experience of negative theology perhaps holds *to* a promise, that of the other, which I must keep because it commits me to speak where negativity ought to lead discourse to its absolute rarefaction'. Yet the tenets of negative theology described above mean that this promise cannot be spoken of neutrally, but only in a fashion already betokening the form of that promise: 'If I therefore speak of the promise, I will not be able to keep any metalinguistic distance from it. Discourse on the promise is a promise in advance; *within* the promise'. This problematizes speech act theory's understanding of the promise, in which, 'like every authentic performative, a promise must be made in the present, in the first person (singular or plural) by one who is capable of saying *I* or *we*, here and now'. Negative theology's apophatic structure of the promise would underscore the finitude and contingency of this *I* or *we*, and disrupt any smooth passage from *I* to *we* that would characterize the community in general (153).

However, if this provisional alliance with negative theology elaborates a refraining from a communitarian model of language, Derrida insists that this refraining not be misconstrued as articulating some 'beyond' of the community – an esoteric community structured around some unspoken or unspeakable secret. Derrida again qualifies a straightforward resemblance between deconstruction and negative theology:

> those who, still today, denounce "deconstruction," for example, with its thinking of differance or the writing of writing as a bastardized resurgence of negative theology [une resurgence abâtardie de la théologie négative], are also those who readily suspect those they call *deconstructionists* of forming a sect, a brotherhood, an esoteric corporation, or, more vulgarly, a clique, a gang, or, I quote, a "mafia." (157/551)

This 'familiar indictment [réquisitoire connu]' (157/552) derives from three assumptions about deconstruction and negative theology: that the negative quality of their discourse, its hesitancy over linguistic adequation, amounts to keeping something for itself; that the indeterminacy of this secret, its lack of effective existence, amounts to it being a sophistic sham whose only function is to attain rhetorical power inside and outside of the academy; and that deconstructionists and negative theologians, even in admitting there is no secret, will not avow this positively as their position, but insist that this avowal cannot be made in any single way, thereby retaining the initial grammatical form of secrecy and hence admitting nothing (157).

Derrida does not straightforwardly contest these charges, but instead uses this 'detour' through the secret to address 'the question of *place* that will henceforth orient my talk' (158). This is an interesting movement, since Derrida will now demonstrate that the negative theology of Pseudo-Dionysius entails a fundamentally Platonic inscription of place, and since this demonstration therefore exemplarizes place as the point of distinction between deconstruction and negative theology – because the topos of place is where the deconstructive reading of negative theology is focused, *even as* it proceeds to express reservations concerning such an anchoring of focus in negative theology. The fact that Derrida reaches this methodological double bind – interrelating deconstruction and negative theology in a complex fashion – through a caricature of objections to deconstruction as an institution – interrelating deconstruction and negative theology in a simple fashion – makes visible the institutional stakes of Derrida's subsequent reading. I will now clarify how this works.

Derrida concludes the first part of his lecture with a reading of Pseudo-Dionysius's argument, in *The Mystical Theology*, that the 'divine mystery' is situated '*beyond* all position', which nonetheless puts this 'beyond' into position by prefacing it with a warning to Timothy (dedicatee of the text) that none of the *Theology* is to be heard by the 'profane' – either those who deny the hyperessentiality of the divine and believe a direct knowledge of Him to be possible, or those who derive their notion of the divine from lower orders of being. 'Beyond', for Pseudo-Dionysius, designates both the absolutely secret place of God, and the apprehension of this absolute secrecy that distinguishes the negative theologian from the profane, and so Derrida states, 'Between this place [of God] and the place of the secret [its keeping by negative theology], between this secret place and the topography of the social bond that must protect the nondivulgence, there must be a certain homology'. This homology would organize the relation between the absolutely secret place of the divine and 'the topology, the initiatory politopology that both organizes the mystical community and makes possible this address to the other, this quasi-pedagogical and mystagogical speech that Dionysius singularly directs to Timothy'. Irrevocably, the absolute Cause in negative theology 'is also the Cause for this community' (159).

Derrida finishes this part of the lecture by elaborating this double function in three aspects of the initiation to this community outlined by Pseudo-Dionysus: priestly knowledge as an intercession between God and the holy institution; the symbology of this institution as representations of the analogical function of any representation of God, and as means of shielding this institution against 'the many'; and the summit of the holy place being where the initiate might contemplate where God dwells, without contemplating God himself. The place is an ambiguous site that confirms the rectitude of negative theology while retaining the necessary distance to postulate this rectitude (160–64).

This final ambiguity marks the 'threshold' of negative theology that concerns the rest of Derrida's lecture. I have emphasized the institutional concerns by which Derrida arrives at this threshold, which can be summarized as an attempt to indicate the politopology or topolitology (160) of negative theology's hyperessentiality (the 'beyond'), the act of which indication would mark an important distinction between negative theology and deconstruction, because it treats negative theology as paradigmatic, or at least suggests reasons for the paradigmatic invocation of negative theology that is presupposed in conjunctions such as 'negative theology and deconstruction'. As for the analogous paradigmatization of deconstruction in such constructions ('Deconstruction and . . . ', 'Derrida and . . . '.), Derrida does not critique this gesture in any aphoristic way, but allows his response to emerge in the reading.

THE THREE PARADIGMS

1: Greek

Derrida outlines three paradigms for negative theology: 'Greek', 'Christian', and 'neither Greek nor Christian'. The first is Platonic negativity, which can be subdivided into two modes. First, the *Republic*'s intimation of the beyond (*epekeina*) is derived from the idea of the Good (*idea tou agathou*) having its place 'beyond being or essence'. However, this 'beyond' is already conceptualized in hyperbolic terms, and hence this mode of negativity 'maintains a sufficiently homogeneous, homologous, or analogous relation between Being and (what is) beyond Being, so that what exceeds the limit can be compared to Being, albeit through the figure of hyperbole' (169) – this mode of negativity enshrines representational adequation.

The second Platonic negativity cannot strictly be called a negativity, and nor, perhaps, can it strictly be called Platonic (170): It concerns the *khōra* (χώρα) in the *Timaeus*.[4] Excerpting from his text 'Khora', which was then a work-in-progress,[5] Derrida stresses that the *khōra*, as the place where Plato's demiurge orders the sensible universe based on an eternal model, is identifiable neither as the eternal model, nor as the derived model of the universe, but is the 'third kind' necessary for the analogical genesis of the universe to take place. *Khōra* is neither the 'Model Form, intelligible and uniformly existent', nor 'the model's Copy, subject to becoming and visible'.[6] If *khōra* is the place where the formation of the copy takes place, then in order for the copying to be unalloyed, it must be 'itself devoid of all those forms which it is about to receive from any quarter'.[7] This place making the analogical genesis possible is therefore also that which disorients the logic of the analogy whereby an eternal model *directly* begets a finite one: 'At the moment, so to speak, when the demiurge organizes the cosmos by cutting, introducing, and impressing the images of the models "in" the *khōra*, the latter must already have been there, as the "there" itself [comme le <<là>> lui-même]', heterogeneous both to 'the eternity of ideas' and 'the becoming of sensible things' (171/566).

Derrida argues that the *Timaeus* addresses this heterogeneity through a double readability. The *Timaeus* both metaphorically figures the *khōra* in a fashion that would maintain its usefulness for philosophy – as 'gold, mother, wet nurse, sieve, recipient, molding stuff, and so on', the reading canonized by Aristotle and legitimating the construal of a certain 'Platonism'[8] – and, in a fashion that interests Derrida more, it lets the name *khōra* designate nothing but 'an irreducible spacing within (but therefore also outside, once the inside is placed outside) Platonism', as something unthinkable by the philosophical framework that, as the space of the analogical inscription, it made possible.[9] It is 'that element in Plato that always resists its assimilation into Platonism'.[10]

This second readability of the *khōra* would finally question the first, as what John Sallis terms its 'counterstress',[11] by showing that the *metaphorically-expressible* negativity of the first readability is a negativity already predicated on what the *khōra* has made possible (on the analogically approachable distinction between the sensible and the intelligible), and hence this negative metaphorics is already within the mode of thinking for which the *khōra* gives place, and has nothing to say about the *khōra* (171–72).[12] But this does not mean the second negativity is any more 'literal' in how it invokes the *khōra*, because its valuation of the receptivity of the *khōra*, even though that receptivity is not intrinsically metaphorical, necessitates some figuration of that receptivity. One must find a way to figure the *khōra* as space without content, but this would not entail metaphorizing its 'literal' meaning, because to presuppose its literal meaning would be to mistake the *khōra* as the space engendering analogical possibility, for an effect of that possibility thus engendered. The *khōra* already 'introduces a dissociation or a différance in the literal meaning that it makes possible, thus forcing one to take tropic detours that are no longer rhetorical figures' (173). They are no longer rhetorical figures because understanding them as such would short-change how they are oriented toward a rupture in analogy that rhetoric must overlook.

Confronted by the problem and also the insight offered by this self-defeating discourse, Plato suggests as a rule of thumb that 'If one wishes to respect the absolute singularity of the *khora* (there is only one *khora*, even if it can be the pure multiplicity of places [si elle peut être pure multiplicité de lieux]), *it is necessary always to refer to it in the same way*' (173/569) – not to give it the same name, but to address myself to it in the same way. *Khōra* therefore names an injunction rather than an object, or exposes the injunction typically forgotten in the metaphoricity of naming – *khōra* is only 'apprehensible by a kind of bastard reasoning by the aid of non-sensation, barely an object of belief'.[13] Plato does not invent the word, but invests an existing Greek word, which concretely names a place,[14] with this injunction to think the abyssal history of precisely that kind of naming.[15] What is seemingly added to *khōra* is thereby situated at its source. Plato's gesture is therefore deconstructive, inscribing a trace and a promise in the body of this language (174), indissociable from and yet irreducible to the system of which it is part.

2: Christian

Derrida states that apprehending the second, Christian paradigm of negative theology needs to reckon with the translation of this thinking of the *khōra*, which is not theological, into 'what one calls the *via negativa* in its Christian moment' (174). Apprehending the second paradigm entails understanding the *khōra* as a (theological) paradigm for the first time. This is partly because the criteria that consolidate paradigmaticity presuppose an inferential thinking that is 'foreign to the *khora*', which gives nothing (175), whilst as a version of abstraction such thinking chimes with the negativity modelled on the 'beyond' of the Good presented in the *Republic*:

> Even if one wanted to describe "what happens" in terms of structures and relations, it would be necessary to recognize that what happens between [the experience of the *khōra* and Christian apophasis] is, perhaps, precisely the event of the event, history, the thinking of an essential "having-taken-place," of a revelation, of an order and a promise, of an anthropo-theologicalization that – despite the extreme rigor of the negative hyperbole – seems to take command once again, closer still to the *agathon* than to the *khora*. (175)

The passage from the experience of the *khōra* to the apophasis of negative theology is not a discovery, but the effect of a fundamentally *institutional* displacement of the experience of the *khōra* by the more hospitable negativity formulated through the *agathon* of the *Republic*. Such displacement, perhaps, makes it possible to think in these paradigmatic terms.

Having announced three paradigms of negative theology, Derrida's attention to these paradigms has the effect of questioning the paradigm as a premise. Even at the risk of undermining his own argument, he thereby retains a fidelity to the experience of *khōra* even as he discusses its almost inevitable eclipse. The relation of the Christian theology of Pseudo-Dionysius to the experience of the *khōra* is the superimposition by the former of a paradigm-giving inflection upon the latter: 'Even if this Good [the term in which 'God' is figured] is called formless (like the *khora*), this time it is what gives form' (175). The Christian apophasis requires this paradigm-giving inflection, which is not given by the *khōra*, just as much as affirmative theology does. Hence a certain paradigmaticity remains between, allowing the translation between cataphatic theology (the *via affirmativa*) and apophatic theology (the *via negativa*) in Pseudo-Dionysius's system.[16] As Hent de Vries notes, 'These different conceptions of the religious and the theological – as virtual almost-absence and as virtual fullest presence – presuppose each other, point to each other, call each other forth, and, finally, collapse into each other'.[17] Specifically, the cataphatic-apophatic translation retains this model of *agathon*: 'An experience must still guide the apophasis toward excellence, not allow it to say just anything, and prevent it from manipulating its negations like empty and purely mechanical phrases' (176).

This retention ensures that a Christian negative theology could not be negative in the manner of the experience of the *khōra*, but is hierarchical, attributive, and institutional.[18] The retention is borne by 'prayer', which for Pseudo-Dionysius names a confluence of two traits: the address to the other as other, no more than the imploration that 'the other hear the prayer'; and the praise or celebration (*hymnein*) that carries the imploration. Derrida argues that, unlike the former ('prayer in itself'), the latter trait (praise) must be minimally attributive and hence affirmative – it 'preserves an irreducible relation to attribution', and hence 'qualifies God and *determines* prayer, *determines* the other, the One to whom it addresses itself', and distinguishes itself through this determination. Praise *institutes* the prayer, predicating, albeit minimally, the apostrophe of 'prayer in itself', and to deny this distinction (the distinction *between* praise and prayer, and the distinction *of* the Christian prayer) 'is to refuse the essential quality of prayer to every invocation that would not be Christian'. This refusal, Derrida suggests, is perhaps characteristic of 'Christians in general', as well as Pseudo-Dionysius (177).

The difference between cataphatic and apophatic theology, therefore, would not resemble the difference between the model of negativity given in the *Republic* (from the *agathon*) and the negativity termed *khōra*. 'Negative theology' actually would name the *dissimulated* replacement of a model by an experience of negativity, which actually retains the organizing, hierarchical, and institutional structure of that model: Any resemblance between apophasis and the experience of the *khōra* is a 'displacement [déplacement]' (185/582). This is evident most starkly in prayer, whose retention between cataphatic and apophatic codes makes possible the unchanging institutional preoccupation of Pseudo-Dionysius's theology – Pseudo-Dionysius being one example among many (even extending to 'Christians in general'). The institutional retention in prayer organizes the remainder of this section of Derrida's lecture: He argues that the *khōra* is replaced and displaced by a figure more akin to a sieve – 'un crible' (584)[19] – both in Pseudo-Dionysius and Meister Eckhart.

The apophasis of Meister Eckhart, for Derrida, is based on 'a certain value of unveiling, of laying bare, of truth as what is beyond clothing': The 'rule', 'law', and 'axiomatic' of this apophasis is that 'one must go beyond the veil or the clothing' (179–80), perceiving this multiplied trope of veiling to be common to affirmative theology, whether Christian or pagan, and in doing so enacting a 'principle of demultiplication of voices and discourses, of disappropriation and reappropriation of utterances' (178). This approach would demultiply affirmative theology's symbolic plethora by showing its common contingency.

Going beyond this symbolism does not entail finding the right word(s), as this would fall back into the Word of/as God realm of affirmative theology. Instead it is about acknowledging that there is a sort of incipient logical error in the symbologies' presupposition that it is a question of a perceiving subject simply being cognizant of the significance of a given object: As Eckhart writes in 'Quasi stella matutina', 'Whoever knows but one creature would not need to ponder any sermon, for every creature is full of God and is a book' (181).[20] Eckhart's apophasis critiques the notion that we can at once *be* creatures and *perceive* the essence of creatures, and hence his sermon's 'pedagogical necessity and initiatory virtue' is that it 'supplements, not so much the Word, which has no need for it, as the inability to read the authentic "book" that we are, as creatures, and the adverbiality [l'adverbialité] we should be as a result' (181/578). The 'adverb' in question is *quasi* ('als', 'as', 'beside'), and Eckhart states that we should be 'an ad-verb to the Word', guided by the light of the Word. For this guidance, Eckhart prays to 'the Father and the same Word and the Holy Spirit. Amen' (181).[21] Derrida gives this example to indicate Eckhart's awareness of, and attempt to transcend, an 'institutional politics of interpretation', a politics that would institute itself through an ersatz unveiling of truth and a pretended multiplicity: 'A predicate can always conceal [cacher] another predicate, or even the nakedness of an absence of predicate, the way the veil of a garment – sometimes indispensable – may both dissimulate and make visible the very thing that it dissimulates – and render it attractive at the same time' (179/576).

To assume that the symbol or veil, by dint of concealing *something*, must be concealing the truth – this would be a definition of institutional interpretation that, importantly, entails a reduction of alterity to this symbolic model: 'Hence the voice of an utterance can conceal another, which it then appears to quote without quoting it, presenting itself as another form, namely, as a quotation of the other' (179). It is too easy and tempting to assume that what lies or appears to lie behind the symbol or veil is heterogeneous to that symbol. The insight of Eckhart's adverbiality, although it retains the institutional form of prayer's invocation of the Trinity, is an insight into the good conscience of the institution of interpretation.

This commentary on Eckhart's quasi-institutional hermeneutic allows Derrida to read a properly institutional trajectory in Pseudo-Dionysius's apophasis. This comes out of the difference between Eckhart's lack of direct apostrophe of God in the prayer that closes his sermon, and Pseudo-Dionysius's apostrophic commencement of *The Mystical Theology*, 'the prayer that prepares the theologemes of the *via negativa*' (181). Thus, Pseudo-Dionysius:

> Trinity!! Higher than any being, any divinity, any goodness! Guide of Christians in the wisdom of heaven! Lead us up beyond unknowing and light, up to the farthest, highest peak of mystic scripture, where the mysteries of God's Word lie simple, absolute and unchangeable in the brilliant darkness of a hidden silence. [. . .]
> For this I pray; and Timothy, my friend . . . look for the sight of the mysterious things. (181–82)[22]

Pseudo-Dionysius's apostrophe is a prayer according with the matrix of prayer in itself and praise already outlined. However, it also makes possible a prayer that takes the form of an apostrophe to Timothy, the dedicatee of the *Theology*. Pseudo-Dionysius's initiation of Timothy requires that there be a continuity between the two apostrophes: In order for the *Theology* to initiate Timothy, 'it must *lead* him on the paths to which Dionysius himself has prayed to God to lead him, or more literally to *direct* him in a straight (*ithunon*) line' (182). The change of addressee between the two apostrophes somehow must not entail a turn away from the first: 'It is in fact because [Pseudo-Dionysius] does not turn away from God that he can turn toward Timothy and *pass from one address to the other without changing direction*' (182). Pseudo-Dionysius's text therefore stands, impossibly, 'in the spacing of the *apostrophe* that *turns* the discourse *away* in the *same* direction' (182).

Furthermore, the apostrophe is not only addressed to Timothy, but is addressed to him *as* disciple – as the model for how anyone reading this text 'should be, in our souls, if we read this text as it should be read, rightly, in the proper direction, correctly' (182). The rightness of interpretation becomes possible through the apostrophe's iterability in this text – the apostrophe's capacity to retain its integrity despite its displacement from God, to Timothy, to all readers in principle: 'There is text because there is this iteration [Il y a du texte parce qu'il y a cette itération]' (182/579–80). The actuality of Pseudo-Dionysius's text, and its readers, is 'instituted from the future' (182–83) figured in his prayer. Its achievement will have been to elevate Timothy and a fortiori all its readers to the place and time in which 'the mysteries of God's Word lie simple, absolute and unchangeable in the brilliant darkness of a hidden silence'. This is the text's promise to those who read it aright, and 'the coming of this future [. . .] is the event of this promise' (183).

Derrida opposes this *institution* of the future – which is the institution of a state of grace through interpretative rectitude, and a prescription of the event based on this rectitude – to the experience of the *khōra*, because this nexus of institution sees Pseudo-Dionysius's apophasis 'put[ting] itself in motion', situating the place of itself as that of the hyphen uniting the 'anthropotheological dimension' (183). The apophasis situates itself analogously to the *khōra*, but the logic subtending such analogy has the effect of already making a paradigm or metaphor of the *khōra*, and hence follows from the model the *khōra* makes possible, but nowhere gives. The text participates in the metaphorical displacement of the *khōra* (that of a certain Aristotelian 'Platonism'), and it is still exposed to the second 'readability' of the *khōra*.

This displacement is shown in the privilege Pseudo-Dionysius affords the figure of the seal when describing the consistent trace of divinity in the 'text of creation':

> There are numerous impressions of the seal and these all have a share in the original prototype; it is the same whole seal in each of the impressions and none participates in only a part.
>
> However, the nonparticipation of the all-creative Godhead rises far beyond all these figures. (184)[23]

Although Pseudo-Dionysius disqualifies the analogy in an apophatic gesture, the seal remains a privileged figure because the differences between its material inscriptions can by analogy explain the value of the interpretive rectitude of the initiated as a heightened 'receptivity' to the divine 'seal': 'Maybe someone will say that the seal is not totally identical in all the reproductions of it. My answer is that this is not because of the seal itself, which gives completely and identically to each. The substances which receive the seal are different' (184).[24] The more virginal the receptive substance, the more true and unmistakeable the impression of the seal, 'But if the material is lacking in this receptivity, this would be the cause of its mistaken or unclear imprint or of whatever else results from the unreceptivity of its participation'.[25]

For Pseudo-Dionysius, one must not mistake the variability of substances receiving the seal for a variety of seals thus received: this would be a cataphatic multiplication of figures. Instead, one must understand that this variability itself proves the appropriateness of the apophatic position: 'For the truth is that everything divine and even everything revealed to us is known only by way of whatever share of them is granted. Their actual nature, what they are ultimately in their own source and ground, is beyond all intellect and all being and all knowledge'.[26] By analogy with the text of creation, 'In reality there is no exact likeness between caused and cause, for the caused carry within themselves only such images of their originating sources as are possible for them, whereas the causes themselves are located in a realm transcending the caused, according to the argument regarding their source'.[27] Pseudo-Dionysius asks his readers to see beyond the apparent multiplicity of (imprinted) forms, to see that there is something beyond intellectualization which accounts for these forms; this step would be their initiation. It would also approach something like the *khōra* in acknowledging that the sense of creation, and the perception of this sense, must admit to something heterogeneous to this perceptible sense.

However, Pseudo-Dionysius (and Eckhart) continue to limit this heterogeneity, framing both perceptible sense and that which is heterogeneous to it in relation to God: 'Beyond the Trinity, if one can say this, beyond the multiplicity of images, beyond the created place, the *impassivity without form* [*l'impassibilité sans forme*] that the *Timaeus* attributed, if one can still say this, to the *khōra*, is here found to suit God alone' (185/583). The striving for the intellectual passage beyond being as given – to think the trace of (divine) nonbeing in what is given to intellectualization – is to think of the place of the given as a threshold 'to give access to what is no longer a place', as 'the antechamber of the temple' (186). This relativization of place (as the place of what is given, the place where an apophatic theology must institute itself) has what Derrida calls 'an extraordinary consequence: place is being [le lieu, c'est l'être]. What finds itself reduced to the condition of threshold is being itself, being as place' (186/584). Being is relative, situated and the correct means of orienting oneself in this threshold is to *see* this contingency but, at the same time and in the same place, to see oneself seeing it contingently:

> The soul, which exercises its power in the eye, allows one to see what is not, what is not present; it "works in nonbeing and so follows God who works in nonbeing." Guided by this *psychē*, the eye thus passes the threshold of being toward nonbeing in order to see what does not present itself. Eckhart compares the eye to a sieve. Things must be "sifted." This sieve is not one figure among others; it tells the difference between being and nonbeing, it discerns this difference, it allows one to see it, but as the eye itself. There is no text, above all no sermon, no preaching is possible, without the invention of such a filter. (186)

The final displacement, or paradigmatization, of the *khōra* in this Christian schema would be the invention of an interpretive 'receptacle', a receptacle that gives form through a prior axiomatics or filtering system. The dispensation offered by this anthropo-theological figure of the sieve is, Derrida suggests, indispensable to any institution of interpretation. It describes, for instance, the insistence *of* and *on* paradigmaticity Derrida's work reads in Hägglund, Miller, and Laclau.[28]

3: Other

Derrida's final paradigm for negative theology concerns Heidegger's distinction-making reinscriptions of the *khōra*. Heidegger suggests that the *khōra* names Plato's failure fully to think the place (*Ort*), but that this ultimate failure nonetheless bears the trace of the suggestion of the full thinking of the place to Plato. However, the material inscription of the *khōra* is what 'would, in truth, have only prepared (*vorbereitet*) the way for the Cartesian interpretation of space as *extensio* (*Ausdehnung*)' (187). Of this judgement, Derrida remarks, 'Elsewhere [ailleurs] I have tried to show what is problematic and reductive about this perspective' (187/585). Concluding this chapter, I suggest a reading of this 'elsewhere'.

For Heidegger, Plato's *khōra* designates a germane but unfulfilled movement toward thinking 'a wholly other place (*nach dem ganz anderen Ort*) of Being, as against the place of beings' (187). Heidegger is interested in the unrealized trace of the *khōra* (as opposed to the merely Cartesian account of space[29]), and so his thinking here is situated 'in and beyond a Platonic or Neoplatonic tradition' (188). However, there remains the danger that Heidegger's account be understood as fundamentally Christian (for 'Being' read 'God', for 'the place of beings' read 'the text of creation'), and therefore, on Heidegger's own terms, not philosophical. As a theology, Christianity is a 'science of faith or of divine speech', a science of the revelation of God (*Offenbarung*). To theology, Heidegger opposes ontotheology or theiology, which 'concerns the supreme being, the being par excellence, the ultimate foundation or *causa sui* in its divinity', and hence concerns 'manifestation or the possibility of Being's revealing itself' (188): *Offenbarkeit*, the place for an *Offenbarung*. Theology is a science that presupposes things whose very possibility is what ontotheology or theiology, as philosophy, must think. As Derrida paraphrases it in 'Faith and Knowledge', theology is the 'discourse on God, faith or revelation', whereas theiology is the 'discourse on being-divine, on the essence and the divinity of the divine'.[30]

Derrida relates two instances in which Heidegger tries to avoid using the word 'Being' in a manner such that it would be analogous with the revealed God of theology. To avoid this analogy, Heidegger proposes only to use the word 'Being' citationally, and so not to confuse it with an object: 'Not to avoid *mentioning* it, as certain speech act theorists who distinguish between mention and use would say, but to avoid using it. [...] [T]o refrain from using it normally, if one can say that, without placing it in quotation marks or under erasure' (189).

The first instance, in 'The Question of Being', is Heidegger's proposition to write the word 'Being' under a cruciform erasure (*kreuzweise Durchstreichung*), to stress that you have to decipher 'Being' in order to read it. The word 'must be deciphered under a typography that is spatialized, spaced or spacing, printed over' (189). Importantly, this crossing out is not a conventional or abstract negation: 'Heidegger makes it point to (*zeigen*) the four regions (*Gegenden*) of what he here and elsewhere calls the fourfold (*Geviert*): earth and sky, mortals and divinities' (190). Under this erasure, 'Being' ceases to be an object, and becomes a kind of spacing: Hence, one might read in the word 'Being' the meaning of 'Being', and the appearance of the *Geviert* therein. Moreover, the cross gathers: It can only be intelligible as a cross given the 'place of crossing' (*Ort de Durchkreuzung*), which is 'an indivisible topos' (sometimes called an empty set) and so connotes the simplicity (the 'point', from which Heidegger's *Ort* derives its meaning) 'toward which everything converges and comes together' (190). But this possibility of gathering has an equally ancient history, as a, or even the, 'negative appearance of [...] erasure'. The place of crossing is most commonly understood as a negative inflection. For Heidegger, the negative appearance of the *Geviert* must be thought, but can only be thought, like 'Being', under erasure – because only a thinking under erasure can approach the *Ort* of the nothing that would be the origin of negativity. In Derrida's reading, Heidegger's crossing out of 'Being' gives the possibility of thinking the place in which negation, apparently something originary, originates: It is therefore the passage from *Offenbarung* to *Offenbarkeit*. Avoiding using the word 'normally' is necessary to a philosophy whose task is to think the place where what is normal is given.

Whilst this example shows Heidegger attempting to avoid using the word 'Being' in a quasi-theological, revealed sense, the second instance, from the transcription of a 1951 seminar at the University of Zurich, concerns Heidegger's avoidance of 'Being' in a hypothetical text on the subject of God: 'If I *were* yet *to write* a theology – to which I sometimes feel inclined – the word 'Being' *would* not occur in it' (191).[31] However, Derrida states, at this moment, the transcription of Heidegger's prescription of hypothetical avoidance means that something happens that problematizes the prescription – 'Being' occurs in a discourse on theology: 'Heidegger allows the word "Being" to appear; he does not use it, but mentions it without erasure when he is indeed speaking of theology, the very theology he is tempted to write' (191).

Although Derrida does not explicitly state this, it seems that the reason Heidegger then gives for his hypothetical prescription (that his theology would not contain an occurrence of 'Being') actually depends upon the prescription's pre-inscription of and by 'Being'. That is, Heidegger states that faith does not require the thought of Being, because Being cannot be said to be the ground and essence of God (to imbue God with Being would be to speak of God in a revealed, theological sense). And yet, the experience that makes possible the revelation of God to man (the *Offenbarkeit* for the *Offenbarung* of God) does occur in the dimension of Being: 'Here, the dimension of Being opens to the experience of God who is not or whose being is neither essence nor ground' (192). So, just as Heidegger's hypothetical prescription required the citational, material inscription of the 'Being' that the prescription would proscribe, his explanation of it testifies to that inscription's trace in the *Offenbarkeit*, which makes possible any theology.

Derrida suggests that the relation between 'Being' and the dimension of Being is analogous here to the relation between the figure of the 'sieve' and the 'antechamber' in his second paradigm of negative theology. This analogy allows Derrida to doubt whether Heidegger did not, in fact, write the theology with 'Being' that he tried to proscribe: 'Since [Heidegger] recognizes that God announces himself to experience in the "dimension of Being," what difference is there between writing a theology and writing on Being, of Being, as Heidegger never stopped doing?' (192). Combining the two instances of avoidance just analyzed, to recall Heidegger's generative gesture of *cros*sing out 'Being' in 'The Question of Being', Derrida can then ask:

> Most of all, when he writes the word "Being" under and in the place (*Ort*) of a deletion in the form of a cross? Did Heidegger not write what he says he would have liked to write, a theology *without* the word "Being"? But did he not also write what he says should not be written, what should not have been written, namely a theology that is opened, governed, taken over by the word "Being"? (192).

Heidegger's avoidances inscribe in his text not simply the opposite of his stated intention, but the space in which that opposition can arise: 'He wrote, with and without the word "Being," a theology with and without God' (192). Here, again, at the point or *Ort* of a paradigm's prescriptive institution, Derrida's reading shows a trace of an experience of the *khōra* heterogeneous to, but possibilizing, that institution.

This is the end of Derrida's lecture, and not quite the end. He offers a 'P.S'. that takes the form of a prayer: 'One more word to conclude, I beg you to forgive me for it [je vous prie de me le pardonner]' (193/593). Derrida notes that Heidegger's transcribed prescription, although sharing a pedagogic and psychagogic value with Pseudo-Dionysius's prayer that apostrophizes both God and Timothy (in that both texts teach the correct orientation of thinking), does not take the apostrophic form of Pseudo-Dionysius's text: 'Unlike Dionysius, he never says "you" [toi]: either to God or to a disciple or to a reader' (194/593).

For Derrida, there are two readings of the non-apostrophic form of Heidegger's text. The first is that it excludes the apostrophic movement of faith – prayer, such as that which possibilizes Pseudo-Dionysius's theology. For Heidegger, this apostrophic mode marks the point at which 'thinking as such' becomes impossible, organizing it in advance around a construed addressee (194). By implication, thinking as such can only be accomplished in a mode that relinquishes the apostrophe: Heidegger's non-apostrophic form therefore 'confirms the predominance of a theoretical, "constative," even propositional form (in the third person present indicative: *S* is *P*) at least in the rhetoric of a text that nevertheless powerfully challenges the determination of truth linked to this theoreticism and to this judicative form' (194).

However, the non-apostrophe, on a second reading, may also indicate not some supersession or philosophical demarcation of the form of prayer, but a wavering on the threshold of the questions that this form might ask of philosophy – its apostrophic relation to philosophy. And it is at this point that Derrida's lecture subtly folds back on itself, replies to itself, apostrophizes itself, in the form of a *pli* – a fold or re-mark:

> Are there criteria external to the event itself that would allow one to decide whether Dionysius, for example, distorted or rather accomplished the essence of prayer by quoting it, and first of all by writing it for Timothy? Does one have the right [droit] to think that, as pure address, on the edge of silence, foreign to every code and to every rite, hence to every repetition, prayer should never be turned away from its present by a notation or by the movement of apostrophe, by a multiplication of addresses? (194/594)[32]

The criteria and the right referred to here correspond to the constative mode that Derrida's reading has had to privilege in its examination of the paradigmatic inscriptions upon the spacing opened by the *khōra*. Does the idea of thinking the *khōra* in the *right way* not take the form of the pure constative, a grammar that would be entirely neutral and without the minimally performative inflection of the apostrophe? De Vries states:

> Derrida's repeated reference to the Platonic *chōra* evokes and keeps open a "possibility" – less or more than a possibility, in the philosophical, metaphysical sense of this word – that escapes the possibility, indeed the possibilizing function of Meister Eckhart's threshold (*Vorbürge*, or *parvis*) and the Heideggerian

dimension of being whose revealability (*Offenbarkeit*) precedes and enables all revelation (*Offenbarung*). The repeated invocation of the motif of *chōra* points beyond the "possibility" for which Derrida, most prominently in *Specters of Marx*, reserves the name of messianicity.[33]

This amounts to suggesting that Derrida's *khōra* shares with the apophases that are inadequate to it (necessarily having to paradigmatize or 'sieve' the *khōra* in order to give place to their own negations) a hyperessentializing quality. Derrida has argued here that the apophases of Meister Eckhart, Pseudo-Dionysius, Heidegger, and Plato himself all reach vainly toward the experience of the *khōra* – but by arguing this, is it possible to avoid speaking of the *khōra* in hyperessential terms? As that which possibilizes possibility, the *khōra* would for de Vries ground a minimal predication of the messianic, being both its material substrate and destination.

Derrida's 'P.S'. recognizes this and, more sincerely than not, begs forgiveness for it. It is a *pli* that marks his argument as finally quasi-transcendental: the experience of the *khōra*, to which the negative theological paradigms are inadequate through their paradigmatizations of it, can only be figured as such through an ineluctable paradigmatization. Derrida has instituted the experience of the *khōra* as transcendental of the paradigms of negative theology; his final gesture here is to re-mark this institution and its quasi-transcendentalism. With de Vries, the messianic, too, becomes a paradigm of negative theology, in the sense that it gives itself place vis-à-vis the *khōra* and orients itself toward an incalculability necessarily rendered 'quasi-' by that paradigmatic giving place.

In this reading, the paradigms we saw in the previous chapter imposed upon Derrida by Hägglund, Miller, and Laclau are made to fold back on themselves by the very thing they constitute as a paradigm, evincing something of the motility of deconstruction itself. This very process is both analyzed and exemplified in 'How to Avoid Speaking', and if we can specify the reason this text became for Derrida about 'the institution of interpretation', then it surely lies in the apprehension of this double movement – the two 'readabilities' of Derrida's text, like Plato's before it. Derrida's concluding remarks acknowledge the necessity and urgency both of the apophatic paradigms he has analyzed, and that of the *khōra*, which gave place to this analysis:

> Does one have the right to think that, as pure address, on the edge of silence, foreign to every code and to every rite, hence to every repetition, prayer should never be turned away from its present by a notation or by the movement of apostrophe, by a multiplication of addresses? [. . .] Perhaps there would be no prayer, no pure possibility of prayer, without what we make out as a threat or a contamination: writing, the code, repetition, analogy or the (at least apparent)

Dénégations 183

multiplicity of addresses, initiation. [. . .] [If] there were no supplement, if quotation did not bend [*pliait*] prayer, if prayer did not bend [*pliait*], if it did not submit [*se pliait*] to writing, would a theiology be possible? Would a theology be possible? (195/595)

To the vain notion of a purely apophatic prayer corresponds the notion that the notion of a purely apophatic prayer is a vain notion. To enumerate the inadequacies and vanities of paradigmatic apophases in relation to some putative non-paradigm making the former possible is an analysis that risks arrogating to itself the very vantage point from which these failures can be categorized. And this would be one more example of the *khōra*'s displacement by a hierarchizing 'sieve', even as this analysis sought distinction from those displacements through the demonstration of this exemplarity. Derrida acknowledges this in the same stroke as indicating these vain paradigms' necessity. The necessity of the *pli* of the apophatic prayer is also the necessity of re-marking as a quasi-transcendental the transcendental constatation of the *khōra* in relation to which the history of the apophatic *pli* was described.

The institution of interpretation discovered in 'How to Avoid Speaking' is not only a constatation of the interpretive institutions in and of the *khōra* that the apophatic paradigms cannot help but inscribe. It also performs this ineluctable institutional inscription, as Derrida defines it in 'Mochlos': 'An institution is not merely a few walls or some outer structures surrounding, protecting, guaranteeing, or restricting the freedom of our work; it is also and already the structure of our interpretation [c'est aussi et déjà la structure de notre interprétation]'.[34] Institutional 'refraining' cannot be done at the outset, and nor is it a single act: It is neither incipient nor final, but a vigilance in series: 'Deconstruction cannot be applied and cannot *not* be applied. So we have to deal with this *aporia*, and this is what deconstruction is about'.[35]

AILLEURS

'How to Avoid Speaking' demonstrates that a deconstructive reading does not take place in some putative 'elsewhere', immune to the logic it purports to discover. Therefore, it is apt that its most trenchant challenge to uncritical institutionalism seems to take place elsewhere, in a text obliquely cited in the lecture – which, when the citation is carefully traced, proves utterly germane to it.

Recounting Heidegger's claim that Plato's *khōra* only succeeds as a propaedeutic to the Cartesian interpretation of space as *extensio*, Derrida remarks, 'Elsewhere [ailleurs] I have tried to show what is problematic and reductive about this perspective' (187/585). Derrida goes on to describe the efforts of Heidegger to avoid such an apparently reductive account of space, a project that entails accounting for the 'wholly other place (*nach dem ganz anderen Ort*) of Being' inchoately intuitable in Plato's *khōra* but whose elaboration was stunted in the Cartesian redescription. What must be avoided for Heidegger is that this place of Being, as wholly other, be construed as a displaced version of God. Hence Heidegger's decision to avoid speaking of 'Being' except citationally and under erasure, to distinguish the revealability of Being from the revealed God, and thereby to distinguish ontotheology or theiology from theology. Derrida frames this decision as that of a speech act theorist: Heidegger is 'not to avoid *mentioning* ['Being'], as certain speech act theorists who distinguish between mention and use would say, but to avoid using it' (189).

Why, in this place and on this *topos*, does Derrida frame Heidegger as a speech act theorist? Why frame Heidegger's paradigm of negative theology with the suggestion that his consonance with negative theology can *precisely* – 'To be more precise still [Précisons encore] (189/588)' – be considered in terms of the use/mention distinction? Leaving aside the question of whether making use of the use/mention distinction entails *using* or *mentioning* it, it is significant that demonstrating the problems with Heidegger's cleavage to this distinction leads Derrida to the *pli* with which he concludes, or post-concludes his lecture, in the apostrophic form of a prayer. This 'P.S.', denoting the post-conclusion, the very last conclusion, the beyond of the conclusion that replies (to) everything that has been said up to now, is also the inversion of the 'S is P' to which, Derrida suggests, his own narrative of corruptive imputations of paradigmaticity to the *khōra* provisionally has maintained, and which would retain the ideal of a pure constative ('the third person present indicative'). But the inversion, the turning away from this ideal or the demonstration of its limited value (the folding back, or *pli*, of its transcendental status in the argument into a quasi-transcendental) is heralded in this reference to the use/mention distinction that governs Heidegger's aporias.

The lecture contains a joke at this point that does not survive the text's translation:

> Précisons encore: non pas de le *mentionner*, comme diraient certains théoriciens des *speech acts* qui distinguent entre *mention* et *use*, mais de l'utiliser. (588)

The translation gives 'certain speech act theorists', but Derrida's phrasing hints at a less general reference, one that invokes (in the third person of the constative, no less) the theorist who wrote the book *Speech Acts*, John R. Searle. The suggestion that Derrida invokes Searle here is substantiated by the fact that Derrida's reading of Searle's use/mention distinction, in 'Limited Inc a b c . . .' is substantially about theology and the *khōra*.

In *Speech Acts*,[36] Searle argues that the use/mention distinction is a straightforward thing to grasp, which has been harmfully obfuscated by various philosophers and logicians (74). The *use* of an expression, its 'normal use', pertains to the particularity referred to by the expression (Searle's example, of course, is 'Socrates was a philosopher', in which 'Socrates' refers to Socrates). The *mention* of an expression is where the expression is used to talk about the expression (Searle's example: '"Socrates" has eight letters', in which 'Socrates' talks about the expression 'Socrates') (73–74).

For Searle, confusion arises when philosophers become fixated on the idea that the mention of an expression entails some supplementation of its use, and therefore that the mention entails the advent of 'a completely new word [. . .] the proper name of the word'. This mistaken view can lead to an untrammelled play of mentioning:

> On this account, the word which begins ['"Socrates" has eight letters'] is not, as you might think, "Socrates", it is ""Socrates"" [because the mentioned word is being mentioned again qua mentioned word]. And the word I just wrote, elusively enough, it not ""Socrates"" but is """Socrates""" which completely new word is yet another proper name of a proper name of a proper name, namely """"Socrates"""". And so on up in a hierarchy of names of names of names . . . (74)

This supplementation errs, for Searle, by contradicting what he calls 'the institution of proper names'. The proper name is not formed for the purposes of mentioning the expression it designates, but to refer to an object even when it is not in itself present. If the object of an expression is a 'stretch of discourse', it can always be presented, and hence does not require a proper name: 'With very few exceptions, such as sacred words or obscenities, if we wish to speak of a word we don't need to name it or otherwise refer to it, we can simply produce (a token of) it'. It suffices for Searle that this tokenistic production of a word be denoted by 'e.g., quotation marks'. This argument against the supplementarity of the mention enshrines the 'institution of proper names', which is nothing less than the institution of a way of speaking of things which are not 'merely' intra-linguistic:

> The whole institution gets its point from the fact that we use words to refer to other objects. A proper name can only be a proper name if there is a genuine difference between the name and the thing named. If they are the same, the notion of naming and referring can have no application. (75)

When Searle writes 'institution' here, he refers to a shared demarcation making possible the transmission of any knowledge that is more than a 'brute fact'. Brute facts are those based in 'simple empirical observations recording sense experiences' (such as '"This stone is next to that stone"' or '"I have a pain'"), whereas 'institutional facts' are those that presuppose 'the existence of certain human institutions', such as '"Mr Smith married Miss Jones'", which presupposes the institution of marriage, or '"Green was convicted of larceny,"' which presupposes a legal system (51). Searle's formula for the institutional fact is '"X counts as Y in context C"' (52). That is, the brute facts of X (particular chemical processes) signify Y (for example, matrimony) in institution C. As with the institution of proper names, what the institution makes possible is analogical intelligibility – but this intelligibility in turn only seems possible because of a prior presupposition of the rectitude and desirability of regulated praxis, that is, of the necessity of institution C. Searle's formula does not question the givenness of the institution in this way, but instead presents it as a kind of receptacle that would sift anthropological factuality itself.

This principle of sifting is operative in Searle's 'institution of proper names', by which he cements the use/mention distinction: 'A proper name is only a proper name if there is a genuine difference between the name and the thing named'. What is the principle of difference by which 'a genuine difference' is differentiated from a fake one? If a proper name names a genuine difference – if a proper name, properly named, names a genuine difference – and this difference is precisely the intellectualizable analogy whereby language can speak about what is outside of it, then what gaps are being bridged here? A 'genuine difference' seems to refer to a difference which is singular, originary, unalloyed, but 'a genuine difference' systematizes this singularity, rendering it iterable, so that the 'genuine difference' between word and object is already grammatical in its very description as not merely grammatical, as 'beyond' grammatical. Here we reach the same conclusion as Derrida's 'P.S.' on Heidegger: Perhaps there is no ideal constative that would not depend on something being done with words; perhaps it is ethically dubious to think that there is.[37]

Negative theology's role in Derrida's parody of Searle's use/mention distinction substantiates this point. In 'Limited Inc a b c . . . ',[38] Derrida refers to this distinction as 'rather laborious and problematical' (79), noting its unjustified appeal to what is 'normal' (for Searle, normality possibilizes institution), and wondering how, if the conventions demarcating mention from use ('e.g., quotation marks') are 'perfectly adequate', there remains a threat of their corruption (82). Derrida tests the use/mention distinction's criteria of normality and perfect adequation through 'a single example', which is the function of the word 'Iter' in the subtitle of his text 'Signature Event Context': 'Parasites. Iter, of Writing: That It Perhaps Does Not Exist'.[39] 'Iter' is, among other things, 'a citation of the fifth of Descartes' *Metaphysical Meditations', De essentiâ rerum materialum; et iterum de Deo, quod existat* (*On the Essence of Material Things; And Likewise of God, That He Exists* – although this translation does not make explicit how 'iterum', translated by the French 'derechef', refers to something taking place *again*). Derrida's citation of Descartes is not only a citation, but a citation of a supplementation: 'The latter part of the title, beginning with *iterum*, is, as is well known, a subsequent addition of Descartes, who thus returned to his original title, repeating and changing it in this way, augmenting and completing it with a supplementary *iterum*' (82–83). Because Descartes already had seemingly demonstrated the existence of God in the third of these *Meditations*, the appearance of 'iterum' in the title of the fifth is complex, because it acknowledges both the rectitude of the prior demonstration, and its need of supplementation: It proposes to demonstrate this rectitude through another demonstration, 'multiplying the demonstrations in view of the same conclusion, concerning the same object' (83).[40]

Descartes's 'iterum' is required in order more fully to demonstrate what is beyond demonstration: that God is 'both *absolutely repeatable and unrepeatable*', that the repeated demonstrations of the existence of God are demonstrations of God as unrepeatable ('unique, irreplaceable, beyond all substitution') (83). God repeatedly can be shown to be unrepeatable, and so the exemplarity of God here 'is both that of the unique and that of the repeatable'. God is exemplarily unique because of a repetition without supplementation, a pure iteration; this is what Descartes's supplementation, 'iterum', conveys.

Citing this supplementation in his subtitle, Derrida substitutes 'of writing' for 'of God', not merely to replace one word with another, but to argue that the demonstration of God's existence produces the possibility of substituting 'of writing' for 'of God'. This is because Descartes's insistence on God's iterable unrepeatability cannot split the use and mention of 'God' in Searle's distinction; doing so would make a decision concerning the relation between 'God' and God (word and object) that would impose a logic extraneous to the law of iterable unrepeatability that Descartes apprehends as ⁽'⁾God⁽'⁾:

> ['Signature Event Context'] names writing in this place where the iterability of the proof (of God's existence) *produces writing*, drawing the name of God (of the infinite Being) into a graphematic drift (*dérive*) that excludes (for instance) any decision as to whether God is more than the name of God, whether the "name of God" refers to God or to the name of God, whether it signifies "normally" or "cites", etc., God being here, *qua* writing, what at the same time renders possible and impossible, probable and improbable oppositions such as that of the "normal" and the citational or the parasitical, the serious and the non-serious, the strict and the non-strict or less strict[.] (83)

The iterable demonstration of the existence of God produces a refusal of any givenness to Searle's distinctions – the distinctions that establish his sense of an 'institution'. Additionally, in Derrida's reading and despite Heidegger's suggestion that Cartesian philosophy merely enshrines the failure of Plato's thinking of the *Ort*, this demonstration's paradoxical outcome has a further effect: an inscription of the trace of the *khōra*, that which does not give distinctions, let alone hierarchizing them, but makes them (im)possible.

Derrida cites his reading of Searle's use/mention distinction in the discussion of Heidegger in 'How to Avoid Speaking'. This citation leads to a trace of the *khōra* precisely where Heidegger might say it is unlikely, even impossible, to be found. This trace is the ultimate refusal of 'genuine difference' subtending even the exemplary attempt to prove the genuine difference of the divine. Finally, the citation is that by which Derrida frames if not his argument's reversal, then at least its *pli*. In this citation, Derrida's argument passes through the unjustifiably preferential form of Searle's philosophy – showing that no preference, even for the possible over the impossible, is justifiable – to frame Heidegger's avoidance of the *use* of Being, his preference not to use Being but 'merely' to *mention* it.

Derrida's citational challenge to the apparatus of Heidegger's avoidance also resists Miller's claim that refraining, in Derrida, is incipient – 'his fundamental and defining act, his ground without ground' – because what Derrida finally shows, in 'How to Avoid Speaking', is that refraining has an institutional history, and even names the history of institution: It is quasi-institutional, not anti-institutional. The lecture's refrain – the history of refraining from speaking *of*, in Plato, Meister Eckhart, Pseudo-Dionysius, and Heidegger – ultimately draws the conclusion that refraining is not a privileged act, but it remains a deconstructible preference.

'Préférance' is the citational name (not a proper name) I give to the schematic in which can be grouped Derrida's works' readings of Hägglund, Miller, and Laclau, and Derrida's excavation of institutional paradigms of interpretation in Platonism, Christian apophasis, Heidegger, Searle, and finally Derrida. What groups these several operations is their focus on the sublimation of basic preferential gestures in all of these texts. When and if Derrida prefers – preferring a Freud without Freudianism,[41] a Plato without Platonism, a messianic without messianism – he is preferring what historicizes and renders contingent the gesture of preferring. He is not preferring not to, but he is thinking about the material, institutional inscription anterior even to that preference. It is not only that Derrida has a 'with-against' (or quasi-) relationship to institutions (like some negative institutionalist), but he is interested in how the distinction between 'with' and 'against', from which the 'with-against' formulation must derive its force, is itself an institutional inscription.

The Cambridge Affair took place according to the scheme *placet/non placet*. Nowhere in the literature is the institutional preference subtending this scheme questioned. Nowhere is it suggested that Derrida's work might question it, except, strangely enough, in the cheat sheet sent to the Duke of Edinburgh recommending a joke about 'the deconstruction of the honorary degree ceremony'. The preference in question is simply that those voting *placet* and *non placet* are responding to the same question: 'Placetne vobis, domini doctores? placetne vobis, magistri?' ('Does it please you, Doctors? Does it please you, Masters?').[42] The answers to this apostrophe take the form of the third person present indicative ('the theoretical, "constative," even propositional form'[43]), and literally mean 'it pleases' and 'it does not please'. Responding to an injunction in a manner whose grammar disavows its status as response, and debating the merits or otherwise of Derrida's work already according to this paradigm, this sublimates what perhaps was really at stake, namely the material inscription of this paradigm.

As Derrida might ask: Does one have the right to render preference *constative*, to forget the institutional privileging of this model? Does one have the right to superimpose the value of the distinction *placet/non placet* upon the a-dialogic form that makes this distinction possible (what I called, in the case of Searle's 'institutions', a shared demarcation)? Should the debate always-already have concerned the motion, 'Derrida (does not) please Cambridge'? Is this a motion at all?

NOTES

1. Derrida, 'Interpretations at War: Kant, the Jew, the German', trans. Moshe Ron and Dana Hollander, Derrida, *Psyche: Inventions of the Other, Volume II*, eds. Peggy Kamuf and Elizabeth Rottenberg (Stanford: Stanford University Press, 2008), 241n.

2. Derrida, 'How to Avoid Speaking: Denials', trans. Ken Frieden and Elizabeth Rottenberg, Derrida, *Psyche: Inventions of the Other, Volume II*, eds. Peggy Kamuf and Elizabeth Rottenberg (Stanford: Stanford University Press, 2008)/'Comment ne pas parler: Dénégations', Derrida, *Psyché: Inventions de l'autre* (Paris: Galilée, 1987).

3. Derrida quotes Meister Eckhart, 'Quasi stella matutina', trans. Frank Tobin, *Meister Eckhart, Teacher and Preacher*, ed. Bernard McGinn et al. (New York: Pluralist Press, 1986), 256–57.

4. Against any straightforward opposition between the *Timaeus* and the *Republic* on this point, see Miriam Leonard, *Athens in Paris: Ancient Greece and the Political in Post-War French Thought* (Oxford: Oxford University Press, 2005), 212–15. Leonard argues, with Derrida in 'Khora', that the non-place of the *khōra* is something like the subject-position Socrates strives for at the beginning of the *Timaeus*, distancing himself from anyone, from the poets to the Sophists, and even his present interlocutors (Timaeus, Kritias, and Hermocrates), who would seek to produce an adequate representation of the ideal community he imagines in the *Republic*. Socrates withdraws from such attempts to give form to place, by implication ascribing to himself

the atopic designation of the *khōra*. But Derrida, Leonard argues, passes over the fact that, despite his withdrawal from its process of actualization, 'Socrates remains the architect of the explicitly anti-democratic constitution of his imagined *Republic*. And it is in the *Republic* more than anywhere else where each citizen will be required to take his allotted place without question or revolt'. Overlooking Socrates's continuing advocacy of autocracy allows Derrida to posit Socrates's withdrawal as 'opening onto the possibility of a democracy to come' (214). There is not space to do anything other than summate this astute critique, but it is surely pertinent that the discussions of the *Republic*, the *Timaeus*, and the *khōra* in 'How to Avoid Speaking' do not once involve Socrates – it would be interesting to think about the reasons for this. Typically, accounts of Derrida's work on the *khōra* have privileged 'Khora' over 'How to Avoid Speaking' (which Leonard's text does not mention), as though the latter were the bastard of the former: the irony of this approach, where the *khōra* is concerned, is the role of 'bastard reasoning' in any attempt to apprehend the *khōra* (see 'How to Avoid Speaking', 171).

5. See Derrida, 'Khora', trans. Ian McLeod, Derrida, *On the Name*, ed. Thomas Dutoit (Stanford: Stanford University Press, 1993).

6. Plato, *Timaeus*, Plato, *Timaeus, Critias, Cleitophon, Menexenus, Epistles*, trans. R. G. Bury (London: William Heinemann, 1929), 113.

7. *Timaeus*, 119. By 'any quarter', Plato disqualifies the *khōra*'s homology with any aspect of the eternal model or with the derived copy: 'For were [the *khōra*] similar to any of the entering forms [the components of the eternal model], on receiving forms of an opposite or wholly different kind, as they arrived, it would copy them badly, through obtruding its own visible shape. Wherefore it is right that the substance which is to receive within itself all the kinds [i.e., the *khōra*] should be void of all forms' (*Timaeus*, 119). The accuracy of the copy, and with it the reason of the universe, is therefore possible only in a place that is heterogeneous to this reason.

8. See 'Khora', 120. See also Hent de Vries, *Philosophy and the Turn to Religion* (Baltimore and London: The Johns Hopkins University Press, 1999), 110: 'Derrida leaves no doubt that Plato's *Timaeus* also has the character of a canonized archive that threatens to vanish behind the countless glosses superimposed on it'.

9. See Paul Allen Miller, 'The Platonic Remainder: Derrida's *Khôra* and the *Corpus Platonicum*', *Derrida and Antiquity*, ed. Miriam Leonard (Oxford: Oxford University Press, 2010), 326: The *Timaeus* is 'an unfinalizable dialogue in which each moment of positing is also a moment of irony and interrogation, of simultaneous acceptance and active separation'. However, the fundamentally analogical structure of Miller's argument – that the *khōra* is synecdochic of Socratic irony in Plato (337–40) – evinces the difficulty of arguing this point. Ironically, *Derrida and Antiquity*'s introduction describes Miller's essay as 'argu[ing] that Derrida's reading of the *Khôra* provides the *blueprint* for a new philosophy of space which sidesteps the traditional opposition between the material and the ideal' – a metaphor decidedly belonging to the first 'readability' of the *khōra* sketched by Derrida, and therefore problematized already by the second. See Miriam Leonard, 'Introduction: "Today, on the Eve of Platonism . . . ,"' *Derrida and Antiquity*, 15 (my italics).

10. 'The Platonic Remainder', 330.

11. John Sallis, *Chorology: On Beginning in Plato's* Timaeus (Bloomington and Indianapolis: Indiana University Press, 1999), 114.
12. See Caputo, *The Prayers and Tears of Jacques Derrida: Religion without Religion* (Bloomington and Indianapolis: Indiana University Press, 1997), 34–38.
13. *Timaeus*, 123.
14. See Caputo, '*Khôra*: Being Serious with Plato', Derrida, *Deconstruction in a Nutshell: a Conversation with Jacques Derrida*, ed. John D. Caputo (New York: Fordham University Press, 1997), 85: 'The word *khôra* is the common Greek noun for a concrete area or place; a *khorion*, for example, is a district or an estate, and *khorismos* is a separation in the sense of a gap or space between. *Khôra* is translated into Latin as *locus* and into French as *lieu*'. Sallis lends less weight to this aspect of the term's nomenclature than Derrida: 'It will be granted that in other texts (and to a lesser degree in other parts of the *Timaeus*) there is justification for translating [χώρα], for instance, as place, as land, as country' (*Chorology*, 116).
15. To understand how this reading differs from a certain Classical tradition, see A. E. Taylor, *A Commentary on Plato's* Timaeus (Oxford: Clarendon Press, 1928), 343. Commenting on the way in which the term χώρα is not the first name given to the 'third kind' in the *Timaeus*, but follows from a series of metaphors beginning with 'receptacle' (ὑποδοχή), Taylor states: 'The name χώρα is not given to the ὑποδοχή until Timaeus has first explained what he takes to be character and function of the ὑποδοχή. If it had first been called χώρα and then described we might have imported something illegitimate into our notion of it on the strength of associations which had already grown up in our minds in connexion with the name'. As Derrida's reading shows, the dualism 'legitimate/illegitimate' imputes a logic that the *khōra* actually puts in question. Similarly, F. M. Cornford's commentary on the *Timaeus* straightaway interprets the *khōra* as a corrective metaphilosophical paradigm: 'We may note here [. . .] that the hitherto unrecognised third factor fills a gap in the scheme which Plato, in the *Republic*, had borrowed from Parmenides'. Although Cornford acknowledges that the *khōra* is 'an absolute blank of nothingness', his account has already offered it as paradigmatic. See Francis MacDonald Cornford, *Plato's Cosmology: The* Timaeus *of Plato translated with a Running Commentary* (London: Routledge, 1937; repr. 2001), 177–78.
16. It is tempting to read cataphatic and apophatic theology as related to the first and second 'readabilities' of the *khōra*, respectively. Cataphatic theology would trade in metaphors or symbols for 'God', whilst apophatic theology would point to the negations entailed by these. However, it is important that for Pseudo-Dionysius, affirmative and negative theology are conceived as being in a dialectical relation that coheres around a shared acceptance of the function of symbols, but not of this function's efficacy. To the descending movement of affirmative theology – which begins with the most congruous representations of God (pertaining to Oneness), before declining and multiplying into Trinitarian representations, Christological representations, and then to representations pertaining to things on earth – is opposed the ascending motility of negative theology, which proceeds from the mundane incongruous to the celestial most-congruous, but aims to exceed the starting-point of the cataphatic trajectory by reaching the hyperessential apposite, which would not be representable

or communicable in any way. For Pseudo-Dionysius, any symbol of God should be interpreted according to both the affirmative and negative modes, but both modes are from the start in agreement both about the nature of the symbol, and about a given symbol's place in the hierarchy whose poles are incongruity and apposition. Such assumptions are not shared – and, indeed, are put into question – between the two 'readabilities' of the *khōra* in the *Timaeus*. (See Paul Rorem, *Pseudo-Dionysius: A Commentary on the Texts and an Introduction to Their Influence* (New York and Oxford: Oxford University Press, 1993), 194–205; especially 199–204.)

17. *Philosophy and the Turn to Religion*, 89.

18. See *Prayers and Tears*, 35: 'Derrida holds that, however upwardly mobile this "hyperbolism", the Good [*agathon*] nonetheless maintains at least an analogical community and continuity with Being and knowledge'.

19. 'Crible' can also mean 'riddle', accentuating the sense in which this 'sieve' is interpretive.

20. Derrida quotes 'Quasi stella matutina', 259.

21. Derrida quotes 'Quasi stella matutina', 259.

22. Derrida quotes Pseudo-Dionysius, *The Mystical Theology*, *Pseudo-Dionysius: The Complete Works*, trans. Colm Luibhéid (London: SPCK, 1987), 135: §997A–1000A.

23. Derrida quotes Pseudo-Dionysius, *The Divine Names*, *Pseudo-Dionysius: The Complete Works*, 62–63: §644A.

24. Derrida quotes *The Divine Names*, 63: §644B.

25. *The Divine Names*, 63: §644C.

26. *The Divine Names*, 63: §645A.

27. *The Divine Names*, 64: §645D.

28. In 'Mochlos', Derrida states: 'The interpretation of a theorem, poem, philosopheme, or theologeme is only produced by simultaneously proposing an institutional model [un modèle institutionnel], either by consolidating an existing one that enables the interpretation, or by constituting a new one in accordance with this interpretation. Declared or clandestine, this proposal calls for the politics of a community of interpreters gathered around this text, and at the same time of a global society, a civil society with or without a State, a veritable regime enabling the inscription of that community [l'inscription de cette communauté]' (101/422).

29. For Cartesian *extensio* in relation to the *Timaeus*, see Catherine Wilson, 'Soul, Body and World: Plato's *Timaeus* and Descartes' *Meditations*', *Platonism at the Origins of Modernity: Studies on Platonism and Early Modern Philosophy*, eds. Douglas Hedley and Sarah Hutton (Dordrecht: Springer, 2008), 182–84.

30. 'Faith and Knowledge', 53.

31. Derrida quotes Heidegger, *Seminare*, Heidegger, *Gesamtausgabe*, Vol. 15 (Frankfurt a/M: Klostermann, 1986), 436–37.

32. For an account of the *pli* in Derrida's writing, see Marian Hobson, *Jacques Derrida: Opening lines* (London and New York: Routledge, 1998), 67–72. Hobson argues that the doubling entailed by this movement 'resembles dialectic but is not dialectic, for there is no subsumption, *Aufhebung*, *relève*, as Derrida sometimes translates the German word, that is, remainderless synthesis of the two poles, but instead,

replication of the splitting off' (68). In what follows, I try to indicate that Derrida's conclusion to 'How to Avoid Speaking' draws attention to the necessity of this replication to his own argument: his reading of negative theological paradigms in relation to the *khōra* itself must ascribe an anterior paradigmaticity to the *khōra*, even as he analyzes posterior ascriptions of the same in these paradigms.

33. *Philosophy and the Turn to Religion*, 109.
34. 'Mochlos, 102/424.
35. '*As if* I were Dead', 218.
36. John R. Searle, *Speech Acts: An Essay in the Philosophy of Language* (Cambridge: Cambridge University Press, 1970).
37. Unfortunately, there is not space to consider, in relation to the problems of Searle's 'genuineness' (and for that matter in relation to Pseudo-Dionysius and Meister Eckhart), the privilege afforded the use/mention distinction in the extraordinarily-named model of 'semantic ascent' postulated by Willard Van Orman Quine, noteworthy signatory of Barry Smith's letter to the *Times* during the Cambridge Affair. At the conclusion of *Word and Object*, Quine writes:

> The strategy of semantic ascent is that it carries the discussion into a domain where both parties are better agreed on the objects (viz. words) and on the main terms concerning them. Words, or their inscriptions, unlike points, miles, classes, and the rest, are tangible objects of the size so popular in the marketplace, where men of unlike conceptual schemes communicate at their best. The strategy is one of ascending to a common part of two fundamentally disparate conceptual schemes, the better to discuss the disparate foundations. No wonder it helps in philosophy. Quine, *Word and Object* (Cambridge, MA and London: The MIT Press, 1960; repr. 2013), 251.

The 'ascent' in question correlates with the reduction of the intangible elements of intangible objects; the goal, presumably, is that the geographer, the mathematician, and the philosopher all mean the same thing when they use the word 'mile' – that they could settle on what the 'genuine difference' is between 'mile' and mile. Quine nowhere questions his own recourse to the trope of 'ascent' as a means of expressing this.

38. Derrida, 'Limited Inc a b c . . . ', trans. Samuel Weber, Derrida, *Limited Inc* (Evanston, IL: Northwestern University Press, 1988).
39. Derrida, 'Signature Event Context', *Limited Inc*, 13.
40. For the methodological supplementation of the third ('the causal argument') by the fifth ('the *a priori* argument'), see Stephen Gaukroger, *Descartes: An Intellectual Biography* (Oxford: Clarendon Press, 1995), 197–99.
41. Derrida states: 'I prefer in Freud the partial, regional, and minor analyses, the most venturesome soundings. These breaches and openings sometimes reorganize, at least virtually, the entire field of knowledge'. He prefers all this to the 'grand conceptual framework' of psychoanalysis, which he regards as a provisional assemblage 'cobbled together to be used against a philosophy of consciousness, of transparent and fully responsible intentionality' – an assemblage that perhaps has no reason to survive. The 'breaching' of psychoanalysis, in both senses of the genitive, provides it for Derrida with its force; 'an invincible force', that 'always involves the reaffirmation of

a reason "without alibi," whether theological or metaphysical'. Being 'without alibi', in this sense, entails a heterogeneity to Hägglund's, Miller's, and Laclau's readings: 'The very aim, and I do say the *aim*, of the psychoanalytic revolution is the only one not to rest, not to seek refuge, in principle, in what I call a theological or humanist alibi'. See Derrida and Roudinesco, *For What Tomorrow . . . : A Dialogue*, trans. Jeff Fort (Stanford: Stanford University Press, 2004), 72–73.

    42. *OED* entry, 'Placet'.

    43. 'How to Avoid Speaking', 194.

Afterword

My initial interest in the Cambridge Affair was piqued when I was an undergraduate. For some reason, it was one of the first aspects of Derrida's career I learned about. Discovering the Affair whilst studying in a department that also preferred to keep Derrida at arm's length produced an early conviction that here was a philosopher who was constantly getting himself disbarred from academic life. Of course, this wasn't strictly the case, but every time I see a term like 'hauntology' in an academic text that indicates nothing of its embeddedness in Derrida's thought more broadly, I wonder whether the 'post-theory' humanities have their own forms of censorship for those whose ideas they claim to have assimilated.

My research into the Affair was initially motivated by two assumptions that proved naïve. The first was that I would discover terrible things about Derrida's opponents and their attempts to have him excommunicated as a philosopher. I did not, and although some of those who were 'there' have intimated that there were things going on behind the scenes, as it were, I am only interested here in arguments people were happy to publish under their own names. This is not to say that the debate wasn't provocative, robust, and sometimes outright hostile – it was all of those things, because it isn't every day that one tries to determine the very essence, if there is one, of philosophy.

The second assumption is rather more difficult to describe, partly because I only belatedly realized I was working under it. It was basically that the *placet* and *non placet* positions would map neatly onto present-day 'progressive' and 'reactionary' viewpoints concerning the university and the kinds of work it endorses. And yet I'm unable to escape the conviction that the contemporary heirs to the *non placet* position at its most intransigent are actually those who, in the name of a certain 'progressive' outlook, seek to 'No Platform' others, as though proximity to disagreeable ideas endorses them or otherwise allows a certain contamination to spread. It is no great leap from the jarringly unionized descriptors of philosophy used by the *non placet* flysheets to the uncritical and absolutist consensus model on which No Platforming as a communicable idea is based. It is, therefore, sadly ironic that one current myth about Derrida's work is that it is part of a canon of texts that has contributed to a widespread loss of scepticism on the left and the rise of identity politics.

In his interview about the Cambridge Affair, Derrida outlines several ways it might one day be analyzed. There would be a number of avenues for classical historical analyses of the controversy: a renewal or displacement of old philosophical disagreements between English/empiricist/analytical and Continental/French/German schools; an encounter between models of the university that historically have obtained and 'contemporary historical forces'; and a conflict between philosophy in its traditional self-understanding and the perceived threats posed thereto by 'professionalization'. Other histories might focalize: the media's involvement and the attendant technologies by which, for example, Barry Smith was able to mobilize the countersignatories of his letter to the *Times*; the emergence of a more or less agreed-upon university model in the West that Smith's letter presupposes; and antecedents to the Affair in other declarations *non placet* at Oxford and Cambridge. A political historian might address why the nomination for the same honorary degree of a committed 'Marxist' or conservative would not, in all likelihood, have aroused as much 'anger and disquiet'; and a historian of institutions would need to consider the synecdochal or otherwise overdetermined function of a university such as Cambridge both in England and across the Anglo-American university system.

A philosophical history of the Affair 'would see in what has just happened the projection of a disarticulated and overcondensed figure (metaphor, metonymy or synecdoche), amplified out of all proportions, onto a huge media screen [...] a figure representing a crucial philosophical moment'. But a history of the Affair should not pass over the fact that Cambridge 'was able to organize a public debate, in full daylight, or almost'.[1]

These hypothetical projects have in common an absence of reference to Derrida's work specifically. Derrida suggests that to analyze the Affair in terms of Derrida (to consider it as the 'Derrida Affair') would entail a certain risk: 'If there had been a "Derrida affair," and should its micro-history still deserve the attention of the historian of tomorrow, which I doubt, then to approach it one would need to pull on some tenuous and rather peculiar threads [S'il y avait eu une "affaire Derrida", et dont la micrologie méritât elle-même d'intéresser encore l'historien de demain, ce dont je doute, il faudrait, pour s'en approcher, tirer des fils ténus et singuliers]', to work out the conditions for this particular reception of this particular philosopher.

Derrida states that he has, in the weeks following the Affair, applied himself to this task.²

The interview, and this book, ends here, with the image of Derrida writing about this episode in the reception-history of his work. I do not claim to have undertaken this project from which Derrida himself abstained, but I hope to have indicated some of the ways in which an understanding of deconstruction is pertinent to the Cambridge Affair.

NOTES

1. *'Honoris Causa'*, 417–18.
2. *'Honoris Causa'*, 419/Johnson MS.

Bibliography

ARCHIVES AND UNPUBLISHED TEXTS

Cambridge University Library Manuscripts and University Archives

Cambridge Degr. H. 2A (part 1).
Cambridge Degr. H. 2A (part 2).
EAD/GBR/0265/VOTES 8.

Special Collections and Archives, University of California, Irvine Libraries

Irvine, Box 120: Folder 10.
Irvine, Box 144: Folder 4.
Irvine, Box 62: Folder 2.

Other

Unpublished French text of Derrida's '*Honoris Causa*' interview, provided to the author by Christopher Johnson: 'Johnson MS'.

PRIMARY TEXTS

Placet

'First *placet* flysheet', 'Second *placet* flysheet', 'Third *placet* flysheet', *Cambridge University Reporter* (Wednesday, May 20, 1992), Vol. 122, No. 29.

Baldwin, Thomas, 'Anglo-Saxon Platitudes?', *Cambridge Review*, Vol. 114, No. 2320 (February 1993).
Jeanneret, Marian, 'Opinio Regina Mundi?', *Cambridge Review*, Vol. 113, No. 2318 (October 1992).
Lash, Nicholas, 'Occasions of Contempt', *Cambridge Review*, Vol. 114, No. 2320 (February 1993).
Norris, Christopher, 'Of an Apoplectic Tone Recently Adopted in Philosophy', *Cambridge Review*, Vol. 113, No. 2318 (October 1992).
Prendergast, Christopher, 'Off Limits. Derrida in Cambridge', *Cambridge Review*, Vol. 113, No. 2318 (October 1992).
Prendergast, Christopher, 'On Yawns and the Effortless Superiority of a Cambridge Man', *Cambridge Review*, Vol. 114, No. 2320 (February 1993).
'The Derrida affair', *THES*, No. 1018 (Friday, May 8, 1992).
Thomas, Susannah, 'Media, Derrida and Cambridge', *Cambridge Review*, Vol. 113, No. 2318 (October 1992).

Non placet

'First *non placet* flysheet', 'Second *non placet* flysheet', *Cambridge University Reporter* (Wednesday, May 20, 1992), Vol. 122, No. 29.
Denyer, Nicholas, 'Anglo-Saxon Platitudes', *Cambridge Review*, Vol. 114, No. 2321 (June 1993).
Denyer, Nicholas, 'The Charms of Jacques Derrida', *Cambridge Review*, Vol. 113, No. 2318 (October 1992).
Diggle, James, *Cambridge Orations, 1982–1993: A Selection* (Cambridge: Cambridge University Press, 1994).
Erskine-Hill, Howard, 'Viewpoint: Howard Erskine-Hill', *Cambridge Review*, Vol. 113, No. 2319 (December 1992).
Hebblethwaite, Brian, 'Derrida Non Placet', *Cambridge Review*, Vol. 113, No. 2318 (October 1992).
Sims, Jeffrey, 'Revisiting the Derrida Affair with Barry Smith', *Sophia*, Vol. 38, No. 2 (September/October 1999).
Smith, Barry et al., 'Derrida Degree a Question of Honour', Derrida, *Points...: Interviews, 1974–1994*, ed. Elisabeth Weber, trans. Peggy Kamuf et al. (Stanford: Stanford University Press, 1995).

WORKS BY DERRIDA

'A Certain Impossible Possibility of Saying the Event', trans. Gila Walker, *Critical Inquiry*, 33 (Winter 2007).
A Taste for the Secret (with Maurizio Ferraris), trans. Giacomo Donis, eds. Giacomo Donis and David Webb (Cambridge: Polity, 2001).
Acts of Literature, ed. Derek Attridge (London: Routledge, 1992).
Acts of Religion, ed. Gil Anidjar (New York and Oxford: Routledge, 2002).

'Allocution proférée à l'Université de Coimbra', *Derrida à Coimbra/Derrida em Coimbra*, coord. Fernanda Bernardo (Viseu: Palimage Editores, 2005), 39–43.
Archive Fever: A Freudian Impression, trans. Eric Prenowitz (Chicago and London: University of Chicago Press, 1998).
'*As if* I Were Dead: An Interview with Jacques Derrida', *Applying: To Derrida*, eds. John Brannigan, Ruth Robbins, Julian Wolfreys (Basingstoke: Macmillan, 1996), 212–26.
Athens, Still Remains: The Photographs of Jean-François Bonhomme, trans. Pascale-Anne Brault and Michael Naas (New York: Fordham University Press, 2010).
Cosmopolitanism and Forgiveness, trans. Mark Dooley and Michael Hughes (London and New York: Routledge, 2001; repr. 2005).
The Death Penalty, Volume I, eds. Geoffrey Bennington, Marc Crépon, Thomas Dutoit, trans. Peggy Kamuf (Chicago and London: University of Chicago Press, 2014).
De la grammatologie (Paris: Les Éditions de Minuit, 1967).
De quoi demain...: Dialogue (with Élisabeth Roudinesco) (Paris: Flammarion, 2001).
'Derniers mots', *Rue Descartes*, Vol. 2, No. 48 (2005), 6–7.
Dissemination, trans. Barbara Johnson (London: The Athlone Press, 1981).
Du droit à la philosophie (Paris: Galilée, 1990).
L'Écriture et la différence (Paris: Éditions du Seuil, 1967).
Eyes of the University: Right to Philosophy 2, trans. Jan Plug et al. (Stanford: Stanford University Press, 2002).
La faculté de juger (Paris: Les Éditions de Minuit, 1985).
'following theory: Jacques Derrida', *life.after.theory*, eds. Michael Payne and John Schad (London and New York: Continuum, 2003; repr. 2004), 1–51.
For What Tomorrow...: A Dialogue (with Élisabeth Roudinesco), trans. Jeff Fort (Stanford: Stanford University Press, 2004).
'The Future of the Profession or the Unconditional University (Thanks to the "Humanities", What *Could Take Place* Tomorrow)', trans. Peggy Kamuf, *Derrida Downunder*, eds. Laurence Simmons and Heather Worth (Palmerston North: Dunmore Press, 2001), 233–48.
'Given Time: The Time of the King', trans. Peggy Kamuf, *Critical Inquiry*, 18 (Winter 1992), 161–87.
Glas, trans. John P. Leavey and Richard Rand (Lincoln, NE and London: University of Nebraska Press, 1986).
'Hostipitality', trans. Barry Stocker and Forbes Morlock, *Angelaki*, Vol. 5, No. 3 (December 2000), 3–18.
'Interview: Choreographies: Jacques Derrida and Christie V. McDonald', trans. McDonald, *Diacritics*, Vol. 12, No. 2 (Summer 1982), 66–76.
Limited Inc (Evanston, IL: Northwestern University Press, 1988).
'Living On • Border Lines', trans. James Hulbert, Harold Bloom et al., *Deconstruction and Criticism* (New York: Continuum, 1979), 75–176.
Marges de la philosophie (Paris: Les Éditions de Minuit, 1972).
Margins of Philosophy, trans. Alan Bass (Chicago: University of Chicago Press, 1982; repr. 1984).
Of Grammatology, Corrected Edition, trans. Gayatri Chakravorty Spivak (Baltimore and London: The Johns Hopkins University Press, 1974; repr. 1997).

Of Hospitality: Anne Dufourmantelle invites Jacques Derrida to respond, trans. Rachel Bowlby (Stanford: Stanford University Press, 2000).
'On a Newly Arisen Apocalyptic Tone in Philosophy', trans. John P. Leavey, *Raising the Tone of Philosophy: Late Essays by Immanuel Kant, Transformative Critique by Jacques Derrida*, ed. Peter Fenves (Baltimore and London: The Johns Hopkins University Press, 1993), 117–72.
On the Name, ed. Thomas Dutoit (Stanford: Stanford University Press, 1993).
Paper Machine, trans. Rachel Bowlby (Stanford: Stanford University Press, 2005).
Parages (Paris: Galilée, 1986).
Points de suspension: Entretiens, ed. Elisabeth Weber (Paris: Galilée, 1992).
'Politics and Friendship: An Interview with Jacques Derrida', *The Althusserian Legacy*, eds. E. Ann Kaplan and Michael Sprinker (London and New York: Verso, 1993), 183–231.
Politiques de l'amitié suivi de l'oreille de Heidegger (Paris: Galilée, 1994).
The Politics of Friendship, trans. George Collins (London and New York: Verso, 1997; repr. 2005).
'Proverb: "He that would pun..."', trans. John P. Leavey, *Glossary*, ed. John P. Leavey (Lincoln, NE and London: University of Nebraska Press, 1986), 17–20.
Psyché: Inventions de l'autre (Paris: Galilée, 1987).
Psyche: Inventions of the Other, Volume 1, eds. Peggy Kamuf and Elizabeth Rottenberg (Stanford: Stanford University Press, 2007).
Psyche: Inventions of the Other, Volume II, eds. Peggy Kamuf and Elizabeth Rottenberg (Stanford: Stanford University Press, 2008).
Resistances of Psychoanalysis, trans. Peggy Kamuf, Pascale-Anne Brault, Michael Naas (Stanford: Stanford University Press, 1998).
Rogues: Two Essays on Reason, trans. Pascale-Anne Brault and Michael Naas (Stanford: Stanford University Press, 2005).
Spectres de Marx: L'État de la dette, le travail du deuil et la nouvelle Internationale (Paris: Galilée, 1993).
Specters of Marx: The State of the Debt, The Work of Mourning and the New International, trans. Peggy Kamuf (New York and London: Routledge, 1994; repr. 2011).
'Structure, Sign, and Play in the Discourse of the Human Sciences', trans. Richard Macksey and Eugenio Donato, *The Structuralist Controversy: The Languages of Criticism and the Sciences of Man*, eds. Richard Macksey and Eugenio Donato (Baltimore and London: The Johns Hopkins University Press, 1972; repr. 1977), 247–64.
'The Villanova Roundtable: A Conversation with Jacques Derrida', *Deconstruction in a Nutshell: A Conversation with Jacques Derrida*, ed. John D. Caputo (New York: Fordham University Press, 1997), 3–28.
'What Is a "Relevant" Translation?', trans. Lawrence Venuti, *Critical Inquiry*, Vol. 27, No. 2 (Winter 2001), 174–200.
Who's Afraid of Philosophy?: Right to Philosophy 1, trans. Jan Plug et al. (Stanford: Stanford University Press, 2002).
Without Alibi, ed. and trans. Peggy Kamuf (Stanford: Stanford University Press, 2002).

The Work of Mourning, eds. Pascale-Anne Brault and Michael Naas (Chicago and London: University of Chicago Press, 2001).
'The "World" of the Enlightenment to Come (Exception, Calculation, Sovereignty)', trans. Pascale-Anne Brault and Michael Naas, *Research in Phenomenology*, 33 (2003), 9–52.

OTHER TEXTS

Abrams, M. H., 'The Deconstructive Angel', *Contemporary Literary Criticism: Modernism Through Poststructuralism*, ed. Robert Con Davis (New York and London: Longman, 1986), 553–64.
Abrams, M. H., 'Rationality and Imagination in Cultural History', *Critical Inquiry*, Vol. 2, No. 3 (Spring 1976), 447–64.
Agamben, Giorgio, *Potentialities: Collected Essays in Philosophy*, ed. and trans. Daniel Heller-Roazen (Stanford: Stanford University Press, 1999), 243–74.
Anderson, Nicole, 'Free-play? Fair-play!: Defending Derrida', *Social Semiotics*, Vol. 16, No. 3 (September 2006), 407–20.
Arendt, Hannah, *The Life of the Mind, One: Thinking*, ed. Mary McCarthy (London: Secker & Warburg, 1978).
Aristotle, *The Metaphysics, Books I–IX*, trans. Hugh Tredennick (London: William Heinemann, 1933).
Aristotle, *Poetics*, trans. Margaret E. Hubbard, *Classical Literary Criticism* (Oxford: Oxford University Press, 1972; repr. 2008).
Aristotle, *Poetics*, trans. Anthony Kenny (Oxford: Oxford University Press, 2013).
Arnold, Bruce, *Margaret Thatcher: A Study in Power* (London: Hamish Hamilton, 1984).
Attridge, Derek, 'Review of Martin Hägglund, *Radical Atheism: Derrida and the Time of Life*', *Derrida Today*, Vol. 2, No. 2 (November 2009), 271–81.
Attridge, Derek, *Reading and Responsibility: Deconstruction's Traces* (Edinburgh: Edinburgh University Press, 2010).
Augustine, *Confessions*, trans. Henry Chadwick (Oxford: Oxford University Press, 1992; repr. 1998, 2008).
Saint Augustine, *Confessions*, trans. Louis de Mondadon, ed. André Mandouze (Paris: Éditions Pierre Horay, 1982).
Augustine, *Confessions*, trans. Richard Sydney Pine-Coffin (London: Penguin, 1961; repr. 1963).
Saint Augustine, *Confessions*, trans. Robert Arnauld d'Andilly, *Choix d'ouvrages mystiques*, ed. Jean Alexandre C. Buchon (Paris, 1835).
Augustine, *St. Augustine's Confessions, with an English Translation by William Watts, Volume II* (London: William Heinemann, 1912; repr. 1946).
Augustine, *The Confessions of Saint Augustine*, trans. Francis Joseph Sheed (London: Sheed & Ward, 1943).
Augustine, *The Confessions of Saint Augustine. In the translation of Sir Tobie Matthew, Kt.*, ed. Roger Hudleston (London: Burns Oates and Washbourne, 1923).

Augustine, *The Confessions of St. Augustine*, trans. Edward Bouverie Pusey (London and Toronto: J. M. Dent & Sons, 1907; repr. 1932).
Ayer, A. J., *Language, Truth and Logic, Volume 1 of the Palgrave Macmillan Archive Edition of A. J. AYER: WRITINGS ON PHILOSOPHY* (Basingstoke and New York: Palgrave Macmillan, 2004).
Ayer, A. J., *Probability and Evidence, Volume 3 of the Palgrave Macmillan Archive Edition of A. J. AYER: WRITINGS ON PHILOSOPHY* (Basingstoke and New York: Palgrave Macmillan, 2004).
Ayer, A. J., *The Central Questions of Philosophy, Volume 7 of the Palgrave Macmillan Archive Edition of A. J. AYER: WRITINGS ON PHILOSOPHY* (Basingstoke and New York: Palgrave Macmillan, 2004).
Bari, Shahidha K., *Keats and Philosophy: The Life of Sensations* (New York and London: Routledge, 2012).
Baring, Edward, *The Young Derrida and French Philosophy, 1945–1968* (Cambridge: Cambridge University Press, 2011).
Bennington, Geoffrey, 'Hap', *Oxford Literary Review*, Vol. 36, No. 2 (December 2014), 170–74.
Bloom, Harold, et al., *Deconstruction and Criticism* (New York: Continuum, 1979).
Bowlby, Rachel, 'Domestication', *Deconstruction: A Reader*, ed. Martin McQuillan (Edinburgh: Edinburgh University Press, 2000), 304–10.
Bull, Malcolm, *Anti-Nietzsche* (London and New York: Verso, 2011).
Caputo, John D., 'Deconstruction in a Nutshell: The Very Idea(!)', Derrida, *Deconstruction in a Nutshell: A Conversation with Jacques Derrida*, ed. John D. Caputo (New York: Fordham University Press, 1997), 31–48.
Caputo, John D., 'Derrida and the Trace of Religion', *A Companion to Derrida*, eds. Zeynep Direk and Leonard Lawlor (Chichester: Wiley Blackwell, 2014), 464–79.
Caputo, John D., '*Khôra*: Being Serious with Plato', Derrida, *Deconstruction in a Nutshell: A Conversation with Jacques Derrida*, ed. John D. Caputo (New York: Fordham University Press, 1997), 71–105.
Caputo, John D., *More Radical Hermeneutics: On Not Knowing Who We Are* (Bloomington and Indianapolis: Indiana University Press, 2000).
Caputo, John D., *The Prayers and Tears of Jacques Derrida: Religion without Religion* (Bloomington and Indianapolis: Indiana University Press, 1997).
Caputo, John D., 'The Return of Anti-Religion: From Radical Atheism to Radical Theology', *Journal for Cultural and Religious Theory*, Vol. 11, No. 2 (Spring 2011), 32–125.
Casey, John, 'Much ado about the man who believes in nothing', *Daily Mail*, May 16, 1992.
Castagnoli, Luca, *Ancient Self-Refutation: The Logic and History of the Self-Refutation Argument from Democritus to Augustine* (Cambridge: Cambridge University Press, 2010).
Collini, Stefan, *English Pasts: Essays in History and Culture* (Oxford: Oxford University Press, 1999; repr. 2003).
Collini, Stefan, *What Are Universities For?* (London: Penguin, 2012).
Collins, Jeff, and Bill Mayblin, *Introducing Derrida: A Graphic Guide* (London: Icon, 2011).

Cornford, Francis MacDonald, *Plato's Cosmology: The* Timaeus *of Plato translated with a Running Commentary* (London: Routledge, 1937; repr. 2001).
Critchley, Simon, 'Derrida: the reader', *Derrida's Legacies: Literature and Philosophy*, eds. Simon Glendinning and Robert Eaglestone (London and New York: Routledge, 2008), 1–11.
Critchley, Simon, 'Derrida's Influence on Philosophy... And On My Work', *German Law Journal*, Vol. 6, No. 1 (2005), 25–29.
Culler, Jonathan, *On Deconstruction: Theory and Criticism after Structuralism, 25th Anniversary Edition* (London and New York: Routledge, 2008).
Currie, Mark, *About Time: Narrative, Fiction and the Philosophy of Time* (Edinburgh: Edinburgh University Press, 2007).
Currie, Mark, *The Invention of Deconstruction* (Basingstoke: Palgrave Macmillan, 2013).
Currie, Mark, *The Unexpected: Narrative Temporality and the Philosophy of Surprise* (Edinburgh: Edinburgh University Press, 2013).
D'Cruz, Carolyn, *Identity Politics in Deconstruction: Calculating with the Incalculable* (Aldershot and Burlington, VT: Ashgate, 2008).
de Vries, Hent, *Philosophy and the Turn to Religion* (Baltimore and London: The Johns Hopkins University Press, 1999).
Deleuze, Gilles, *Essays Critical and Clinical*, trans. David W. Smith and Michael A. Greco (London and New York: Verso, 1998).
Deleuze, Gilles, *Critique et clinique* (Les Éditions de Minuit, 1993).
Deutscher, Penelope, *How to Read Derrida* (New York and London: W. W. Norton & Company, 2005; repr. 2006).
Docherty, Thomas, *For the University: Democracy and the Future of the Institution* (London and New York: Bloomsbury Academic, 2011).
Docherty, Thomas, *The English Question, or Academic Freedoms* (Eastbourne and Portland, OR: Sussex Academic Press, 2008).
Dorey, Peter, 'The legacy of Thatcherism for education policies: markets, managerialism and malice (towards teachers)', *The Legacy of Thatcherism: Assessing and Exploring Thatcherite Social and Economic Policies*, eds. Stephen Farrall and Colin Hay (Oxford: Oxford University Press, 2014), 108–35.
Dummett, Michael, *Frege: Philosophy of Mathematics* (London: Duckworth, 1991).
Dunne, Éamonn, *Reading Theory Now: An ABC of Good Reading with J. Hillis Miller* (New York and London: Bloomsbury, 2013).
Eagleton, Terry, '*Derrida: A Biography* by Benoît Peeters – review', http://www.theguardian.com/books/2012/nov/14/derrida-biography-benoit-peeters-review.
Eagleton, Terry, *Literary Theory: An Introduction (Second Edition)* (Oxford: Blackwell, 1996).
Eagleton, Terry, *The Function of Criticism: From* The Spectator *to Post-Structuralism* (London: Verso, 1984).
Eckhart, Meister, 'Quasi stella matutina', trans. Frank Tobin, *Meister Eckhart, Teacher and Preacher*, ed. Bernard McGinn et al. (New York: Pluralist Press, 1986).
Education Reform Act 1988 (London: Her Majesty's Stationery Office, 1989).
[Ehrmann, Jacques], *'Textes' suivi de* La Mort de la littérature (Paris: L'Herne, 1971).

Ellis, John M., *Against Deconstruction* (Princeton and Guildford: Princeton University Press, 1989).

Feltz, Vanessa, 'Philosophy made for spin-doctors', *Daily Express*, October 12, 2004.

Fenves, Peter, 'Introduction: The Topicality of Tone', *Raising the Tone of Philosophy: Late Essays by Immanuel Kant, Transformative Critique by Jacques Derrida*, ed. Peter Fenves (Baltimore and London: The Johns Hopkins University Press, 1993), 1–48.

Ferretter, Luke, *Towards a Christian Literary Theory* (Basingstoke: Palgrave Macmillan, 2003).

Fichte, Johann Gottlieb, 'On the Nature of the Scholar and its Manifestations: Lectures Delivered at Erlangen 1805', *Johann Gottlieb Fichte's Popular Works*, trans. William Smith (London: Trübner, 1873).

Fichte, Johann Gottlieb, *Ueber das Wesen des Gelehrten, und seine Erscheinungen im Gebiete der Freiheit. In öffentlichen Vorlesungen, gehalten zu Erlangen, im Sommer-Halbjahre 1805* (Berlin: In der Himburgischen Bucchandlung, 1806).

Gasché, Rodolphe, *The Tain of the Mirror: Derrida and the Philosophy of Reflection* (Cambridge, MA and London: Harvard University Press, 1986; repr. 1997).

Gaston, Sean, *Derrida and Disinterest* (London and New York: Continuum, 2005).

Gaukroger, Stephen, *Descartes: An Intellectual Biography* (Oxford: Clarendon Press, 1995).

Gildea, Niall, 'Roger Scruton's Daughters', *Influence and Inheritance in Feminist English Studies*, eds. Emily J. Hogg and Clara Jones (Basingstoke and New York: Palgrave Macmillan, 2015), 80–94.

Glendinning, Simon, *Derrida: A Very Short Introduction* (Oxford: Oxford University Press, 2011).

Gould, Julius, *The Attack on Higher Education: Marxist and Radical Penetration. Report of a Study Group of the Institute for the Study of Conflict* (London: The Institute for the Study of Conflict, 1977).

Grant, Edward, *Much Ado About Nothing: Theories of space and vacuum from the Middle Ages to the Scientific Revolution* (Cambridge: Cambridge University Press, 1981).

Groys, Boris, *Introduction to Antiphilosophy*, trans. David Fernbach (London and New York: Verso, 2012).

Guyer, Paul, 'Free Play and True Well-Being: Herder's Critique of Kant's Aesthetics', *Journal of Aesthetics and Art Criticism*, Vol. 65, No. 4 (Autumn 2007), 353–68.

Guyer, Paul, 'Gerard and Kant: Influence and Opposition', *Journal of Scottish Philosophy*, Vol. 9, No. 1 (2011), 59–93.

Haffenden, John, 'Introduction', William Empson, *Argufying: Essays on Literature and Culture*, ed. John Haffenden (London: Chatto and Windus, 1987).

Haffenden, John, *William Empson, Volume I: Among the Mandarins* (Oxford: Oxford University Press, 2005).

Hägglund, Martin, 'Derrida's Radical Atheism', *A Companion to Derrida*, eds. Zeynep Direk and Leonard Lawlor (Chichester: Wiley Blackwell, 2014), 166–78.

Hägglund, Martin, *Dying for Time: Proust, Woolf, Nabokov* (Cambridge, MA and London: Harvard University Press, 2012).

Hägglund, Martin, 'On Chronolibido: A Response to Rabaté and Johnston', *Derrida Today*, Vol. 6, No. 2 (November 2013), 182–96.
Hägglund, Martin, *Radical Atheism: Derrida and the Time of Life* (Stanford: Stanford University Press, 2008).
Hägglund, Martin, 'Radical Atheist Materialism: A Critique of Meillassoux', *The Speculative Turn: Continental Materialism and Realism*, eds. Levi Bryant, Nick Srnicek, Graham Harman (Melbourne: re.press, 2011), 114–29.
Hägglund, Martin, 'The Arche-Materiality of Time: Deconstruction, evolution and speculative materialism', *Theory After 'Theory'*, eds. Jane Elliott and Derek Attridge (Oxford and New York: Routledge, 2011), 265–77.
Hebblethwaite, Brian, 'A critique of Don Cupitt's Christian Buddhism', Hebblethwaite, *Ethics and Religion in a Pluralistic Age* (Edinburgh: T&T Clark, 1997).
Hebblethwaite, Brian, '"True" and "False" in Christology', *The Philosophical Frontiers of Christian Theology: Essays Presented to D. M. MacKinnon*, eds. Brian Hebblethwaite and Stewart Sutherland (Cambridge: Cambridge University Press, 1982), 227–38.
Heidegger, Martin, 'The Concept of Time', trans. William McNeill, Heidegger, *The Concept of Time/Der Begriff der Zeit* (Oxford: Blackwell, 1992).
Heidegger, Martin, *Die Grundbegriffe der Metaphysik. Welt – Endlichkeit – Einsamkeit, Gesamtausgabe, Band 29/30* (Frankfurt am Main: Vittorio Klostermann, 1983).
Heidegger, Martin, *Fundamental Concepts of Metaphysics*, trans. William McNeill and Nicholas Walker (Bloomington and Indianapolis: Indiana University Press, 1995).
Heidegger, Martin, *Seminare*, Heidegger, *Gesamtausgabe*, Vol. 15 (Frankfurt a/M: Klostermann, 1986).
Hill, Leslie, *The Cambridge Introduction to Jacques Derrida* (Cambridge: Cambridge University Press, 2007).
Hobson, Marian, *Jacques Derrida: Opening lines* (London and New York: Routledge, 1998).
Hofstadter, Richard, *The Paranoid Style in American Politics and Other Essays* (London: Cape, 1966).
Holden, James, 'Biographical Note', *life.after.theory*, eds. Michael Payne and John Schad (London and New York: Continuum, 2003; repr. 2004), 1–2.
Holmes, Martin, *The First Thatcher Government 1979–1983: Contemporary Conservatism and Economic Change* (Brighton: Harvester Press, 1985).
Horace, *Satires, Epistles, and Ars Poetics*, trans. H. Rushton Fairclough (London: William Heinemann, 1947).
Johnson, Barbara, *Freedom and Interpretation: The Oxford Amnesty Lectures 1992*, ed. Johnson (New York: Basic Books, 1993).
Johnson, Barbara, *A World of Difference* (Baltimore and London: The Johns Hopkins University Press, 1987).
Johnson, Christopher, *System and Writing in the Philosophy of Jacques Derrida* (Cambridge and New York: Cambridge University Press, 1993).
Jones, Aubrey, *Britain's Economy: The Roots of Stagnation* (Cambridge: Cambridge University Press, 1985).

Kant, Immanuel, 'An answer to the question: What is enlightenment?', Kant, *Practical Philosophy*, ed. and trans. Mary J. Gregor (Cambridge: Cambridge University Press, 1996), 11–22.
Kant, Immanuel, 'Conjectural Beginning of Human History', Kant, *Toward Perpetual Peace and Other Writings on Politics, Peace, and History*, trans. David L. Colclasure, ed. Pauline Kleingeld (New Haven and London: Yale University Press, 2006), 24–36.
Kant, Immanuel Kant, 'Mutmasslicher Anfang der Menschengeschichte', *Kant's gesammelte Schriften VIII*, ed. The Royal Prussian Academy of Sciences (Berlin: Georg Reimer, 1912).
Kant, Immanuel, 'On a Newly Arisen Superior Tone in Philosophy', trans. Peter Fenves, *Raising the Tone of Philosophy: Late Essays by Immanuel Kant, Transformative Critique by Jacques Derrida*, ed. Peter Fenves (Baltimore and London: The Johns Hopkins University Press, 1993), 51–82.
Kant, Immanuel, 'On a Newly Raging Spirit of Domination in Philosophy', trans. Peter Fenves, *Raising the Tone of Philosophy: Late Essays by Immanuel Kant, Transformative Critique by Jacques Derrida*, ed. Peter Fenves (Baltimore and London: The Johns Hopkins University Press, 1993), 105–6.
Kant, Immanuel, *The Conflict of the Faculties*, trans. Mary J. Gregor/*Der Streit der Fakultäten* (Lincoln, NE and London: University of Nebraska Press, 1979; repr. 1992).
Kant, Immanuel, *Thoughts on the True Estimation of Living Forces* (*Selected Passages*), *Kant's Inaugural Dissertation and Early Writings on Space*, trans. John Handyside (Chicago and London: Open Court, 1928).
Kant, Immanuel, 'Toward Perpetual Peace: A Philosophical Sketch', *Toward Perpetual Peace and Other Writings on Politics, Peace, and History*, trans. David L. Colclasure, ed. Pauline Kleingeld (New Haven and London: Yale University Press, 2006), 67–109.
Kant, Immanuel, 'Von einem neuerdings erhobenen vornehmen Ton in der Philosophie', *Kant's gesammelte Schriften Bande VIII*, ed. The Royal Prussian Academy of Sciences (Berlin: Georg Reimer, 1912).
Kant, Immanuel, 'Vorarbeit zu Von einem neuerdings erhobenen vornehmen Ton in der Philosophie', *Kant's gesammelte Schriften, Bande XXIII*, ed. The German Academy of Sciences in Berlin (Berlin: Walter de Gruyter & Co., 1955).
Kant, Immanuel, *Zum ewigen Frieden, Kant's gesammelte Schriften Bande VIII*, ed. The Royal Prussian Academy of Sciences (Berlin: Georg Reimer, 1912).
Krieger, Murray, *Arts on the Level: The Fall of the Elite Object* (Knoxville: University of Tennessee Press, 1981).
Krieger, Murray, *Poetic Presence and Illusion: Essays in Critical History and Theory* (Baltimore and London: The Johns Hopkins University Press, 1979).
Krieger, Murray, *Theory of Criticism: A Tradition and Its System* (Baltimore and London: The Johns Hopkins University Press, 1976).
Krieger, Murray, *Words about Words about Words: Theory, Criticism, and the Literary Text* (Baltimore and London: The Johns Hopkins University Press, 1988).
Laclau, Ernesto, 'Is Radical Atheism a Good Name for Deconstruction?', *diacritics*, Vol. 38, Nos. 1–2 (Spring/Summer 2008), 180–89.

Laclau, Ernesto, '"The Time Is Out of Joint,"' Laclau, *Emancipation(s)* (London and New York: Verso, 1996), 66–83.

Laclau, Ernesto and Chantal Mouffe, *Hegemony and Socialist Strategy: Towards a Radical Democratic Politics, Second Edition* (London and New York: Verso, 2001).

Leith, William, 'Now you read it, now you don't', *Independent on Sunday*, May 17, 1992.

Leonard, Miriam, *Athens in Paris: Ancient Greece and the Political in Post-War French Thought* (Oxford: Oxford University Press, 2005).

Leonard, Miriam, 'Introduction: "Today, on the Eve of Platonism..."', *Derrida and Antiquity*, ed. Miriam Leonard (Oxford: Oxford University Press, 2010), 1–16.

Lewis, Geoffrey, *Lord Hailsham: A Life* (London: Pimlico, 1998).

Maley, Willy, '*À Propos* of Marx, Attribute to Derrida: A Note on a Note in *Margins of Philosophy*', *Deconstruction Reading Politics*, ed. Martin McQuillan (Basingstoke and New York: Palgrave Macmillan, 2008), 178–96.

Malpas, Jeff, *Heidegger and the Thinking of Place: Explorations in the Topology of Being* (Cambridge, MA and London: The MIT Press, 2012).

Malpas, Jeff, *Place and Experience: A Philosophical Topography* (Cambridge: Cambridge University Press, 1999).

Mansfield, Nick, 'Refusing Defeatism: Derrida, Decision and Absolute Risk', *Social Semiotics*, Vol. 16, No. 3 (September 2006), 473–83.

Mason, Richard (ed.), *Cambridge Minds* (Cambridge: Cambridge University Press, 1994; repr. 1998).

Mehlman, Jeffrey, *Adventures in the French Trade: Fragments Toward a Life* (Stanford: Stanford University Press, 2010).

Meillassoux, Quentin, *After Finitude: An Essay on the Necessity of Contingency*, trans. Ray Brassier (London and New York: Continuum, 2008; repr. 2011).

Mellor, D. H., *Matters of Metaphysics* (Cambridge: Cambridge University Press, 1991).

Melville, Herman, 'Bartleby, The Scrivener', *Melville's Short Novels*, ed. Dan McCall (New York and London: W. W. Norton & Company, 2002).

Mikics, David, *Who Was Jacques Derrida?: An Intellectual Biography* (New Haven and London: Yale University Press, 2009).

Miller, J. Hillis, *For Derrida* (New York: Fordham University Press, 2009).

Miller, J. Hillis, 'Interview: For the Reader-to-Come', Éamonn Dunne, *J. Hillis Miller and the Possibilities of Reading: Literature After Deconstruction* (New York and London: Continuum, 2010), 123–40.

Miller, J. Hillis, '*Jeu*', *Reading Derrida's* Of Grammatology, eds. Sean Gaston and Ian Maclachlan (London and New York: Continuum, 2011), 43–47.

Miller, Paul Allen, 'The Platonic Remainder: Derrida's *Khôra* and the *Corpus Platonicum*', *Derrida and Antiquity*, ed. Miriam Leonard (Oxford: Oxford University Press, 2010), 321–41.

Monk, Ray, 'Is Jacques a Cambridge Chap?', *Independent*, May 15, 1992.

Morse, Ruth, and Stefan Collini, 'Reflections on "The Derrida Affair,"' *The Cambridge Review*, Vol. 113, No. 2318 (October 1992).

Mulderrig, Jane, *The Language of Education Policy: from Thatcher to Blair* (Saarbrücken: VDM Verlag Dr. Müller, 2009).

Naas, Michael, 'An Atheism That (*Dieu merci!*) Still Leaves Something to Be Desired', *CR: The New Centennial Review*, Vol. 9, No. 1 (Spring 2009), 45–68.
Naas, Michael, *Derrida From Now On* (New York: Fordham University Press, 2008).
Nancy, Jean-Luc, *La pensée dérobée* (Paris: Galilée, 2001).
Nancy, Jean-Luc, *A Finite Thinking*, ed. Simon Sparks (Stanford: Stanford University Press, 2002).
Neumann, Harry, 'Civic Piety and Socratic Atheism: An Interpretation of Strauss' Socrates and Aristophanes', *Independent Journal of Philosophy*, Vol. 2 (1978), 33–37.
Nightingale, Andrea, *Once Out of Nature: Augustine on Time and the Body* (Chicago and London: University of Chicago Press, 2011).
Norris, Christopher, 'Deconstruction, Ontology, and Philosophy of Science: Derrida on Aristotle', *Questioning Derrida: with his replies on philosophy*, ed. Michel Meyer (Aldershot: Ashgate, 2001), 39–65.
Norris, Christopher, 'Hawking contra Philosophy', *Philosophy Now* 82 (January/February 2011).
Norris, Christopher, 'Philosophy as *Not* Just a "Kind of Writing": Derrida and the claim of reason', *Redrawing the Lines: analytic philosophy, deconstruction, and literary theory*, ed. Reed Way Dasenbrock (Minneapolis: University of Minnesota Press, 1989), 189–203.
Norris, Christopher, *Uncritical Theory: Postmodernism, Intellectuals and the Gulf War* (London: Lawrence & Wishart, 1992).
Novalis, *Das Allgemeine Brouillon: Materialien zur Enzyklopädistik 1798/1799* (Hamburg: Felix Meiner Verlag, 1993).
Novalis, *Notes for a Romantic Encyclopaedia: Das Allgemeine Brouillon*, ed. and trans. David W. Wood (Albany: SUNY Press, 2007).
O'Sullivan, Michael, 'L'Université sans profession (the University without profession): The Privilege of the Conflict of the Faculties', *Parallax*, Vol. 12, No. 3 (2006), 112–24.
Orchard, Vivienne, 'The "GREPH" movement: philosophical and historical perspectives' (unpublished doctoral thesis: Queen Mary, University of London, 2002).
Orchard, Vivienne, *Jacques Derrida and the Institution of French Philosophy* (London: Legenda, 2011).
Peeters, Benoît, *Derrida* (Paris: Flammarion, 2010).
Peeters, Benôit, *Derrida: A Biography*, trans. Andrew Brown (Cambridge and Malden, MA: Polity, 2013).
Pelikan, Jaroslav, *The Mystery of Continuity: Time and History, Memory and Eternity in the Thought of Saint Augustine* (Charlottesville: University Press of Virginia, 1986).
Peters, Michael A., 'The University and the Future of the Humanities', Michael A. Peters and Gert Biesta, *Derrida, Deconstruction, and the Politics of Pedagogy* (New York: Peter Lang, 2009).
Phillips, Adam, 'On Eating, and Preferring Not To', Phillips, *Promises, Promises: Essays on Literature and Psychoanalysis* (London: Faber & Faber, 2000).
Plato, *Clitophon*, ed. and trans. S. R. Slings (Cambridge: Cambridge University Press, 1999).

Plato, *Timaeus*, Plato, *Timaeus, Critias, Cleitophon, Menexenus, Epistles*, trans. R. G. Bury (London: William Heinemann, 1929).
Powell, Jason, *Jacques Derrida: A Biography* (London and New York: Continuum, 2006).
Pseudo-Dionysius, *The Divine Names, Pseudo-Dionysius: The Complete Works*, trans. Colm Luibhéid (London: SPCK, 1987).
Pseudo-Dionysius, *The Mystical Theology, Pseudo-Dionysius: The Complete Works*, trans. Colm Luibhéid (London: SPCK, 1987).
Quine, Willard Van Orman, *Word and Object* (Cambridge, MA and London: The MIT Press, 1960; repr. 2013).
Rampley, Matthew, *Nietzsche, Aesthetics and Modernity* (Cambridge: Cambridge University Press, 2000).
Rancière, Jacques, 'The Aesthetic Dimension: Aesthetics, Politics, Knowledge', *Critical Inquiry*, Vol. 36, No. 1 (Autumn 2009), 1–19.
Rand, Richard (ed.), *Logomachia: The Conflict of the Faculties* (Lincoln, NE and London: University of Nebraska Press, 1992).
Rapaport, Herman, *The Theory Mess: Deconstruction in Eclipse* (New York and Chichester: Columbia University Press, 2001).
Readings, Bill, *The University in Ruins* (Harvard: Harvard University Press, 1996; repr. 1999).
Resident Members of the University 1992/1993 (*The Cambridge Review Special Issue*).
Ricks, Christopher, 'In theory', *London Review of Books*, Vol. 3, No. 7 (April 16, 1981), 3–6.
Ricks, Christopher, 'John Crowe Ransom, *Selected Essays*', Ricks, *Reviewery* (London: Penguin, 2003).
Riddell, Peter, *The Thatcher Era and its Legacy* (Oxford and Cambridge, MA: Blackwell, 1989; repr. 1991).
Ronell, Avital, *Crack Wars: Literature Addiction Mania* (Urbana and Chicago: University of Illinois Press, 1992; repr. 2004).
Ronen, Ruth, *Aesthetics of Anxiety* (Albany: SUNY Press, 2009).
Ronen, Ruth, *Possible worlds in literary theory* (Cambridge: Cambridge University Press, 1994).
Rorem, Paul, *Pseudo-Dionysius: A Commentary on the Texts and an Introduction to Their Influence* (New York and Oxford: Oxford University Press, 1993).
Rorty, Richard, *Consequences of Pragmatism* (Brighton: Harvester Press, 1982).
Rorty, Richard, *Essays on Heidegger and Others* (Cambridge: Cambridge University Press, 1991).
Rorty, Richard, 'Is Derrida a Quasi-Transcendental Philosopher? (Review of Geoffrey Bennington and Jacques Derrida, *Jacques Derrida*)', *Contemporary Literature*, Vol. 36, No. 1 (Spring 1995), 173–200.
Rorty, Richard, 'Two Meanings of "Logocentrism": a reply to Norris', *Redrawing the Lines: analytic philosophy, deconstruction, and literary theory*, ed. Reed Way Dasenbrock (Minneapolis: University of Minnesota Press, 1989), 204–16.
Rose, Jacqueline, *Why War?—Psychoanalysis, Politics, and the Return to Melanie Klein* (Oxford and Cambridge, MA: Blackwell, 1993).

Rosenzweig, Franz, *Understanding the Sick and the Healthy: A View of World, Man, and God*, ed. Nahum N. Glatzer (Cambridge, MA and London: Harvard University Press, 1999).

Royle, Nicholas, 'The Private Parts of Jesus Christ', *Writing the Bodies of Christ*, ed. John Schad (Aldershot: Ashgate, 2001), 159–76.

Ryan, Desmond, 'The Thatcher Government's Attack on Higher Education in Historical Perspective', *New Left Review*, No. 227 (January/February 1998), 3–32.

Sallis, John, *Chorology: On Beginning in Plato's* Timaeus (Bloomington and Indianapolis: Indiana University Press, 1999).

Salusbury, Matthew, *Thatcherism Goes to College: The Conservative Assault on Higher Education* (London: Canary Press, 1989).

Scruton, Roger, 'The Idea of a University', *American Spectator*, Vol. 43, No. 7 (September 2010), 50–52.

Searle, John R., *Speech Acts: An Essay in the Philosophy of Language* (Cambridge: Cambridge University Press, 1970).

Searle, John R., 'The World Turned Upside Down', *Working Through Derrida*, ed. Gary Brent Madison (Evanston, IL: Northwestern University Press, 1993), 170–88.

Shell, Susan Meld, *Kant and the Limits of Autonomy* (Cambridge, MA and London: Harvard University Press, 2009).

Sloterdijk, Peter, *Bubbles: microspherology*, trans. Wieland Hoban (Los Angeles: Semiotext[e], 2011).

Sloterdijk, Peter, *Neither Sun nor Death* (with Hans-Jürgen Heinrichs), trans. Steve Corcoran (Los Angeles: Semiotext[e], 2011).

Sloterdijk, Peter, *The Art of Philosophy: Wisdom as a Practice*, trans. Karen Margolis (New York: Columbia University Press, 2012).

Smith, Anna Marie, *New Right discourse on race and sexuality: Britain, 1968–1990* (Cambridge: Cambridge University Press, 1994).

Smith, James K. A., *Jacques Derrida: Live Theory* (New York and London: Continuum, 2005).

Sokoloff, William W., 'Between Justice and Legality: Derrida on Decision', *Political Research Quarterly*, Vol. 58, No. 2 (June 2005), 341–52.

Statutes and Ordinances of the University of Cambridge: And Passages from Acts of Parliament Relating to the University (Cambridge: Cambridge University Press, 2014).

Tallis, Raymond, 'Sokal and Bricmont: Is this the beginning of the end of the dark ages in the humanities?' *PN Review*, Vol. 25, No. 6 (June 1999), 35–42.

Taylor, A. E., *A Commentary on Plato's* Timaeus (Oxford: Clarendon Press, 1928).

Taylor, Charles, *Sources of the Self: The Making of the Modern Identity* (Cambridge: Cambridge University Press, 1989).

Taylor, Charles, *The Ethics of Authenticity* (Cambridge, MA and London: Harvard University Press, 1991; repr. 2003).

Terdiman, Richard, 'Given memory: on mnemonic coercion, reproduction and invention', *Memory Cultures: Memory, Subjectivity, and Recognition* eds. Susannah Radstone and Katharine Hodgkin (New Brunswick: Transaction, 2005; repr. 2009), 186–201.

Teske, Roland J., *Paradoxes of Time in Saint Augustine (The Aquinas Lecture, 1996)* (Milwaukee: Marquette University Press, 1996).
Thompson, Michael, *Rubbish Theory* (Oxford: Oxford University Press, 1979).
Thomson, Alex, *Deconstruction and Democracy: Derrida's Politics of Friendship* (London and New York: Continuum, 2005).
Turner, Alwyn W., *A Classless Society: Britain in the 1990s* (London: Aurum Press, 2013).
Ward, Graham, 'Why Is Derrida Important for Theology?', *Theology*, Vol. 95 (1992), 263–70.
Weber, Samuel, *Institution and Interpretation. Expanded Edition* (Stanford: Stanford University Press, 2001).
Wills, Garry, *Augustine's* Confessions*: A Biography* (Princeton and Oxford: Princeton University Press, 2011).
Wilson, Catherine, 'Soul, Body and World: Plato's *Timaeus* and Descartes' *Meditations*', *Platonism at the Origins of Modernity: Studies on Platonism and Early Modern Philosophy*, eds. Douglas Hedley and Sarah Hutton (Dordrecht: Springer, 2008), 177–92.
Wittgenstein, Ludwig, *Tractatus Logico-Philosophicus*, trans. D. F. Pears and B. F. McGuinness (London and New York: Routledge, 2001).
Wood, Sarah, *Derrida's* Writing and Difference*: A Reader's Guide* (London and New York: Continuum, 2009).
Wortham, Simon Morgan, *Counter-Institutions: Jacques Derrida and the Question of the University* (New York: Fordham University Press, 2006).
Youngerman, Mark, 'Murray Krieger. *The Institution of Theory*', *International Studies in Philosophy*, Vol. 28, No. 4 (1996).
Žižek, Slavoj, 'The Real of Sexual Difference', *Reading Seminar XX: Lacan's Major Work on Love, Knowledge, and Feminine Sexuality*, eds. Suzanne Barnard and Bruce Fink (Albany: SUNY Press, 2002), 57–66.
Zlomislic, Marko, *Jacques Derrida's Aporetic Ethics* (Lanham, MD and Plymouth: Lexington Books, 2007).

Index

Aristotle, 91–92, 95–96, 171, 176
Augustine, 96–102, 107, 118n67
Ayer, A. J., 94

Baldwin, Thomas, 25–26, 28
Bull, Malcolm, 132–33

Caputo, John D., 41n63, 150–52, 162n24, 162n27, 191n14
Collini, Stefan, 8, 47, 77
Currie, Mark, 98–99

Deleuze, Gilles, 157–58
de Man, Paul, 8, 11, 20, 33
Denyer, Nicholas, 17–18, 26–28
Derrida, Jacques: the archive, 88–89; CIPH and GREPH, 53, 71n29, 153–53; deconstruction and negative theology, 165–89; 'free play', 5–6, 17, 18, 51–52, 54, 60–68; *Of Grammatology*, 40n52, 42n76, 42n77; hospitality, 151–52, 158, 163n45; 'How to Avoid Speaking: Denials', 160, 165–89; 'Living On • Border Lines', 52–61; *Politics of Friendship*, 85, 96; reading of Kant, 23–24; reading of Lévi-Strauss, 27–28; sovereignty, 89–90; the university, 6–9, 37n12, 48, 60, 92–93, 104, 119n84, 138, 139n12, 153–54, 195
Descartes, René, 186–88
Diggle, James, 21, 33–35, 43n91
Dummett, Michael, 130–33

Eagleton, Terry, 8–9, 10, 24, 41n70
Ehrmann, Jacques, 54–55, 72n42
Ellis, John M., 17, 38n26
Empson, William, 25, 42n73, 42n74
Erskine-Hill, Howard, 32–33, 42n83–42n84

Fichte, Johann Gottlieb: *On the Nature of the Scholar*, 81–84, 110–14
flysheets, 12–16, 80, 188–89; first *non placet*, 13–14, 19, 48–50, 66–68, 79–81, 85–91, 94–96, 101–2, 103, 109–10, 113–14, 128, 135–36, 138; first *placet*, 12, 48; second *non placet*, 14–15, 49–50, 66–68, 128, 135, 138; second *placet*, 12, 48–50; third *placet*, 12–13

Gasché, Rodolphe, 56
general election of 1992, 4–5, 8, 10

Hägglund, Martin, 78–79, 145–52, 160, 161n16, 162n24, 162n27, 178, 182, 188
Hebblethwaite, Brian, 4–5, 20–21, 23, 28–29, 38n28, 51, 67, 73n65, 129–31, 133–34
Heidegger, Martin, 101, 107, 122–27, 178–88
Hobson, Marian, 16–17, 62, 77, 192–93n32

Jeanneret, Marian. *See* Hobson, Marian
Johnson, Barbara, 36n7, 140n18
Johnson, Christopher, 42n79, 52, 77

Kant, Immanuel, 22, 61–68, 75n83, 81, 92–93, 102–9, 114n13, 120n90, 120n93; *The Conflict of the Faculties*, 4, 50–51, 65–68, 102, 104–5
Krieger, Murray, 52, 132–33

Laclau, Ernesto, 135–36, 145–46, 159–60, 178, 182, 188
Lash, Nicholas, 28–30

Major, John, 4, 140n20
Malpas, Jeff, 77, 118–19n75, 121–22
McCann, Graham, 128–34
Meillassoux, Quentin, 100–1, 118n74, 149
Meister Eckhart, 165, 166–67, 174–75, 177, 181–82, 188
Mellor, D. H., 32, 84
Melville, Herman: 'Bartleby, The Scrivener', 156–58, 164n47
Miller, J. Hillis, 69n19, 145–46, 153–58, 160, 178, 182, 188

Negative theology, 165–88
Norris, Christopher, 22–25, 49, 95
Novalis, 47, 81, 95, 114n13, 122–27

Plato, 78–79, 105, 178, 182; *Khōra*, 170–88, 189–90n4, 190n7, 190n9, 191n14, 191n15, 191–92n16
Prendergast, Christopher, 18–20, 30–32
Pseudo-Dionysius, 165, 169–70, 173–77, 181–82, 188, 191–92n16

Ronen, Ruth, 75n76, 91–94
Rorty, Richard, 23, 41n63
Rose, Jacqueline, 134–37
Ryan, Desmond, 136–38

Searle, John R., 20, 70n21, 75n84, 184–88, 193n37
Sloterdijk, Peter, 81, 84, 103, 115n20, 120n89
Smith, Barry, 39n49; letter to the *Times*, 15–16, 17, 26, 33, 39n45, 70n21, 193n37

Tallis, Raymond, 16, 69n16
Taylor, Charles, 51–52, 60–64, 67, 74n68
Thatcher, Margaret, 8, 121, 127–38, 140n20, 141n30

Von Hardenberg, Georg Philipp Friedrich Freiherr. *See* Novalis
Von Hochheim, Eckhart. *See* Meister Eckhart

About the Author

Niall Gildea is researcher and writer. He has taught Literature and Philosophy in a number of universities in the United Kingdom.

www.ingramcontent.com/pod-product-compliance
Lightning Source LLC
Chambersburg PA
CBHW032041300426
44117CB00009B/1150